Carta de Pedro vaz caminha so=
bre o descobrimento da terra nova
q̃ fez Pedro álbes. feita na Ilha da
vera Cruz em o 1.º de Março de
_1500_   Gaveta 8.ª

Maço 2.º —— N.º 8.

Aquer esta junta huma copia para
melhor inteligencia deste originale

Transcripto no L. 43 da Reforma
dos Documentos das Gavetas   L 43

We love you!
Dr. Susan Sterling-Fishe
Ha-Gotcha!
SFS

Virgin Territory

WOMEN, GENDER, AND HISTORY IN CONTEMPORARY BRAZILIAN ART

NATIONAL MUSEUM OF WOMEN IN THE ARTS

CURATED BY
SUSAN FISHER STERLING
BERTA SICHEL
FRANKLIN ESPATH PEDROSO

National Museum
of Women in the Arts
1250 New York Avenue, N.W.
Washington, D.C. 20005
www.nmwa.org

Project Director:
Susan Fisher Sterling
Project Coordinator:
Britta Konau
Publication Director:
Laureen Schipsi
Publication Assistants:
Corynne A. Hill, Sarah Hall,
and Elizabeth Olson

Except where otherwise
indicated, translations were
provided by Albert G. Bork.

Prepared for publication
by Archetype Press,
Washington, D.C.
Project Director:
Diane Maddex
Assistant Editor:
Gretchen Smith Mui
Designer: Robert L. Wiser
Editorial Assistants:
Carol Peters
and Wendy A. Jordan

Printed and bound in Canada

ISBN 0-940979-47-0
(hardcover)
ISBN 0-940979-48-9
(paperback)

Essay credits

Pages 56–57: Translation by
Sophié Athié.
Pages 60–61: Excerpted and
adapted from Panorama '99
(São Paulo: Museu de Arte
Moderna, 1999), 293.
Pages 62–65: Excerpted and
adapted from "The Art of
Anna Bella Geiger: A Sense
of Constellation," in Anna
Bella Geiger: Constelações
(Rio de Janeiro: Museu
de Arte Moderna, 1996),
76–78.
Pages 68–69: Excerpted and
adapted from "De fora para
dentro/de dentro para fora,"
in Lápis, 1997.
Pages 74–75: Excerpted and
adapted from "Laura Lima:
The Artist as Predator," Trans,
vol. 8 (2000), 237–42.
Pages 86–87: Excerpted and
adapted from Nazareth
Pacheco: Jóais (São Paulo:
Fundaçao Bienal de São
Paulo, 1998).
Pages 92–93: Adapted
from Rosana Paulino, Album
de desenho (São Paulo:
Galeria Adriana Penteado,
1997), 19; translation by Yara
Nagelschmidt.
Page 101: Excerpted and
adapted from Miguel Rio
Branco (Rio de Janeiro: Museu
de Arte Moderna, 1996); trans-
lation by Peter Lines Morris.
Pages 102–4: Excerpted from
"Recapturing History: The
(Un)official Story in Contem-
porary Latin American Art,"
Art Journal, vol. 51, no 4.
(Winter 1992), 69–80.

Pages 106–8: Excerpted
from "Valeska Soares,"
BOMB Magazine (Winter
2001), 52–53.
Pages 110–11: Excerpted and
adapted from "Carmen
Miranda: Bananas Is My Business," in O Cinema Brasileiro:
de O Pagador de promessas
a Central do Brasil (The Films
from Brazil: From The Given
Word to Central Station), ed.
Amir Labaki (São Paulo:
PubliFolha, 1998), 175–79.
Pages 116–19: Excerpted and
adapted from "Travel Chroni-
cles: The Work of Adriana
Varejão," in New Histories
(Boston: Institute of Contem-
porary Art, 1996).
Pages 130–37: Adapted from
"Algunas consideraciones
sobre identidades étnicas
y racismo en Brasil," Revista
de Cultura Brasileña, no. 1
(March 1998), 69–86.
Pages 138–43: Translation
by Michael Reade, Erika
Benincasa, Alfred MacAdam,
and Nadine Fajerman.
Pages 146–57: Excerpted and
adapted from Robert Stam,
Tropical Multiculturalism: A
Comparative History of Race
in Brazilian Cinema and
Culture (Durham: Duke
University Press, 1997).

Photography credits

Denise Andrade: 93, 94, 95,
141, 142
César Barreto: 4
Mário Carneiro: 149
Chan Chao: 48, 49
Guido Cosulich: 156
Fernando Duarte: 148
Lauro Escorel: 151
Rômulo Fialdini: 123
Galeria Brito Cimino: 43
Galeria Casa Triângulo: 139

Luis Gomes: 88–89
Highcliffe Album–
Instituto Moreira Salles: 6
Luiz Hossaka: 8 top
Epaminondas Lima: 38
Estate of Humberto Mauro:
80, 81
José Medeiros: 154
Vicente de Mello: 24, 77, 116,
117, 118, 131, 144–45
Walter Morgenthaler: 22
Edgard Moura: 147
Jean Claude Planchet: 28, 62
Rio Filme: 40, 111
Lula Rodrigues: 63
Murilo Sales: 153
José António Silva: 8, 20
Tiago Veloso: 156
José António Ventura: 149
Women Make Movies: 7, 48,
49, 111

Display images

Page 1: Giovanni Batista
Ramusio, detail of Brasil,
1557; hand-colored engraving;
15 × 10⅝ in. (38 × 27 cm);
Collection BancoSantos,
São Paulo
Page 2: Marc Ferrez (1843–
1923), Indienne Tobá, Brazil,
1870–99 (see page 133)
Page 3: Rosana Paulino,
Drawing from Models series,
1996–98 (see page 93)
Page 4: Johann Moritz
Rugendas (1802–58),
Floresta Virgem (Native
Forest), ca. 1830; oil
on canvas; 24¾ × 19⅝ in.
(63 × 50 cm); Collection
Maria Cecília and Paulo
Geyer/Museu Imperial,
Rio de Janeiro
Page 5: Adriana Varejão,
Detail of Testemunhas
Oculares X, Y e Z (Eye
Witnesses X, Y and Z), 1997
(see page 116)
Page 6: Jean Baptiste Debret

(1768–1848), detail of Mulher
Negra Vendendo Folhas
de Bananeira (Negro Woman
Selling Banana Leaves), n.d.;
watercolor on paper;
7 × 8⅛ in. (17.8 × 20.6 cm);
Highcliffe Album, Acervo;
Collection Instituto Moreira
Salles, Rio de Janeiro
Page 7: Helena Solberg,
Carmen Miranda: Bananas
Is My Business, 1995
(see page 111)
Pages 8–9: Detail of last
page of Carta de Pero Vaz
de Caminha, 1500; manu-
script; Instituto dos Arquivos
Nacionais, Torre do Tombo,
Lisbon
Pages 12–13: Regina Silveira,
Detail of Monudentro (Inside
the Monument), 986–87/
2001 (see page 103)
Pages 16–17: Theodore Galle
and Jean van der Straet,
America, 1589 (see page 21)
Pages 46–47: Anna Bella
Geiger, Am. Latina, 1977
(see page 62)
Pages 120–21: Frans Post
(1592–1680), Engenho
(Sugar Plantation), n.d.
(see page 127)
Pages 158–59: Sylvio Back,
Yndio do Brasil (Our Indians),
1995 (see page 52)

***Virgin Territory: Women, Gen-
der, and History in Contemporary Brazilian Art*** is organized
by the National Museum of
Women in the Arts in collaboration with BrasilConnects.

BrasilConnects is an independent non-governmental organization that supports Brazilian
culture and ecology and
emphasizes the human dimension of Brazil's development.

■ *Virgin Territory*, an exhibition of contemporary art commemorating the 500th anniversary of the first Portuguese encounter with Brazil, is the National Museum of Women in the Arts's second exhibition of Brazilian art. As an example of continued and successful cross-cultural dialogue, it would not have been possible without the vision and enthusiasm of many individuals and organizations. First and foremost, we are extremely grateful to BrasilConnects for its generous support of the exhibition, its accompanying catalogue, and related education programs. It has done a great deal over the past several years to bring Brazilian art, past and present, to wider public attention both in Brazil and abroad. We therefore express our gratitude to Edemar Cid Ferreira, president of BrasilConnects, for his interest and involvement, as well as to Emilio Kalil, project director, for his valuable assistance in all aspects of the exhibition's planning.

We also recognize the early efforts of Fausto M. Godoy, now minister counselor, Brazilian Embassy, Tokyo, who, as the coordinator for international itinerary, first proposed working with NMWA on an exhibition of contemporary art. In addition, Franklin Espath Pedroso, associate chief curator of BrasilConnects, developed a working partnership with NMWA that was of the highest caliber—a true meeting of arts and minds. We also thank Nina Hokka, assistant to the chief curator, and Elisio Yamada, curatorial assistant, for their expertise in facilitating the exhibition. The efforts of Marifé Hernández in carrying out this BrasilConnects program in the United States are much appreciated.

On behalf of the NMWA board and staff, I also thank His Excellency Rubens A. Barbosa, the ambassador of Brazil, and Mrs. Maria Ignez Barbosa, for the personal interest they have shown in the exhibition. We also appreciate the encouragment and support of Renato de Assumpção Faria, cultural counselor.

Deserving of distinct recognition as well is Berta Sichel, director of the Film and Video Department, Museo Nacional Centro de Arte Reina Sofia in Madrid, who as co-curator of the exhibition brought

Acknowledgments

NANCY RISQUE ROHRBACH

DIRECTOR

expertise, humor, and a passion for Brazilian art. In addition to her contributions to the exhibition and the catalogue, she was instrumental in developing the catalogue's selection of four essays that offer additional food for thought about Brazilian life and culture. To Pedro P. Geiger, Suely Rolnik, Giralda Seyferth, and Robert Stam, we express warmest thanks for their illuminating contributions. Thanks are also due all of the curators, critics, and artists who wrote, or enabled us to reprint, articles and excerpts about the artists in the catalogue. Throughout this process, translator Albert G. Bork was a tremendous asset, and Berta Sichel also thanks Lorna Scott Fox for her assistance. For the editing, design, and production of this beautiful volume, we wish to recognize Archetype Press of Washington, D.C.

Those who kindly loaned works for the exhibition deserve our profound gratitude. They include the artists; Museum of Modern Art, Rio de Janeiro; Museum of Contemporary Art, Niterói; Museum of Modern Art Library, New York; Aperture; Funarte; RioFilme; Women Make Movies; Graziela Strina de Arruda; Moisés and Diana Berezdivin; Celia S. de Birbragher; Daniela and Patrice de Camaret; Frances Marinho; José Antonio Marton; Patricia Phelps de Cisneros; Plinio de Toledo Arruda; Ricardo Trevisan; Galeria Brito Cimino, São Paulo; Galeria Camargo Vilaça, São Paulo; Galeria Casa Triângulo, São Paulo; Galeria Thomas Cohn, São Paulo; Galeria Luisa Strina, São Paulo; and D'Amelio Terras Gallery, New York.

Finally, my appreciation goes to the staff of the National Museum of Women in the Arts, especially to Susan Fisher Sterling, our chief curator, who developed the exhibition concept and saw it through to completion with intelligence and enthusiasm. She and her NMWA colleagues have once again brought a significant and challenging exhibition of contemporary art to fruition at the museum, and we are truly thankful for their efforts. ■

Acknowledgments

NANCY RISQUE ROHRBACH, DIRECTOR

11

BrasilConnects Statement

EDEMAR CID FERREIRA

PRESIDENT, BRASILCONNECTS

14

Preface

RUBENS A. BARBOSA

AMBASSADOR OF BRAZIL

15

CURATORS' ESSAYS

Introduction

BY FRANKLIN ESPATH PEDROSO

18

Virgin Territory

BY SUSAN FISHER STERLING

20

The History of the Present

BY BERTA SICHEL

34

THE ARTISTS

Silvana Afram
Mulheres Negras

BY SILVANA AFRAM

48

Sylvio Back
Barracks Indians

BY SYLVIO BACK

50

Brígida Baltar
Transient Dialogues

BY ANIA CORCILIUS

54

Anna Barros
Short Tales: Saci-Si

BY ANNA BARROS

56

Sandra Cinto
Endless Night

BY LISETTE LAGNADO

58

Oriana Duarte
Noumenon: The Thing-in-Itself

BY MOACIR DOS ANJOS

60

Anna Bella Geiger
A Sense of Constellation

BY FERNANDO COCCHIARALE

62

Sandra Kogut
Video Confessions

BY IVANA BENTES

66

Sonia Labouriau
From Without to Within/
From Within to Without

BY RICARDO BASBAUM

68

Nelson Leirner
The Miracle of the
Multiplication of Images

BY AGNALDO FARIAS

70

Laura Lima
The Artist as Predator

BY RICARDO BASBAUM

74

Anna Maria Maiolino
Rice and Beans

BY BERTA SICHEL

76

Humberto Mauro
O descobrimento do Brasil

BY HERNANI HEFFNER

80

Beth Moysés
Memory of Affection
BY KATIA CANTON
82

Mônica Nador
Transformations of Place
BY TADEU CHIARELLI
84

Nazareth Pacheco
A Lacerating Reality
BY TADEU CHIARELLI
86

Lygia Pape
My Work in Marginal Cinema
BY LYGIA PAPE
90

Rosana Paulino
Women and Their Bodies
BY ARACY AMARAL
92

Rosângela Rennó
Vera Cruz
BY ROSÂNGELA RENNÓ
96

Miguel Rio Branco
Door into Darkness
BY MIGUEL RIO BRANCO
AND LIGIA CANONGIA
98

Regina Silveira
Recapturing History
BY SUSANA TORRUELLA LEVAL
102

Valeska Soares
Intoxication
BY VIK MUNIZ
106

Helena Solberg
Bananas Is My Business
BY ARNALDO JABOR
110

Janaína Tschäpe
Fables for a Body in Pieces
BY CELSO FIORAVANTE
112

Adriana Varejão
Travel Chronicles
BY RINA CARVAJAL
116

SOURCEBOOK ESSAYS

Geographic Contingencies.
Space and Memory
BY PEDRO P. GEIGER
122

Ethnic Identities in Brazil
BY GIRALDA SEYFERTH
130

Beyond the Identity Principle:
The Anthropophagy Formula
BY SUELY ROLNIK
138

Brazilian Cinema:
Race and Representation
BY ROBERT STAM
146

CHECKLIST & BIOGRAPHIES

Checklist of the Exhibition
160

Artist Biographies
163

Notes
172

Contributors
176

■ *Virgin Territory* comes to the capital of the United States under the auspices of the National Museum of Women in the Arts, a thoroughly modern institution founded to explore the female consciousness so critical to contemporary society. This is not the first exhibition of Brazilian art at the museum. In the 1990s *UltraModern: The Art of Contemporary Brazil* revealed to the North American public the leading role women have played in Brazilian culture. After all, modern art in Brazil originated in 1917 with a show of the work of Anita Malfatti, who sojourned in New York before giving birth to the most provocative paintings of her era. That foray into modernism continued with Tarsila do Amaral's anthropophagic paintings, made a stop for Maria Martins's surrealist sculpture—she was also Duchamp's muse and Mondrian's patron—and is multiplied fivefold in the artists' works presented in the current exhibition.

BrasilConnects Statement

E D E M A R   C I D   F E R R E I R A

P R E S I D E N T ,   B R A S I L C O N N E C T S

The exhibition *Virgin Territory* has its roots in the *Rediscovery Exhibition*, which was presented in São Paulo from April 23 to September 10, 2000, to commemorate the quincentenary of the discovery of Brazil, celebrated on April 22, 2000. Its subjects ranged from the arts to the humanities, from the first evidence of human occupation of Brazil to today's installation art. It encompassed exhibitions of indigenous vessels and ceremonial art, Afro-Brazilian art and artifacts, baroque liturgical art, neoclassical and nineteenth-century paintings and sculpture, modern and contemporary art, and popular and outsider art, as well as travelers' diaries, including the first letter describing the new territory: Pero Vaz de Caminha's letter of 1500. The *Rediscovery Exhibition* offered a portrait of the shaping of a nation. It was visited by 1.9 million persons during its six-month run and by another million in other Brazilian cities. Still others experienced it in Lisbon, Santiago, and Buenos Aires, where elements of the original exhibition were shown.

In an era when international relations are strengthened by means of electronic communications, there is still nothing that can take the place of the actual, physical work of art. The north-south dialogue between the creators—which always precedes political understanding between peoples—will be clear from the exhibition. ■

BrasilConnects
Culture & Ecology

■ During the commemoration of the 500th anniversary of the arrival of the first Portuguese in Brazil, celebrated in 2000, a series of expressive events permitted reflection on several aspects of Brazilian culture, history, and society. Over the last five centuries, Brazil—a country with continental dimensions—has received ethnic and cultural contributions from all over the world. Adding to its indigenous, Portuguese, and African elements—the foundations of our national identity—people have come from the Middle East, other regions of Europe, and the Far East. The Latin and Mediterranean character of the Portuguese settlers instigated this extraordinary blending of people and cultures with the potential to achieve great intermixture, making Brazil not only a "melting pot" but also a "melted pot."

The cultural vigor and dynamism generated by such a blending can be appreciated in the exhibition *Virgin Territory*, which is a splendid allegorical reflection on our background and identity. It gathers together some of the most exceptional Brazilian female artists of the moment, along with four male artists. Equally important is the fact that the exhibition is being held at the National Museum of Women in the Arts, one of the most prestigious cultural spaces in Washington.

Preface

RUBENS A. BARBOSA

AMBASSADOR OF BRAZIL

In fact, it has become a tradition for the National Museum of Women in the Arts to host contemporary Brazilian artists. In 1994 the excellent exhibition *UltraModern* took place here. *Virgin Territory* refocuses, updates, and enhances the body of Brazilian art in the third millennium.

I would like to mention my appreciation for the support received from the museum's chair and founder, Wilhelmina Cole Holladay; the director, Nancy Risque Rohrbach; and especially the chief curator, Susan Fisher Sterling, who knows so well how to identify the richness of Brazilian art from the modernist movement to postmodern times. I also want to acknowledge the invaluable cooperation of Edemar Cid Ferreira, president of BrasilConnects.

I am confident that *Virgin Territory*, by bringing to the attention of the American public several aspects of contemporary Brazilian art, will foster a greater knowledge about Brazilian culture and life and will be an important element in strengthening the traditional ties of friendship between Brazil and the United States. ■

CURATORS'

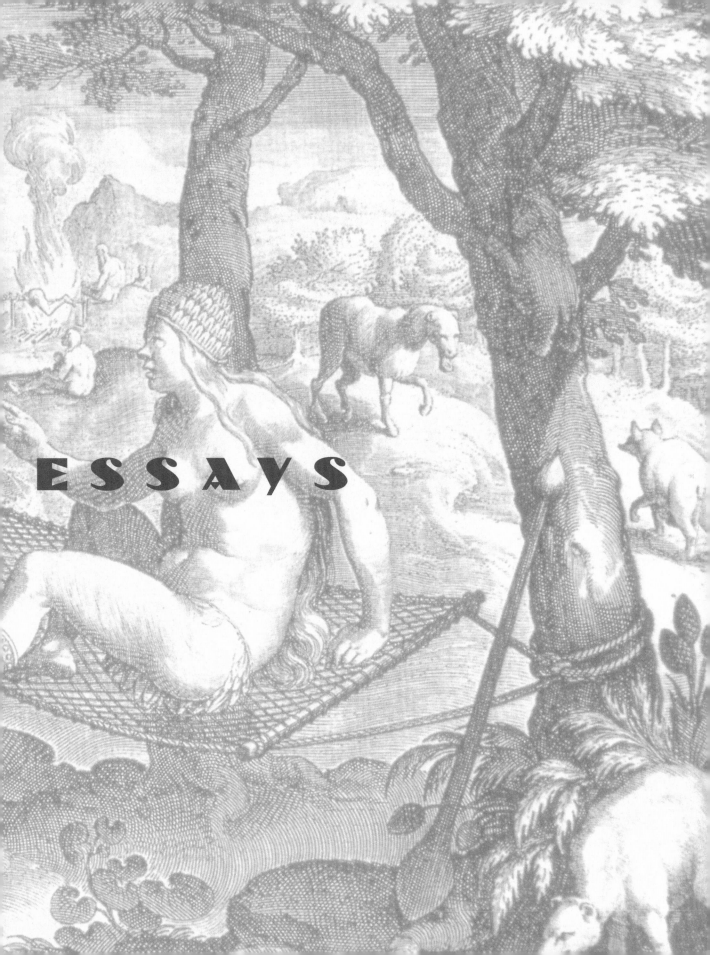

ESSAYS

Introduction

BY FRANKLIN ESPATH PEDROSO

I asked no other thing—
No other—was denied—
I offered Being—for it—
The Mighty Merchant sneered—

Brazil? He twirled a Button—
Without a glance my way—
"But—Madam—is there nothing else—
That We can show—Today?"

Emily Dickinson[1]

Intimate Maps

Each artist is the cartographer of her own inner universe—exploring it, deciphering it, and measuring it with her own intimate coordinates that give it meaning, coherence, consistency. By displaying together the individual universes of two dozen artists in *Virgin Territory*, our intention is to present a star chart of contemporary Brazilian art. Here are worlds that overlap, interpenetrate, talk to one another, and then return to their own spheres, enriched and strengthened. These are the constellations, governed by their own inimitable designs, that make up a significant quadrant of the celestial vault of Brazilian art.

Earth (terra) is a feminine noun in Portuguese. The earth is the mother from whom we are born and on whom we move—a concrete, palpable presence whose essence is mysterious, unfathomable, in a word, feminine. The scientific geographer studies and describes the earth's surface, its physical features, climates, soils, vegetation, and the relationship between the natural environment and humans. The artistic geographer analyzes and describes the epidermis of the soul, describing emotional depths, psychological climates, moods, pleasures and displeasures, and the relationship between the artist and the artistic milieu where she belongs and the society in which she grows. That is why priority has been given to women artists in this exhibition; although some of the exhibitors are men, they are men who are deeply involved with women's issues.

Brazil, a male-dominated society, has numbered women among its major artists since the early twentieth century. Indeed, women have played a critically important role in various movements and moments in the history of Brazilian art, particularly from Modern Art Week in 1922 on: artists like Anita Malfatti, Djanira da Motta e Silva, Tarsila do Amaral, Maria Martins, Mary Vieira, Judith Lauand, Maria Leontina, Lygia Pape, Lygia Clark, Mira Schendel, and Iole de Freitas, to mention just a few. Since the so-called '80s Generation, so many women artists have come into prominence that it would take a very long list to name them all. Women have also made major contributions to Brazilian printmaking.

Discovering Brazil

The *Rediscovery Exhibition* (April 23 to September 10, 2000) was the largest artistic and cultural event ever held in Brazil. Divided into modules of equal importance, the exhibition made it possible for the first time to see the nation's diverse artistic and cultural forms of expression placed democratically side by side, avoiding the pitfall of privileging "high" art over "popular" art or of relegating the work of native Brazilians and inmates of psychiatric institutions to the condition of picturesque curiosities. Since that monumental exposition came to an end, BrasilConnects has held a number of exhibitions that, although dwarfed by the original event, are still impressive. In this way the organization has continued to assert and publicize Brazilian art not only in Brazil but also abroad, preparing new exhibitions that highlight specific aspects of the nation's art. Through this succession of discoveries and rediscoveries, Brazilians learn more about themselves and other countries get to know the best of our artistic work, which is increasingly gaining recognition and acclaim on the international art circuit.

The *Virgin Territory* exhibition at the National Museum of Women in the Arts is particularly important to us for two reasons. First, it is highly gratifying to collaborate with a museum dedicated to highlighting women's contributions because the accomplishment of women artists in Brazil is closer in importance to that of their male peers than is the case in most countries in the Northern Hemisphere and Europe. Second, there is a deep affinity between the United States and Brazil, which ensures that the exhibition will be received with much interest by the American public and the intellectual community. The empathy between the two countries is the product of a cultural identification, of an awareness of mutual interests derived from cultural as well as commercial interchange. This exhibition offers a significant opportunity to balance this interchange by showing to Americans the work of some of the most provocative artists working today in Brazil—an opportunity also for the United States to discover Brazil. ∎

Opposite top:

Frans Post (1592–1680)

Cachoeira de Paulo Afonso (Paulo Afonso Waterfall), 1647

Oil on panel

23¼ × 18⅛ in. (59 × 46 cm)

Museu de Arte de São Paulo Assis Chateaubriand, São Paulo

Opposite bottom:

Guillaume D'Isle and Johann Justin Gebauer

América das Sudliche . . . , 1753

12⅝ × 16⅛ in. (32 × 41 cm)

Hand-colored engraving

Collection BancoSantos, São Paulo

The Master Narrative

On Monday, March 9, 1500, a fleet of thirteen vessels commanded by Pedro Álvares Cabral sailed out of Tejo, Portugal, bound for Calicut, India. Vasco da Gama had prepared the sailing instructions for the voyage, which would lead the fleet from the Canary Islands to Cape Verde then south-southwest, sailing close to the wind, to the Cape of Good Hope. On Wednesday, April 21, Cabral's chronicler, Pero Vaz de Caminha, wrote, "On that day, at the hour of vespers, we saw land! First of all a great mountain, very high and round, and other ranges, much lower, to the south; then a lowland, with great forests: the captain named the peak Monte Pascoal (Easter Mountain) and the land, Terra da Vera Cruz (Land of the True Cross)."[1]

The letter then goes on to record that Cabral, unsure whether he had discovered a continent or a large island, ordered his vessels to sail toward the shore. On the morning of April 23 they entered the mouth of a river. Nicolau Coelho was sent ashore, becoming the first Portuguese known to set foot on

The letter from Pero Vaz to Dom Manuel I of Portugal represents what some historians call Brazil's "birth certificate," the first chapter in its history,[3] although more correctly it represents the birth of Brazil's colonial or modern history. In this diaristic letter to his sovereign, Pero Vaz set forth his observations of the first encounter of two radically different cultures in a safe, freshwater anchorage along a calm South American beach, with all the features of an unsullied Garden of Eden.[4]

Like other reports coming back from the New World, Pero Vaz's was informed in part by a desire to obtain the king's favor, in part by his excitement about this new land, and in part by his belief that the company had located the Terrestrial Paradise that medieval cosmographers had long featured at the top of their maps.[5] Although the breadth of the new fourth continent would not be known until Spaniard Vasco Núñez de Balboa reached the Pacific Ocean in 1513, and the physical space of Brazil's interior would not be legally claimed and agreed on until 1750, Pero Vaz and his compatriots viewed

Virgin Territory

BY   SUSAN   FISHER   STERLING

the soil of Brazil. He saw a large number of "Indians," all naked and peaceable, and spoke with them. A second encounter occurred ten leagues to the north when two of the aboriginals canoed out to the Portuguese fleet. Cabral ordered them dressed from head to foot and sent them back to shore.

On April 26, Low Sunday, mass was sung before an altar in the wilderness by Frei Henriques Soares de Coimbra. The natives sat in rapt attention and respectful silence, leading the Portuguese to believe they were ripe for conversion to Christianity. After mass Cabral called a meeting at which it was agreed that the fleet's supply ship should be sent back to Portugal with news of the discovery. It was also agreed that they would not take any natives with them by force but rather leave two of Cabral's men with the Indians to learn the language. Lacking a *padrão* (stone pillar), Cabral had the ship's carpenters construct a wooden cross to symbolize taking possession of the territory. The cross was raised on May 1, 1500, and the following day the fleet set sail for the Cape of Good Hope.[2]

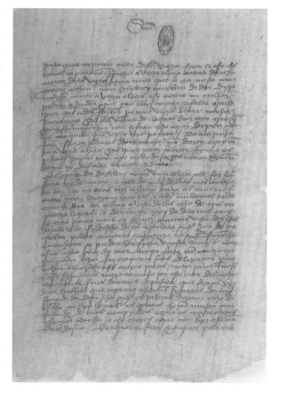

Above:

Theodore Galle and

Jean van der Straet

America, 1589

Engraving

7 1/8 × 10 1/8 in.

(18.2 × 27 cm)

Bibliothèque Mazarine, Paris

Opposite:

First page of *Carta de Pero*

Vaz de Caminha, 1500

Manuscript

Instituto dos Arquivos

Nacionais, Torre do Tombo,

Lisbon, Portugal

the new virgin territory as heaven on earth, the land of the True Cross. In the best Christian sense it was an *orbis alterius*—another world.[6]

The Metaphor: Networking Difference

There is more to this story, however—five hundred one years more, to be precise, for Brazil is still living with the consequences of that moment of "discovery." The quincentenary of Cabral's expedition offers the unique opportunity to look back, with postcolonial eyes, to an important if lesser known encounter with the New World.

A defined historical moment, similar to Columbus's claiming of "the Indies" for Spain on the isle of Trinidad in 1492, the 500th anniversary of Cabral's encounter with *terra brasilieras* offers the opportunity for one nation to come to terms with itself. Claimed by the Portuguese ("the other" Iberians), its territory already anticipated and prescribed by the 1494 Treaty of Tordesillas, Brazil experienced a historical trajectory that was nuanced differently from that of the Spanish American colonies.[7]

As the historian Peter Winn has noted, "Unlike the Spanish conquistadors, the Portuguese who landed on Brazil's tropical coast in the sixteenth century found no cities to conquer, treasures to despoil, or mines to exploit. Instead they encountered virgin forests with the red dyewood that gave Brazil its name. . . ."[8] As a colonial power, Portugal was soon to impel a new form and future on the Brazilian *orbis alterius*, including its aboriginal inhabitants; its soon-to-arrive colonial planters; its African slaves, who eventually numbered more than seven million; and its immigrant farm and industrial workers, who arrived in the late nineteenth and early twentieth centuries from Europe, the Middle East, and Japan.

Through a succession of metaphorical musings on this "claiming" of Brazil, the exhibition *Virgin Territory* began to take on form. Looking back on Cabral's voyage as the singular event that began the implantation within the modern historical consciousness of what would first become the colony, then the empire, and finally the republic of Brazil,

I began to consider the richness of contemporary works by Brazilian women artists, and some men as well, that could be seen within the context of coming to terms with other worlds.

From the start it was also my intention to propose a contemporary repositioning of the master narrative and its presumption of possession. This exhibition, as its title suggests, posits an ongoing relationship between the notion of *virgin*—generally seen as female, untouched, and pure—and *territory*—which denotes male possession and domination. Imagining this relationship as one that operates first as a "discovery" at the margins of the known world and then unfolds through time, what began in conquest can end in a very different sense of place, whether its location is contemporary Brazil or some future yet unknown.

Using Bracha Lichtenberg Ettlinger and Griselda Pollock's theories of the female matrix as a signifier for "a model for human situations and processes in which the *non-I* is not an intruder but a partner in difference," I determined to move beyond the dualities of oppositional thinking—such as self-other, love-hate, here-there, now-then—to "a symbol of the coexistence in one space of two bodies, two subjectivities whose encounter at this moment is not either/or. . . ."[9] I also intended to show that the matrix extends "as do all these metaphors of sexual difference to other Others—issues of race, immigration, diaspora, genocide [all of which] are tangled at the moment around the lack of means to signify other possible relations between different subjects—I and *non-I*."[10]

Beginning with the conceptual maps of Anna Bella Geiger and the postmodern history paintings of Adriana Varejão, I set out four interconnected and open-ended lines of thought, linked by the form and content of the artists' work, that would offer negotiable alterities—embodiments of otherness—to the master narrative. The first of these envisions the New World as a virgin land—a beautiful, untouched (read: primitive), and exotic place

to be conquered and colonized. The second meditates on mapping as a means of staking out or claiming territory: the creation of physical and mental boundaries that can be retained or retooled with the passage of time and history. The third contemplates the importance of religion, Catholicism in particular, in prescribing a new social sphere in which to operate. The fourth speculates on the mixing of cultures and races—*mestiço* in Portuguese—as the basis of a new social order. Like the four directions of a compass, these ideas provided my bearings.

By applying the matrixial line to these four ideas, the exhibition's premise also began to correspond with constructions of "otherness" recently made in postcolonial theory. Acknowledging that the world is in the midst of what the cultural critic Thomas McEvilley defined as the long aftermath of cultural readjustment to decolonization, *Virgin Territory* ascribes to current curatorial practice in contemporary art recognizing the importance of territorial and temporal continuities and discontinuities in the wake of colonialism.[11]

Again the goal here is to move beyond polarities—to move away from social dependency theory and the dualities of center/periphery, hegemony/subordination, global/local used in describing Latin America's relationship to European colonialism and dominance by the United States. Beginning in the late 1960s this theory enabled art historians and cultural critics to carve out a space for Latin American art that recognized yet resisted marginalization by First World powers. In doing so, they provided a platform for art and theory today that values not one pole or the other but rather multiple realities that cycle one on another, intermixing along the way. Using terms such as *hybridity, transculturation,* and *mestizage,* European and U.S. exhibitions over the past ten years—such as *Transcontinental* (1990), *America: Bride of the Sun* (1992), *News from Post America–Aperto '93/Venice Biennale* (1993), *Latin American Artists of the Twentieth Century* (1993), *Re-aligning Vision: Alternative Currents in South American Drawing* (1997), *Sense of Place* (1997), and most recently *UltraBaroque* (2001) and *Versions del Sur* (2001)—are predicated on a sense of exchange and value where globalization and national (and individual) fragmentation coexist, cross over, combine, and reconstitute.

Joseph Leon Righini
(ca. 1820–1884)
Rio na Floresta Brasileira, Pará (River in the Brazilian Forest, Pará), 1872
Oil on canvas
16⅛ × 23¼ in. (41 × 59 cm)
Collection Maria Cecília and Paulo Geyer/Museu Imperial, Rio de Janeiro

Brazil's Postmodern Alterities

In her essay "The History of the Present" in this catalogue, Berta Sichel, co-curator of the exhibition, asks the rhetorical question: "Why do we keep harking back to the consequences of bygone power relationships that are surely irrelevant to the present day?" She answers that these relationships "may only seem unimportant for our times. In fact, it is the engagement with European imperialism and its transformation within a postcolonial society that has given color and identity to the very nature of contemporary societies. Brazil is no exception."

Recognizing this phase of Brazil's existence, the twenty-five artists in the exhibition *Virgin Territory* offer diverse artistic alterities to master narratives. These are expressions that are syntactically inflected by local as well as global concerns, grounded in history yet very much of the present day. Encompassing paintings, sculpture, installation, film, and new media, the works constitute rewritings, remappings, and reinventions of history and place. They are assemblages of positions that transgress borders, fragment identities, politicize the corporeal, exorcise the territorial, and disrupt smooth narration. So, while each work is categorized by theme in this essay, they can and often do refer to, step over, and intersect with the other themes and artworks in the exhibition, enriching the enterprise, as these artists visualize their worlds anew.

The Encounter

Prevailing myths and romantic fantasies that issue from the master narrative comprise the first grouping of works in *Virgin Territory*. Including works by Adriana Varejão, Humberto Mauro, Rosângela Rennó, Sylvio Back, Regina Silveira, Helena Solberg, and Anna Barros, these scenes retell the drama of the New World conquest and question its reigning idealisms. (See Sichel's essay for discussion of several of these artists.)

Opening the curtain on this new first chapter are Adriana Varejão's contemporary baroque history paintings. Created in the guise of Portugal's famed *azulejos* (blue-and-white decorative tiles), these paintings deftly invert the official story of Brazil's conquest using a visual language favored by its Portuguese conquerers. Beginning with her *Figura de Convite* (Entrance Figure) (1997), a baroque

personification of America as a beautiful, white, female nude bids us welcome with open arms and a comely half-smile. As we visually pass beyond her body and the balustrade, however, it becomes evident that the Garden of Eden into which we are being ushered is one where Amerindian cannibals, practicing the rituals of *anthropofagia*, appear to be winning out over the keepers of the Christian faith. In an earlier work, *Proposta para uma catequese: Parte I Diptico: Morte e Esquartejamento* (Proposal for a Catechesis: Part I Diptych: Death and Dismemberment) (1993), these same images are used to pose a particularly pointed question: What is the difference between the violence of Christ's flagellation and eventual crucifixion and the rites of the indigenous tribes of *terra brasilieris?* Already, as we can see in these works, the bloom is off the rose, the apple has been eaten, the wine has been spilled, and the new paradise is lost.

In another pointed reframing of the privileged status accorded to the Portuguese in colonial discourse, Varejão presents the installation *Testemunhas Oculares X, Y e Z* (Eye Witnesses X, Y and Z) (1997). In this work three staid historicist portraits offer a provocative visualization of the popular expression, "Every Brazilian man needs three women in his life. A white woman to bear his heirs, a black woman to cook for him, and a *mulata* to make love to."[12] This summing up of Portuguese colonial elitism, racism, and sexism offers a powerful deconstructive image of the inherent contradiction between Brazilian miscegenist machismo and the country's long-held myth of racial democracy.

Rosângela Rennó takes a different approach to the "discovery" in her video *Vera Cruz* (True Cross) (2000), an imaginary series of vignettes based on Pero Vaz's letter. Playing off important experimental films from an earlier generation, such as Humberto Mauro's *O descobrimento do Brasil* (The Discovery of Brazil) (1937), Rennó's work is laced with ironic intent. A parody of the grand tradition of historical reenactments on the silver screen as well as more serious forms of docudrama, her video consists of forty-four minutes of film that is blank except for an imaginary dialogue set as subtitles at the bottom of the screen. The video, which seems empty at first, is actually an inflected tabula rasa, allowing the potential for

multiple readings. The words on screen, sepia on white, reproduce the look of Pero Vaz's historic letter but cannot bring the viewer back to that moment of encounter except through his or her imagination. Or, more critically, the actual event between Cabral's men and the Indians is hidden from today's field of vision, veiled forever behind colonizing assumptions and their aftermaths. To understand Rennó's artistic commentary, as the curator Dan Cameron once wrote, the viewer must learn to read between the lines.[13]

While Rennó's *Vera Cruz* effectively uses the light of blank film to reference a deep cultural divide, Regina Silveira's shadow play also pushes the limits of representation. Using linear perspective, the revolutionary Renaissance approach to drawing that was ever so new at the time of the conquest, Silveira's postmodern exercise both visually and conceptually arrests and turns back the course of empire. Entitled *Monudentro* (Inside the Monument) (1986–87/2001), this flat black vinyl shadow recasts the meaning of the famous Bandeiras Monument (1920–53), the symbol of São Paulo. Using perspectival distortion to "get inside" the monument's skin, Silveira wittily questions the social as well as physical consequences of the manifest destiny of the *bandeirantes* (expeditionaries) who explored Brazil's interior from the seventeenth through the nineteenth centuries.

With a related penchant for inversion, *Yndio do Brasil* (Our Indians) (1995), by Sylvio Back, Brazil's first postmodern filmmaker, is a powerfully deconstructed work that provides an elaborate reworking of the documentary genre. Using clips from a variety of film types, Back's nonlinear narrative dissects how cultural stereotyping of Brazil's indigenous populations was used to confirm the fantasies of the colonizers from the seventeenth century on. As his work also makes clear, modern filmmaking in Brazil since the 1920s has become a powerful form of image production and destruction. In itself, it perpetuated a colonizing gaze and patriarchal practice that dictated the eventual disappearance of the Indian from the Brazilian landscape. As the film historian David William Foster has recently pointed out, *Yndio do Brasil* is one of a number of efforts since Brazil's return to democracy in 1985 to represent indigenous cultures that evades centuries-old structures of oppression and extermination.[14]

Adriana Varejão
Figura de Convite
(Entrance Figure), 1997
Oil on canvas
78¾ × 78¾ in.
(200 × 200 cm)
Private collection Celia S. de Birbragher

The Map

As with conquest, "the voice of power writes the world, traces meridians, names its great divisions as if the world were so much putty."[15] Understanding this truism and recognizing that there is a long Eurocentric tradition of arbitrarily emphasizing the Northern over the Southern Hemisphere, it is a critical part of Brazilian and Latin American alterity to attempt to orient and then reorient oneself globally and locally. In the works of Anna Bella Geiger, Sandra Cinto, Oriana Duarte, Sandra Kogut, Brígida Baltar, Lygia Pape, and Sonia Labouriau, this process takes on existential dimensions.

In her art Anna Bella Geiger incorporates all the constituent elements that cartographers have used to represent the world since the voyages of discovery. In this reinvented cartography, however, she does not offer the typical coherent vision of global order. Instead, since the early 1970s Geiger's mapping strategies have emphasized geographic fragmentation, elision, and discontinuity, played out in a variety of media. Using these strategies,

she has portrayed Brazil as a place of action and a locus of change and exchange. In her recent *Fronteiriços* (Borderlines) series (1995–present), she fills shallow file drawers with elegantly reconfigured maps of the Southern and Northern Hemispheres. Whether stamped out in encaustic or traced in precious and base metals, her waxen seas are fluid, the continents drift, meridians reposition themselves, and their existence appears poised to continue outside the box. Redefined in this way, these maps present metaphysical speculations about the territorial construction of Brazil's new global sphere.

Using a different medium, Sandra Cinto also maps out new worlds in consonance with a truly enchanted vision of the sublime. In her gallery-size environments she creates dreamlike spaces that seem to go on forever using naive yet elegant line drawings of trees and forests, clouds and stars, cliffs and ladders, candelabras and candles, and sometimes tears. Existing on an uninflected, monochromatic ground, these elements never truly cohere into a single unified whole. The sheer scale of the walls she

Above:

Jerônimo Marini

Orbis Typus Universalis Tabula, ca. 1511

Facsimile; color lithograph (produced 1923)

9⅞ × 13¾ in. (25 × 35 cm)

Fundação Biblioteca Nacional, Rio de Janeiro

Opposite:

Sylvio Back

Yndio do Brasil (Our Indians), 1995

Video version of 35mm film with English subtitles (70 min.)

Courtesy of the artist

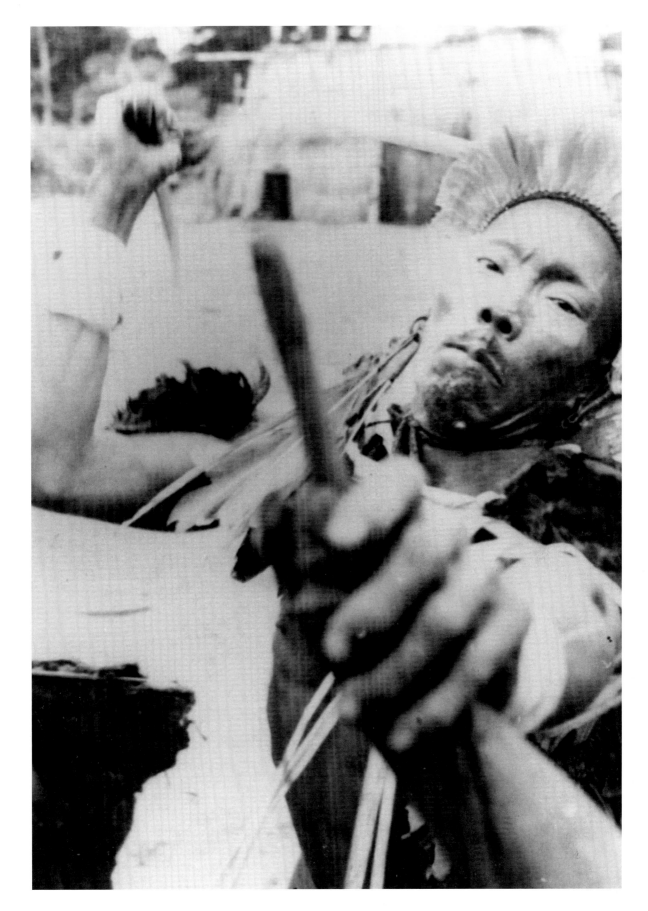

draws on, the distance between the objects, and the transparency of the drawing prevent such fusion. Like constellations in a night sky, her worlds go on beyond the frame and can never truly be colonized except perhaps by the mind's eye.

As a complement to these two artists' works, Oriana Duarte maps pathways as well. Hers, however, represent the real world as she physically moves through villages, towns, and cities from northeastern Brazil to its southern region. In the role of a geographic anthropophagist, she documents each of her visits by performing and videotaping a new version of *Sopa do pedra* (Stone Soup) and by collecting town maps, anthems, pens, and other paraphernalia for her *O gabinete de souvenirs de A coisa em si* (Souvenir Cabinet of the Thing-in-Itself) (1998–2001). The centerpiece of her souvenirs, her video of *Sopa do pedra* (1998), records her ingestion, both physical and artistic, of each specific locale as she cooks and eats broth made from stones she has gathered from the area. In this piece, a concept that gives a new meaning to the term *regional flavor*, Duarte dissolves the geographic borders of exteriority and interiority. Using the cooking pot rather than the machete, she comes not to claim Brazil's mineral wealth, as the *bandeirantes* once did, but to reterritorialize the localities by absorbing their mineral essence into her body.

Another record of an itinerant and ephemeral claiming of territory is Brígida Baltar's digital video disc *A coleta da neblina* (Collecting Mist) (1996–2001), in which the artist documents her dawn forays into the mountains surrounding Rio de Janeiro. Dressed in a specially made bubble-wrap costume, she assumes a quasi-scientific guise and literally takes in the properties of the region by placing vials and beakers of mist in specially constructed pockets or slings. In this practice, one that she has ritualistically observed over a period of years, she relinquishes any claim to scientific objectivity or intent, leaving viewers to ponder the artist's relation to nature and the ineffability of art.

Metaphors of transmutation of the corporeal and territorial are key to the performance-based works of Lygia Pape and Sonia Labouriau. In Pape's well-known film *O Ovo* (The Egg) (1968), the artist's body slowly breaks through a membrane, rectangular rather than ovoid, fused with the motion of the sea and a silent horizon. A reorientation of European modernism in a Brazilian context, the

original version of this work featured samba musicians bursting though the elastic skin, their percussion reaching a crescendo as they entered this new world, passing from one state to another with a new musical beat.[16]

Reflecting a similar attention to a creation-based metaphor for process and elapsed time is Sonia Labouriau's *Pássaros Migratórios* (Migratory Birds) (1992–2001). In this installation she performs a simple sequence of movements over and over again, akin to a musical theme or a bit of sign language. Through this sequencing she creates hundreds of miniature bird sculptures, molded from the natural red pigmented paste that is used for cooking and native to her home region of Minas Gerais. On each day of the installation, one bird is placed in a dish of clear water and dissolves into paste again, thus completing its migratory process.

The Virgin

Another highly charged dimension of difference and alterity is developed in *Virgin Territory*'s third grouping of works. In the art of Valeska Soares, Nazareth Pacheco, Janaína Tschäpe, Laura Lima, Rosana Paulino, and Beth Moysés, gender and sexuality interweave with history, often ending up on the precipice of violence.

Valeska Soares's installation Untitled (from *Strangelove*) (1996), in particular, offers up an elegant yet physically spare commentary on the nature of tainted love. Her vision of love, like the vision of the Garden of Eden or the *orbis alterius* imagined by Pero Vaz, is inviting to the eye but will ultimately prove deadly to the touch. In the series *Strangelove*, she adorns glass hummingbird feeders with exquisite lead flowers and fills two of their three separated chambers with a lovely red nectar made from wine and poison. The viewer, like a bird, is set loose through the maze of glass vessels where the threat of encounter, attraction, betrayal, and death is omnipresent. As signified by the fragile balance between each vessel's vacuum-sealed chambers, for Soares the world of virtue and the world of the senses are coequals from the beginning. And the seal between them may some day break, no matter how difficult and potentially destructive the consummation of their relationship will be.

For Nazareth Pacheco, as for Soares, beauty plays a potentially deadly game. In *Jóais* (Jewelry) (1997–2001), Pacheco has encased beautifully wrought beads, chokers, and pendants in rows on rows of crystal boxes that set off their precious objecthood. On closer inspection, however, the viewer becomes aware that these adornments are made not only of crystals and black jet but also of fish hooks, needles, scalpels, and razor blades. As accoutrements of attraction, these articles recall rosaries, Victorian collars, pearl necklaces, and lace. As ornaments, they play into the need, driven by society's values, for enhancement of the female body through clothes, jewelry, cosmetics, and even plastic surgery. In this sense they can be seen as symbols of submission to a feminine cultural identity that can be dangerous to those who take it upon themselves.

Compared to the work of Soares and Pacheco, Janaína Tschäpe's trio of videos—*He Drowned in Her Eyes as She Called Him to Follow: Wave* (2000), *Medusa* (2000), and *Moss* (2001)—combine gender, sexuality, geography, and myth into a song that once again carries with it the fall from a position of equivocated power. Built on her fascination with maritime voyages and legendary sea creatures, Tschäpe's performance-based videos present women who carry with them an overwhelming sexual power: the siren with her alluring songs of desire; a marooned gorgon with the power to turn men to stone; or the goddess Iemanjá, divinity of the sea, whose interventions on behalf of love and life are a tangible part of Afro-Brazilian *candomblé* spiritualism.

The art and imagery of Rosana Paulino and Beth Moysés clearly reveal that they have sided with a woman's cause when it comes to the trials of the flesh. Paulino created her *Model* drawings (1996–98) specifically to argue that the current ideal of female beauty—symbolized by freakishly proportioned, impossibly thin, light-skinned dolls—is actually the antithesis of femininity as well as physical well-being. Paulino proposes "to draw as an exercise in creation. To enter history in a search for another body. To think about a body that is not so arid, that breathes and throbs strongly because it exists, round, fat, sensual, lazy, lascivious, strong, fearless. It is this body, a source of pleasure, that is sought."[17]

Reacting against a society in which aggression toward women is commonplace, Moysés's art is poised to fight back. From *Luta* (Battle) (1998), which depicts white boxing gloves adorned with wedding lace, to her video *Memória do Afeto* (Memory of Affection) (2000), the artist gives form to her outrage over physical and sexual violence against women, "the issue of the 1990s" in Brazil.[18] Questioning the value of the Judeo-Christian marriage ritual that was first inculcated into the Brazilian social order during colonial times, Moysés exposes the fallacy of *marianismo*, which prescribes a life of humility and self-sacrifice that few woman can afford to live by while machismo, with its aggressive assertion of male chauvinism and violence, goes on unchecked.

Laura Lima's Managed Actions take up the body as a domain for trangressive and potentially ruinous behavior, but in an extreme physical sense different from these other artists' works. In her series entitled *Homem=carne/mulher=carne* (Man= Flesh/Woman=Flesh) (1996–99), Lima sets out to push right up to or even beyond the limits of the body's functional capacity. Often choreographing her performers' actions to the point of exhaustion, her proposals for actions bear no ill will against them, and yet the threat of immobilization, dissolution, or both is often inherent in agreeing to take on her odd, Sisyphean tasks.

The Mix

In this part of *Virgin Territory*, cultural intermixture—*mestiço*—and the transmutations it makes visible in everyday life are articulated through the art of Anna Maria Maiolino, Silvana Afram, Mônica Nador, Nelson Leirner, and Miguel Rio Branco.

Beginning with Maiolino's installation *Arroz & Feijão* (Rice and Beans) (first created in 1979), one of the ritual centers of the home—the dinner table— becomes a place of action and political commentary. In the middle of this space, Maiolino placed a long central table, overlaid it with a black cloth to resemble a catafalque, and set it with dishes containing germinating rice (the grain brought to Brazil by African slaves) and beans (a staple of Iberian cooking). At the four corners of the installation, like the four corners of Brazil, she then set tables with white cloths and empty tableware. In this setting, sustenance, humankind's basic need, confronts scarcity. Created at a time when Brazil was emerging from economic depression but was still ruled by a military regime whose plans for modernization exacerbated the conditions of the unlanded poor, the work mocked the idea that a country of supposedly

Nazareth Pacheco
Untitled, 1997
Crystal beads, needles, and acrylic
19⅝ × 15¾ × 2⅜ in. (50 × 40 × 6 cm)
Collection of Museum of Contemporary Art, Niterói, Brazil

inexhaustible riches cannot feed its people. However, as she suggests, despite the implication of scarcity, the plates germinating with the fruits of the soil hold in themselves the promise of plenty. An assertion of life over death, the installation is a site of renewal, offering a space where humankind can construct or reconstruct its own history and culture.[19]

For the writer and filmmaker Silvana Afram, the artist's stance as social activist is also important. Her film *Mulheres Negras* (Black Women of Brazil) (1986) was one of the earliest contributions to opening up the country's contemporary debate on identity, gender, and racism. In this video Afram presents face-to-face interchanges with women who by their very being dismantle the myth of Brazil as a racial democracy and its failed ideal of societal whitening. Although it is true that racial mixing—miscegenation—has been an accepted pattern in Brazil since colonization began and "passing" is

common, class and culture still play a part. As Afram makes clear, for black women of Brazil deep traces of discrimination exist and are interlinked with poverty in this country that is the world's second largest "African nation."[20]

In the late 1990s Mônica Nador linked her richly decorative painting style to a social cause in her ongoing project *Paredes Pinturas* (Painting Walls) (1997–present). Working in the *favelas* (shantytowns) of Brazil and other countries, including Mexico, Nador brings people together in developing simple home beautification projects. Creating a kind of self-help society, not unlike the Catholic Church's Christian-based communities, evangelical storefronts, or Oludum and Ile Aiyé *bloco afro* Carnival groups, Nador's work bridges gaps between individuals yet stresses the great national divide between the people's activities and the pressing need for more tangible social services for the poor.

Mônica Nador
Untitled, 2000
Site-specific wall painting;
acrylic on wood
Vila Rodhia, São José dos Campos
Courtesy of the artist

In this intermixture that is the realm of the everyday, cultural activism can also pull in the reifying direction of art as a measure of social engagement. In this context Nelson Leirner's witty and ironic resuscitations of common, mass-produced popular icons and other forms of kitsch offer a reorientation of elitist perspectives. In his series *Santa Ceia* (The Last Supper) (1990), for example, he establishes a new and revitalized context for Leonardo da Vinci's icon, so worn out by endless repetition that it has almost ceased to signify. Using the work's desacralization as a source of invention, he enables the viewer to cast a new eye on the homespun objects that bear da Vinci's faint imprint: familiar apostle-boarders, whom the curator Agnaldo Farias describes as "frequent inhabitants of our dining rooms or of the pages of the bibles that our grandmothers so judiciously leave open on the buffet or china cabinets."[21] Reworking each appropriated image through superimpositions, collages, and inversions, Leirner practices a kind of pop cultural transubstantiation. Whether unraveling a cheap tapestry, placing a plaster sculpture in a fish tank, or surrounding a picture postcard with iridescent butterfly wings, Leirner transposes the "fake original" from its marginal status as kitsch into the realm of art. In this way he reinvigorates the "sainted supper," the event at which the ritual transmigration of the wine and the wafer actually began, with a new sense of purpose while he celebrates the inventive variety of popular forms of belief.

With his decidedly baroque sensibility, Miguel Rio Branco, a filmmaker and cinematographer as well as a photographer, restores dignity to common places and difficult situations through his art, lifting for a time their accustomed stigma of banality, immorality, and poverty. His art embraces the prostitutes of Salvador's Maciel district, charnel houses, street children, prisons, boxers from Rio's Academy Santa Rosa, and others who make up the the diaspora of the dispossessed. Supersaturated color, counterpoint cuts and fast edits, dissolving frames and mirrored images, intense chiaroscuro, and other forms of fragmentation make his photographs and slide presentations theatrical, hypnotic, and sensual. The connection to the real moment is blurred, and the viewer's sense of actualized space and time is thrown into the "sphere of enigma . . . another more sensitive universe, re-dimensioned by its subjective poetry."[22] While viewers can physically locate themselves in relation to his pictures, they cannot be so sure how to subjectively judge the appearances of the things they see.

Reconfiguring the Island of Earth

The metaphorical content of the exhibition *Virgin Territory* began with the idea, brought by Brazil's conquerers, that the New World was an *orbis alterius*—a world apart—and ends with the notion that Brazil, as it enters the twenty-first century, is now an integral part of the *orbis terrarum*—this island of earth that is our contemporary global consciousness.

In this new context, *Virgin Territory* offers a series of postmodern world views that reconfigure aspects of Brazil's history and location based on the realignments of gender theory and postcolonial discourse. The artists in *Virgin Territory* chart current renegotiations of issues of power and representation that were introduced into Brazil through Portugal's discovery, and they pose artistic alterities to the Old World's master narratives. With little nostalgia for memories but with a deep sense of history, identity, and locale, they and their works transgress limits and cross borders to establish a new sense of being *in* the world.

A Final Note: About the Sourcebook Essays

Following the essays about the artists represented in *Virgin Territory* are four sourcebook essays that discuss aspects of Brazilian identity from the initial conquest to today's contemporary mix. The first of these, by the cultural geographer Pedro P. Geiger, consists of seven propositions that illuminate defining moments in Brazil's identity formation as seen through cartographic representations and territorial shifts. The second, by the social historian Giralda Seyferth, looks at ethnicity, modernity, and assimilation policies in Brazil as part of a national ideal of social progress in the twentieth century. The third, by the psychologist and art theorist Suely Roelnik, profiles Brazilian *anthropofagia* as a state of being and a psychological practice that redefines power relationships. The fourth, by the film historian Robert Stam, discusses how the cinema stages and represents a multicultural society, especially Afro-Brazilians, indigenous peoples, and women. As points of contact with other disciplines and as considerations of issues of otherness, these essays offer additional background information and add breadth and richness to the curators' essays. ■

"But while we cannot see globalization as a simple extension of imperialism as early globalization theory proposed . . . the engagement of imperial culture by post-colonial societies offers a compelling model for the relationship between the local and the global today."

Bill Ashcroft, *Post-Colonial Transformation*[1]

The History of the Present

BY   BERTA   SICHEL

■ Just as the world as it is now understood cannot be disconnected from European ideological power, the New World was already divided between Spain and Portugal even before it was charted and inhabited. Setting the limits of the Portuguese domain, a papal edict issued two years after Columbus's arrival on a small island in the Bahamas allotted to Spain all land that might be discovered west of an imaginary line—a conceptual boundary that stretched southwest one hundred leagues off the Azores and Cape Verde Islands.

Challenging Spain's dominion of space and for that matter her dominance of vision and language,[2] Pedro Álvares Cabral sighted the coast of Brazil in 1500. A new region was thus introduced onto the world stage, governed by a recent papal dictate, the Treaty of Tordesillas (1494). The key to this expansion was also the key to a new geographical conception of the world: Portugal was endowed with all the land and wealth located up to 370 leagues from the Azores and Cape Verde.

The new boundary sliced through the center of what is now Brazil.

Taking advantage of disputes within the Spanish empire, Portuguese settlers in Brazil gradually infiltrated into the unexplored section of Spanish territory. By the seventeenth century, in defiance of the papal edict, gold and slave hunters—the legendary *bandeirantes*, as these explorers are romantically described in Brazilian history books—were regularly crossing the Tordesillas line. Without the least opposition or struggle, hundreds of square miles of "virgin territory," with all of its natural resources, were incorporated into the Portuguese commonwealth. Why the Spaniards did not attempt to reclaim their lawful property has never been fully explained. Historians believe that they were already overstretched, unable to control existing rebellions against their authority and too absorbed in "civilizing" the "barbarian peoples" who inhabited the many regions of their vast empire to worry about the blank spaces still inaccessible to them.

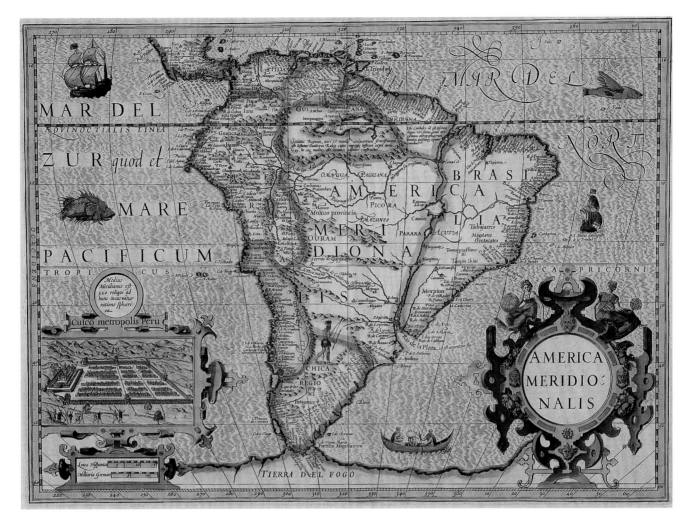

Gerard Mercator
(1512–94), designer
Jodocus Hondius
(1563–1612), editor
América Meridionalis, 1606
Hand-colored engraving
14⅛ × 19¼ in. (36 × 49 cm)
Collection BancoSantos,
São Paulo

One fact is indisputable, however: despite variations in colonial ideology, the experience of colonization created and shaped the identity of all of the settler communities of the Atlantic world, including the United States and Canada. Carving up the continent and overthrowing native civilizations, the imperial powers that colonized the Americas imported their metropolitan set of cultural, social, and religious values and incorporated these into the unfolding narrative of the colonies' newly forming identities. In spite of the differences between mother countries and the varied character of their colonial discourses, by the end of the seventeenth century three trends were consistently evident throughout the New World: a drastic decline in the native population; a growing number of black slaves; and the emergence of a *mestiço* population, the result of the interbreeding of Europeans, Africans, and indigenous peoples.

Brazil was a Portuguese colony for almost four hundred years. Its ethnic and cultural past is extremely diverse; historians who have studied the Portuguese ethos believe that Phoenicians, Romans, Jews, and Arabs all left their mark on its cultural and social structures. The Romans, for example, bequeathed to the Portuguese the structure of their language as well as the organization of certain social institutions, such as Roman law, while the Arabs influenced a large range of cultural activities, from music to architecture. In Brazil the blend was further enriched by indigenous and later African elements. This process resulted in the birth of a new culture, the Brazilian culture.[3] The links among all the knowledge sets of these different genotypes have established an innovative group of connections—rules of inclusion and exclusion—operating on the assumption of the superiority of the colonizer's culture over others. Yet, as many authors have pointed out, the unfamiliar synergy among these miscegenational forces in Brazil may have been the reason why the freshly forged Brazilian identities were so unevenly constructed. In general, it was hard to establish any binding consensus on what these new identities should or should not be.[4]

In light of this historical process, the global question that should be asked today is, Does the issue of colonization involve an intellectual orientation that requires a constant looking back to the past? Why do we keep harking back to the consequences of bygone power relationships that are surely irrelevant to the present day?[5] For Bill Ashcroft, a professor at New South Wales University who has written on postcolonial theory, these relationships may only seem unimportant for our times. In fact, it is the engagement with European imperialism and its transformation within a postcolonial society that has given color and identity to the very nature of contemporary societies. Brazil is no exception.

The Exhibition

Virgin Territory is not a historical exhibition—that is, its purpose is not to display works made in the past and show them as the country's artistic patrimony. It is concerned with the past, however, because of the engagement Ashcroft talks about and also because the past is essential to understanding the present. This exploration of the nature of this engagement, past and present, is certainly one of the most deeply felt of contemporary aesthetic and creative possibilities.

Within this context the danger of historicism—looking back to history as the only determinant of events—also recedes. As a curatorial enterprise, *Virgin Territory* acknowledges that no past can be understood purely on its own terms. It attempts to expose, through artworks from various media, the development of a culture that, like other postcolonial cultures, has had to struggle for its own

statements and systems. The present determines issues of interest in art history, while the past takes on new meanings through works constructed in the particular space that Homi K. Bhabha calls the "third space of enunciation"[6]—the ambivalent space where postcolonial identities always emerged. Going back into one's culture becomes a way of rewriting and reinterpreting the past while intersecting with the present. The past, as Arjun Appadurai says, "is not a land to return to in a simple politics of memory"; rather, it has become a "synchronic warehouse of cultural scenarios."[7] In this context colonial subordination becomes a postcolonial insurrection.

Virgin Territory, a contemporary art project, revives that which has already happened. Infused with a sense of Brazil's roots, which is the exhibition's local focus, *Virgin Territory* addresses a broad range of topics from contemporary global society: cultural interchange, environmental concerns, politics, place, space, religion, and race, among others. The most crucial and perhaps the most intransigent question it poses is how the exhibition disrupts the notion of a static point of view. The artworks selected include elements that in various ways embody the land, the local identity. When museumgoers seat themselves in front of a computer screen in the exhibition gallery and click on Anna Barros's computer animation *Como Pegar um Saci-Si* (How to Catch a Saci-Si) (1998), for example, they will see not just another computer-generated image but also a consummate demonstration of a local mythology. Barros takes advantage of digital technology to speak about home. Using three-dimensional software, she manipulates the idea of Saci, the fabled one-legged black goblin that likes to play tricks. The images that appear on the screen are closer to abstraction than figuration, yet the whirling forms and emphasis on the color red—both important elements of the myth—suggest the question of identity. The mutant Saci-Si underscores the way collective memories can be translated into technological form without losing their authenticity. Through this piece Barros also argues successfully against a common claim that contemporary technological society necessarily lacks historical consciousness.

The 1950s: Decade of Change

If it is true that history advances to the tune of technological progress, imagine Brazil in 1950, at the start of a decade marked by a complex series of transformations in society, politics, and economics that sketched the profile of a nascent new modernity. This decade proved fertile ground for the emergence of refreshing proposals in the arts. Worldwide, the postwar system underwent extraordinary upheavals. Technology lifted off during the process of readjustment of international relations, enabling some underdeveloped countries such as Brazil to attain a reasonable level of industrial modernization within certain limits and in specific sectors.

Under the slogan "Fifty Years in Five," President Juscelino Kubistchek's administration set out a target schedule aimed at updating Brazil and equipping it with core industries and consumer goods. During this period, from 1955 to 1960, Brazilian society acquired a decisively urban character, a result of the government's modernization and expansion policies, tight inflationary controls, and foreign capital investment that underwrote the installation of a new, sophisticated industrial capacity. For the first time but irrevocably the city became the pivot of Brazil's national life, and the mass of city dwellers made themselves heard on the political stage. In his poem *Crescendo num Pais Ultramarinho*, Silviano Santiago related the experiences of a boy on the brink of adolescence in a country that changes day by day, its eyes longingly fixed—no longer on its previous mentor France and all of fusty old Europe, now part of the past—but on the United States.

In Brazilian art the first signs of post–World War II modernization was to be found in the establishment of the Museums of Modern Art in São Paulo and Rio de Janeiro (1948 and 1949) and the inauguration of the São Paulo Bienal (1951). The Bienal was an unprecedented event in Brazil, an art exhibition that attracted serious international attention while at the same time exposing the local artistic community and local public to the latest offerings from abroad. The architecture of the modernist Oscar Niemeyer flourished in conjunction with that of Le Corbusier. Sectors of the São Paulo bourgeoisie even showed themselves nervously willing to finance the Vera Cruz Company, a first step toward the Brazilian dream of a Hollywood-style film industry.

Brazil, in fact, has a century-old tradition of movie making, and by 1900 home-grown productions

Anna Barros
Como Pegar um Saci-Si
(How to Catch a Saci-Si),
1998
Computer animation
Courtesy of the artist

controlled the market. In his essay "Brazilian Cinema: Race and Representation" in this catalogue, Robert Stam, considered the foremost U.S. authority on Brazilian cinema, writes about the development of the film industry and attempts to describe how Brazilian cinema stages and represents a multicultural society. In the process he asks several questions, including, "To what extent have Afro-Brazilians and indigenous Brazilians . . . been able to represent themselves?"

This question is answered in his analysis of "tropical multiculturalism," which examines the history of race in Brazilian cinema and culture[8] and provides a selection of films and videos addressing these themes. Despite its idealization of the European purpose in conquering the New World, Humberto Mauro's *O descobrimento do Brasil* (The Discovery of Brazil) (1937), screened in this exhibition, is an avant-garde film for its

time. In it, unlike most Hollywood films devoted to the "discovery" of America, local tribes speak their own languages. Partially inspired by *The First Mass* (1891), a landmark Brazilian painting by the academic artist Victor Meirelles, and set to music by Heitor Villa-Lobos, the film appropriates the text of the 1500 letter describing the new lands written to the Portuguese king by Pero Vaz de Caminha, the official scribe of the Portuguese fleet.

Indigenous peoples remained the subject of further films produced until the 1930s and then disappeared from the repertoire of Brazilian cinematography for a few decades. In the 1970s, coinciding with the growing awareness of the diversity of cultural expressions, native cultures were brought back to the large screen. These cultures, until now thought to exist outside history, became an active component in the representation of the local.[9]

Sylvio Back's film collage *Yndio do Brasil* (Our Indians) (1995), included in this exhibition, is "a precious anthology of documentary and feature film representation of the Brazilian Indian," according to Stam.[10] Back had worked with the theme before, but here he splices in extracts from several classics: George Dyott's *The River of Doubt* (1913–27), Nelson Pereira dos Santos's *Como era gostoso meu frances* (1975), and Andre Luis Oliveira's *Lenda de Ubirajara* (1975), among others, in addition to several ethnographic films. In the contemporary world, where the visual does not always offer a transparent window, *Yndio do Brasil* is a rarity. Ironic and mordant, it encapsulates the essence and effects of the white European gaze on its indigenous subject.

This transparent space of representation is also evident in *Mulheres Negras* (Black Women of Brazil) (1986), a video by Silvana Afram. Her images consistently tie into her politics and her view of Brazilian society as a racially segregated system. Afram's women, who validate their lives through music and religion, are portrayed through their own experiences and their expressions of that experience.

During the 1950s and 1960s the gradual configuration of a modern urban-industrial complex in Brazil strengthened the links between the domestic social process and the dynamics of the international system. A considerable segment of the country's population was beginning to benefit from a lifestyle that increasingly resembled that of the inhabitants of any major global urban center. As distances became shorter, people grew ever more appreciative of technological conquests, with their speedy repercussions on the "urban imaginary" and the conditions of daily life in large cities. Like other colonial countries, Brazil was sampling—and enjoying—the experiences of cosmopolitanism: theaters, restaurants, tourism, and television, to name a few. By 1950 Brazil was already transmitting regular television broadcasts and embracing the euphoria of the ideology of developmentalism.

In the exhibition *Virgin Territory*, the 1950s is deconstructed through another movie, *Carmen Miranda: Bananas Is My Business* (1995), by Helena Solberg. This film is more than a documentary about Miranda, the "lady in the tutti-frutti hat" who brought to American wartime audiences the seductive rhythm, exoticism, and sensuality of the tropics. Using film clips, home movies, interviews, and scenes of a performance by the drag queen Erick Barreto playing Carmen, Solberg examines the Brazilian colonial discourse from a

Helena Solberg
Carmen Miranda: Bananas Is My Business, 1995
Video version of 35mm film with English subtitles
(92 min.)
Courtesy Women Make Movies

different perspective: Carmen the woman, traveling to the United States at the outbreak of World War II, riding to an imagined geography in order to carve out her own space, yet always remaining an outsider.

Successors to Modernism

The 1950s in Brazil will be remembered not only as the Carmen Miranda decade or the decade of development of industrialism and the formation of an affluent urban society. This was also the decade in which visual art cut its way into the historical present.

Brazilian modern art came under fire with the emergence of the concrete movement in 1952.[11] Two groups were formed: one literary, founded by Décio Pignatari and Haroldo and Augusto de Campos and accompanied by the launch of *Noigrandes* magazine; the other, Ruptura, concerned with the visual arts and attracting painters and sculptors such as Geraldo de Barrios, Waldemar Cordeiro, and Kasmer Fejer. Ruptura initiated a reaction against the subjective premises of one strand of figurative expressionism, corresponding to the most recent trends in North American art. At the same time the group took a stand against, in the words of Cordeiro, "the hedonistic conception of abstract art."

By 1956 the concrete movement's theoretical backdrop was firmly established and the basic formal procedures were clearly stipulated. In December of that year the *Noigrandes* team joined forces with painters and sculptors associated with the movement to mount the *First National Exhibition of Concrete Art*, shown at the São Paulo Museum of Modern Art. Among the participants were the artists Geraldo de Barrios, Amilcar da Castro, Lygia Clark, Waldemar Cordeiro, César Oiticica, Hélio Oiticica, Lygia Pape, Ivan Serpa, Alfredo Volpi, and Franz J. Weissemann. Poets invited as special guests included Ronaldo Azeredo, Augusto and Haroldo de Campos, Waldemar Dias Pino, Ferreira Gullar, and Décio Pignatari.

Today Lygia Clark and Hélio Oiticica are considered by the international artistic community as the founders of Brazil's modernity in contemporary art, an almost natural consequence of the modernization of society. Clark, a student of Burle Marx and later in Paris of Fernand Leger, began her career as a painter but very early began to experiment with other art forms. In 1960 she began her famous *Bichos* series, which were shown the following year at the São Paulo Bienal, and she developed her series of works called *trabalhos vivenciais*, which require public participation. These include *Caminhando* (1963) and *A casa é o corpo* (1968), which together completely abolish the distinction between spaces, from both the artist's and the public's perception. Both Clark and Oiticica are paradigms of contemporary art in the country, even though other Brazilian artists of the same generation do not always concur with this assessment of Oiticica.[12] Unquestionably he was an original: a genial, maverick theorist and a tireless challenger of international art movements. He was also determinedly marginal, more at home in the *favelas* (shantytowns), the samba school, or the underground bars of New York's East Village, where he lived for eight years, than in the salons of the jet set of international art. His radicalism led him to treat art as a form of protest against any kind of repression—intellectual, aesthetic, and, above all, social.[13]

The concrete movement became the object of heated argument. When the show organized in São Paulo opened in Rio de Janeiro in February 1957, the *First National Exhibition of Concrete Art* became the most talked-about event in the city. Mounted in the lobby of the Ministry of Culture, the show included poster-poems presented next to the paintings and sculptures. The posters' design had been overseen by the artist and publicist Hermelindo Fiaminghini, who also participated in the exhibition.[14] The movement received much attention in the press—newspapers and magazines pictured examples of this new direction in art—but the euphoria was short-lived.

From 1964 until the early 1980s, Brazil was plunged into darkness. Although the period of military dictatorship—led by a series of generals beginning with Umberto Castelo Branco—was not as violently repressive as its counterparts in Chile or Argentina, it did sink the country into absolute intellectual poverty.[15]

Artistic activity was not exempt from the new order imposed by the regime. Throughout the 1970s it underwent what the Brazilian curator and art critic Frederico de Moraes called "the cooling of avant-garde activity."[16] Yet if on one hand a visible slowdown occurred, on the other hand artists continued to create art, although in unorthodox forms.

This decade—a period characterized by "the reflective wedge," according to Moraes—may not have been quite so stagnant after all. Reflection continued, but now there was also an incentive to investigate new aesthetic parameters, burrowing into what was happening on the political and social fronts in Brazil.

Although channels of personal expression were blocked, it was during the 1970s that, in consonance with international movements, women in different areas of the arts and humanities started to think about postcolonialism and gender relations. A number of studies, although incipient, began to retrieve buried data, bringing numerous authors to the surface and opening new fields of investigation. Women who in fact played a prominent role during the heyday of modernism, with Tarsila do Amaral as their paradigm, were now even freer to explore and rethink the hegemonic maps of representation that privileged the male gaze and moved toward the postcolonial moment, despite the political situation. In spite of the difficulties of living under the military regime, their voices were articulated both textually and visually, and they were able to take their place in history.[17]

In the field of visual art, women artists along the Rio–São Paulo axis began to make art with a political content, an unprecedented move in those days. Even now these works remain little known or studied, even in Brazil, despite a handful of recent shows attempting to correct the record of that period. Amelia Toledo, Lygia Clark, Lygia Pape, Regina Silveira, Anna Bella Geiger, and Anna Maria Maiolino, among others, resorted to new artistic strategies to denounce both political and gender repression, while broaching issues relating to the representation of the human body.[18] Many of these artists are included in this exhibition, and even if their work has taken a different path today, at the time it indicated an awareness of the need for self-expression within the context of gender politics, not to mention the indisputable politics of social and cultural repression.

Under the yoke of this repression, these women artists were among those who shaped their work into an instrument of protest. The re-creation of Anna Maria Maiolino's installation *Arroz & Feijão* (Rice and Beans) (1979), is of particular interest. Apparently simple, the installation requires little more than four square tables, conventionally set; in the middle of this group is one rectangular table covered in a black cloth with matching black napkins. On the center table lie a number of dishes filled with soil, in which rice and black beans germinate. Created under the military dictatorship in an artist-run alternative space, the piece was thoroughly in keeping with international art movements of the time—conceptual art and *arte povera*—and yet was entirely focused on the local situation and represented the neediness of the Brazilian people on many levels. When it was first shown, it was so real that not many people saw it as art.

Women were not the only ones to aim their work against Brazil's political ills. Hélio Oiticica, Carlos Zilio, Antonio Manuel, and Nelson Leirner did so as well. At the end of the 1960s, Leirner, whose art is included in the exhibition, showed in Brasília an installation entitled *O porco*, a clear allusion to the military regime. It was promptly destroyed by the police.[19]

Another field of artistic exploration—and in some cases explosive politics—in the 1970s was the new technology of video. Despite the fact that the national borders were sealed and news, books, and films were censored, Brazilian artists added video making to the national artistic repertoire, in timely congruence with the international avant-garde. Lacking technical background and predecessors, Brazilian artists rapidly evolved strategies to exploit the new medium. Their fearless adoption of this technology, at that time only cautiously approached in the United States, deserves further study, as does the content of this remarkable output.

Again, women were at the forefront of such new artistic experiments. During this time Anna Bella Geiger, Sônia Andrade, and Leticia Parente produced pieces that earned them international renown. They looked at themselves—their bodies, biographies, daily lives, gender, and identity—raising issues that took more than ten years to be accepted and widely embraced by the art world. Women also used the new medium to create sociopolitical analyses of the myths and facts of patriarchal culture, revealing socioeconomic realities and political ideologies that dominated everyday life. People were beginning to realize that gender, rather than an isolated construct, is dependent on the matrix of the ideological discourses that define nation, sex, race, and class.

Nelson Leirner
Porco Empalhado
(Stuffed Pig), 1996
Wooden crate, stuffed pig,
and ham
33 × 63 × 24 in.
(83 × 159 × 62 cm)
Collection of Pinacoteca
do Estado de São Paulo

In 1975 the exhibition *Video Art*, organized by Suzanne Delehanty for the Institute of Contemporary Art at the University of Pennsylvania, for the first time brought together video works by more than sixty artists, including Vito Acconci, Wolf Vostell, Nam June Paik, and Eleanor Antin, as well as Geiger and Andrade. Geiger, who represented Brazil at the Venice Biennale of 1980, is an unorthodox artist with a repertoire that runs the gamut of video, photography, objects, and installations. *Virgin Territory* includes two videotapes created by Geiger in 1976 in addition to some of her more recent works. *Mapas Elementales nº 1* and *nº 3* (Elemental Maps #1 and #3) (1976) are more than an anecdotal commentary on how Latin America is represented through clichés about race, mysticism, and economic dependency. Featuring a multiplicity of social, ethnic, and cul-

tural ideas condensed with economy of language into three minutes, this videotape, like others in the same series, constitutes a trajectory related to Brazil the place as well as to Brazil the space. To understand a new place or space—even temporarily, as during the time spent viewing an exhibition like *Virgin Territory*—viewers must construct personal points of reference based not only on what they see but also on their intuition and comprehension of the undeclared meaning of words and images.

From the 1970s onward, independent video production grew more sophisticated, opting for an innovative approach to both content and formal language. Following the path of the first video makers, Arthur Omar, Rafael França, Sandra Kogut, and Eder Santos also crossed Brazilian art frontiers with their dense, poetic video works, which soon found

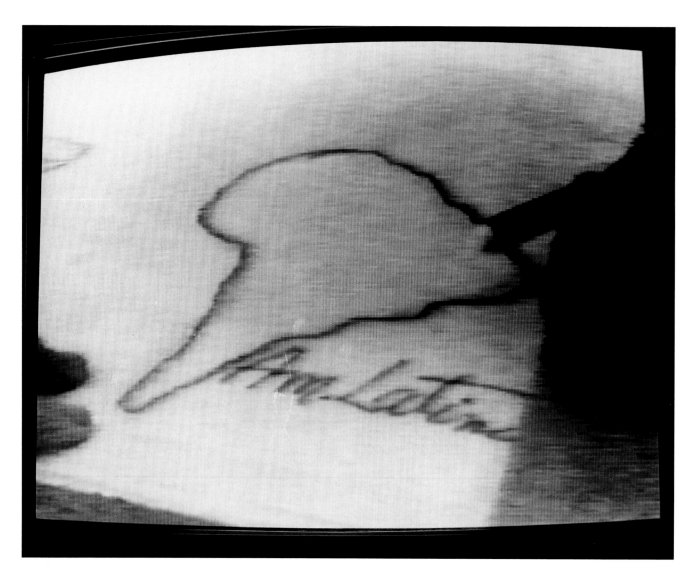

Anna Bella Geiger
Mapas Elementales nº 1
(Elemental Maps #1), 1976
Video (3 min.)
Courtesy of the artist

a place in the collections of the Art Institute of Chicago, Museum of Modern Art in New York, and Centre Georges Pompidou in Paris. Today, however, their works are rarely included in Brazilian and Latin American exhibitions, even though their importance has been widely acknowledged.

A New Global Context

The advent of the 1980s brought a glimmer of hope to this tropical society. President Jimmy Carter's visit in 1978 and the subsequent declaration of political amnesty heralded a softening of the military's repression. With the prospect of imminent democracy, the atmosphere of excitement spread to the art world. São Paulo became Brazil's hegemonic cultural center, and the Bienal, after years of international boycott that had seriously damaged its reputation, resumed its place on the world stage

with a new, more global perspective. Directed by Walter Zanini, an eminent art historian, the 1981 Bienal once more attracted an international audience. Zanini also organized the 1983 Bienal, consolidating the event's strong position and bringing to the country works that had not been seen there before, such as the unforgettable Fluxus show. (Fluxus, a term first used by George Maciunas, implies flow or change and is more a state of mind than a style. Fluxus artists include Dick Higgins, Wolf Wostel, Ben Patterson, and Ben Vautier.)

Under the curatorial wing of the curator and art critic Sheila Leirner, the 1985 Bienal took a different direction. In response to the wave of neo-expressionism that had swept Europe since 1982, it sought to demonstrate that neo-expressionism was not restricted to the First World. A corridor was built in the exhibition building, horizontally bisecting it. On this long wall, hung side by side, were more than three hundred paintings by artists from Sandro Chia to Jörg Immendorf, from the Argentine Guillermo Kuitca to the Brazilian Jorge Guinle. Although this montage baffled the foreign curators attending the event, this parade of paintings made a considerable impression on the up-and-coming generation. Many Brazilian artists now turned their backs on minimalist frugality and the hermeticism of conceptual art, and a spate of painters came to the fore: Daniel Senise, Karen Lambrecht, Beatriz Milhazes, whose work combines a passion for color with a passion for Brazilian popular art, and Adriana Varejão, whose historical paintings evoke the baroque tradition in Brazil and can be seen in *Virgin Territory*. These last two are internationally recognized, featured in major exhibitions, and represented by New York galleries. The galleries' preference for gestural painting was no obstacle to the overnight success of artists working with other media such as Jac Leirner, Leda Catunda, Nina de Moraes, Sérgio Romagnolo, and Mônica Nador, who is represented in this exhibition by a new wall painting and the video document of *Paredes Pinturas* (Painting Walls) (1998–99).[20] At this time such works were seen as breaking away from conventional approaches to pictorial space and prompted a new way of seeing. That generation was also the first to benefit from a system that was, however haltingly, adapting to the rules of a market. Galleries legitimized the works of these young people by showing and selling them. Even so, the leap to the international stage would still take a few years.

By the mid-1980s, primarily because the international art community had put the São Paulo Bienal back on its agenda, American and European curators started to pay attention to a new generation of artists. I recall touring São Paulo around this time with a curator from a European museum. After rushing in and out of countless artists' studios, taking pictures, and collecting catalogues, at last she was sitting, chastened, at a café table. She asked, "How can it be possible to find so many artists, with so many different outlooks, in a remote country with so many social contrasts, and no art market. . . ?" In a 1999 article in the Spanish art magazine *Lápiz*, the Brazilian art critic Aracy Amaral offered a plausible if incomplete answer to the curator's question. The lack of a market, according to

Amaral, gave Brazilian artists "scope for speculation." What is more, scarcity of means, institutional precariousness, the fact that Brazil is actually several countries at the same time, and even the famous phrase uttered by an ex-minister to the effect that Brazilian reality belongs somewhere between Belgium and Biafra, have always constituted positive incentives to innovation and improvisation.

It is no longer necessary to find complete answers to recognize the fact of this innovative outlook. Whether it is a result of the talent for invention that is so strong a feature of Brazilian art, of the need for renovation in the international art market, or of the influence of a well-organized lobby of gallery owners, in the 1990s Brazil erupted onto the global art scene. Supported by a group of international curators, a dozen Brazilians have been exhibiting their work all over the globe: from Vienna to Madrid, from Mexico to Santa Fe, these artists have been drawing more critical attention than most of their Brazilian—or indeed Latin American—contemporaries. *Artforum* magazine in its spring 2001 issue asked, "Is there a Brazilian Fever?" and answered the question affirmatively.

Virgin Territory was conceived amid this feverish and euphoric explosion of creativity. Yet it breaks away from the customary cast of artists. Taking an independent line, it presents a counter-discursive framework that encompasses a bigger picture, introducing artists that have been overlooked by the establishment. By confronting the viewer with "other" artists, the exhibition promotes a culturally "alien" discourse. In this sense it is a subversive exhibition.

Because place is never simply a location, *Virgin Territory* also displays a range of dissimilar sites and spaces of representation in which to experience a specific region of the world in a fluid temporal frame: five hundred years of contemporary history. Here in these works the past, colonial history, tradition, landscape, and identity take on new meanings in the light of current events. As noted earlier, history is always a history of the present. A new map of a virgin territory is now being drawn. Like any other map, it offers the chance to see the whole world in a dynamic state of formation. After all, as the sixteenth-century voyages of discovery made clear, there is no more extreme effect on people's grasp of the nature of the world than its changing representation in maps. ■

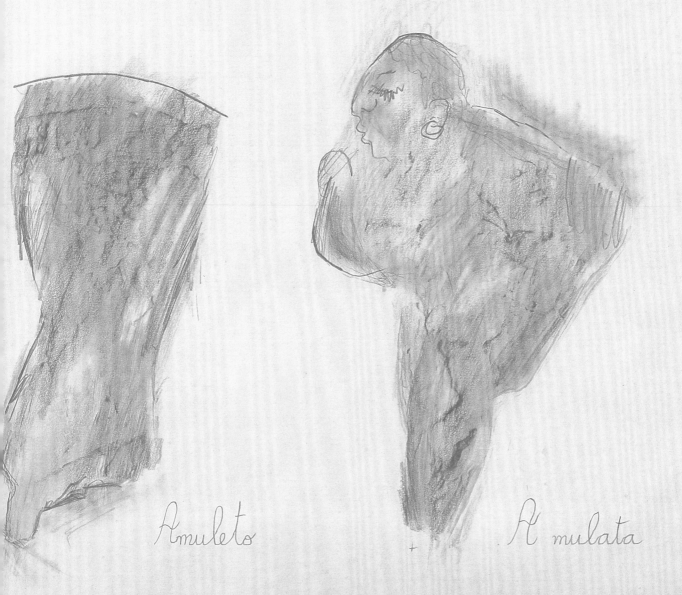

Amuleto

A mulata

THE ARTISTS

A muleta

Am. Latin

■ *Mulheres Negras* (Black Women of Brazil) was conceived for the São Paulo State Council on the Condition of Women (CECF) in 1986 as part of a larger social-action project of the council to highlight different aspects of discrimination against women. At the time, I was part of Lilith Video, a group of women who were also concerned with issues related to women's rights. We produced many videos for the São Paulo CECF, among which was a television series called *Feminino Plural* (Feminine Plural) with five programs a week.

Mulheres Negras was a special video because, although we were a group of white women working on a theme—racism and gender—to which we were sensitive, it did not affect us directly—we did not "feel" it in our own skin. We worked under the thematic coordination of the Black Women's Committee of the CECF.

While writing the script, I immersed myself in the world of Afro-Brazilian gods and goddesses, in the music of the drums and the beat of the *orixás*, in our shameful slavocrat past. One of the aims of this video was to question the myth of a Brazil without racism, looking at the specifics of discrimination against black women in an attempt to reach a wider public.

In this video documentary, black women speak out about their oppression. Despite the official jargon to the contrary, there exists in Brazil a racially segregated class system, where wealth belongs to a small white elite. The women describe how they cope with this discrimination, how they have created ways to validate their lives and experiences through their own music and religion. Using an intense yet sensitive interview-portrait style, the tape celebrates the many faces of black women in Brazil.

When *Mulheres Negras* was exhibited at the first Women's Video Festival in Brasília in 1987, it won first prize and received a standing ovation. I was very touched and had that "mission-accomplished" feeling. It is a small contribution to a cause still to be sorted out—and not only in our country, this immense, multiracial Brazil. ■

Sílvana Afram

Mulheres Negras

BY SILVANA AFRAM

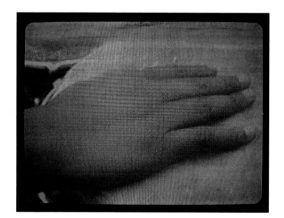

Mulheres Negras
(Black Women of Brazil),
1986
Video with English subtitles
(25 min.)
Courtesy Women Make
Movies

As chance is the mother of so many ideas, the project for the documentary *Yndio do Brasil* (Our Indians) (1995) did not escape the rule or the risk. Although I had visited the "Indian" topic in the 1970s and 1980s in *República Guarani* (Guarani Republic) (1982), a film that recaptures the controversy of a spiritual conquest from 350 years ago, *Yndio do Brasil* includes a dialogue with history, but it is a history contemporaneous with the revolution of twentieth-century cinema. If in *República Guarani* the iconography gives visibility to the adolescence of South America and Brazil, in *Yndio do Brasil* the imagery coincides with a time when cinema was still in its teens.

I was using public and private archives in the United States to research the Brazilian Expeditionary Force in Italy during World War II, the basis for my polemical documentary *Rádio Auriverde* (Radio Brazil) (1991). As I consulted card files, prospected in collections of movie periodicals, spoke to American researchers, cross checked authors, dates, and restored films about Brazil, I unexpectedly began to perceive the existence of an "archive of indigenous film." This archive that was slipping away became an obsession. I was a hostage to it, as time and again it returned as if asking to be rescued from the limbo to which it had been relegated. I had been a tenacious reader about Brazilian cinema, a bookworm in film

Sylvío Back

Barracks Indians

BY SYLVIO BACK

The first film images of Brazil's indigenous population presumably came from *Os Sertões de Mato Grosso* (The Back Woods of Mato Grosso) (1912), by Major Luiz Thomaz Reis,[1] who accompanied General Candido Mariano da Silva Rondon's geopolitical expeditions. Rondon's purpose was not only to extend telegraph lines but also to mark borders and "civilize the backlands."[2] Cinema continued to extract from the indigenous population and attendant mythology images of either pure alienation or preconceived prejudice, and many times they presented a mix of idyllic and ethnocentric usurpation of a culture "lost" by civilization.

The beginnings of *Yndio do Brasil* came while

archives since 1978, when I was baptized with *Revolução de 30* (The 1930 Revolution) (1980).

Following an impetus as vague as it was ambitious, I came to consider a miniseries using old films whose theme would be how cinema sees and hears Indians in all the countries in which they still live. However, I immediately realized that in addition to lacking feasibility given Brazilian production norms, such a series would also demand foreign capital and research in countless countries because the filmography on Indians is worldwide and immeasurable.

The Brazilian Indians might be considered by far the most relished "primitives" in the entire world, as they are the only ones whose survival and culture

Yndio do Brasil (Our Indians), 1995

Video version of 35mm film with English subtitles

(70 min.)

Courtesy of the artist

symbolize an obstinate resistance to the aggression of white society, which as a supporter variously of their disappearance or their integration presents perverse faces of the same coin. From that observation came *Yndio do Brasil,* a look at how cinema—by the journalistic and "scientific" route or mediated by a fictional discourse—has drawn close to and fixed our Indians, their daily life, rituals, idiosyncrasies, and cosmogony.

My researches took four years through the mirage of film titles, both silent and sound, documentary and fiction, unknown and classic, black and white and color, in a wide range of conservation states and ease of access. The investigation took me back to an essential source of my film collage-to-be: the United States, which until then had scarcely been studied. I unearthed an audiovisual history of Brazil, veiled and underground, an unofficial and antiacademic history and thus one almost never taken seriously by the intelligentsia and the media.

Except for schools of communications, Brazilian universities are hostile to cinema even when films are strictly anthropological and ethnographic, not to mention lay or artistic records even more focused

on indigenous peoples. But it is impossible to revisit a country's recent past without using its cinema archives—no matter how compromised those assets are politically, ideologically, or aesthetically. In this photogrammatic womb lies the collective consciousness of the last three generations—all of them movie lovers—regarding our origins. And what is found in the cinema, and reproduced with impunity and enticement, is distorted reflections of the Indian. Certainly influenced by Hollywood's westerns, Brazilian cinema scarred the aura of minority and marginality that mediates between the "savage" and the "noble savage."

A documentary script is usually annihilated by the harsh reality captured by the camera, a fact aggravated when the narrative body is made up of archival material filmed by others. Unlike fiction, in which the script guides the film and the editing, and unlike improvisation, which is self-limiting, in the documentary liberty is apparently cyclopean, broadening the horizon of chance as well as risk. In that regard, the original idea for *Yndio do Brasil* overflowed its banks, invading an un-thought-of territory during the research and regimen of making the film.

Although what seemed in this montage to be a mere juxtaposition of the cinema's countless contradictions, the Brazilian Indian, as framed by us and by foreigners, set off impressive political, ideological, and moral readings. One after the other, newsreels, ethnographic and informational documentaries, movies, stage productions, musicals, institutional and propaganda films—the entire "indigenous" cinema exploited by whites—is the continuation of a paternal-pedagogical conception that goes back to the colonial era's Christian catechizing.

Films from the last eighty years, reviewed at a distance and stripped of their contemporary passions, expose this fact. When decoded on celluloid, Indians—romanticized or demonized by the Church, historians, literature, and the plastic arts—are victims of the same discrimination they have suffered since the so-called discovery of Brazil.

Yndio do Brasil's initial goal was merely to scrutinize the aesthetic and ethical tension between the camera and the Indian. Faced with unexpected film evidence, however, its film components, using sound after 1930, trace the militaristic approaches of the state, the Church, and society, which until the end of the nineteenth century promoted the subduing and massacre of indigenous communities— for example, the "ethnic cleansing" expeditions of the *bugreiros* (Indian civilizers) in the southern states. It was no coincidence that the Rondon Commission, with military inspiration and logistics, formulated a strategy of attraction and pacification in an attempt to integrate and civilize the Indians at the start of the twentieth century. The organized campaigns were authentic military operations in the style of their predecessors, the *bandeirantes* (expeditionaries) and missionaries.

The film ends by testifying to the tragedy of our Indians as a kind of premeditated perpetual motion of physical and mythical death—on which thousands of cinema eyes are always focused—to the point of identifying an imposed barracks culture presiding over their submission during the course of the twentieth century. When surveyed years or decades later by a spectator armed with new criteria of evaluation and a nonideological point of view, films telling the winner's history always become a lampoon. Images never, ever lie. ■

Yndio do Brasil (Our Indians), 1995
Video version of 35mm film with English subtitles
(70 min.)
Courtesy of the artist

■ Brígida Baltar's poetic research projects reflect a particular conception of life, one in which everyday experience and artistic work are combined in a process of permanent experimentation. When Baltar walks up a mountain—equipped with specially designed laboratory glasses and thermos bottles—to collect the early morning mist, or when she chases the ocean breeze on an empty beach, she is investigating the nature of her environment.

Her constant failure to grasp transient substances or atmospheric situations can be seen as an allegory of artistic work itself. At the same time, these vain approaches also act as a metaphor for the intangibility of nature beyond the socially encrypted parameters of reality. Exploring the borderline of materiality and immateriality, she creates a dialogue between the transparent and the opaque, between

Brígida Baltar
Transient Dialogues

BY ANIA CORCILIUS

the wide horizons of an indefinite landscape and her own delicate, small body movements within.

Documentation of these excursions—for example, into the Serra das Araras or Serra dos Órgãos in Rio de Janeiro—has taken the form of photographs, film, and videos, which function in a way that is similar to the performances themselves: they raise questions about what happened rather than present answers. Giving us only an incomplete, fragmentary account of the performance, these different media form separate entities in the context of Baltar's all-encompassing project.

Brígida Baltar regards reality with a mixture of wonder and disturbance. In her work viewers feel as if they were looking at the world in slow motion. What once was familiar to us now seems alien and calls for fresh scrutiny and reappraisal. ■

A coleta da neblina
(Collecting Mist), 1996–2001
DVD projection (3 min.)
Courtesy of the artist

Anna Barros

Short Tales: Sací-Sí

BY ANNA BARROS

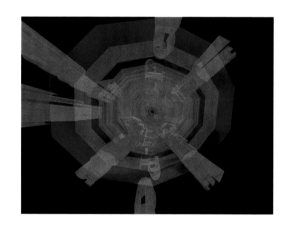

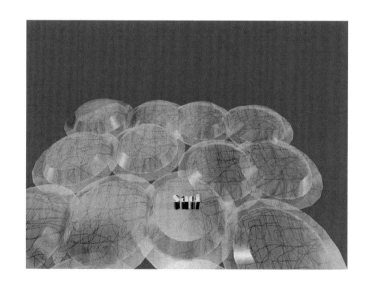

"In every whirlwind there is a Saci inside, for whirlwind making is Saci's main occupation over the world."

Monteiro Lobato

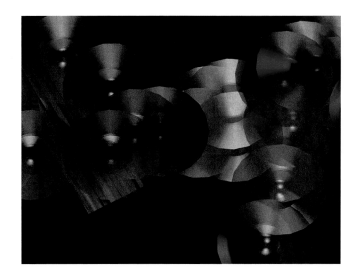

"The type of a sign is memory and delivers a portion of it to future memory."

C. S. Pierce

Como Pegar um Saci-Si
(How to Catch a Saci-Si),
1998
Computer animation
Courtesy of the artist

■ Fairy tales and myths are a child's first, subconscious contact with art. Saci-Pererê, a Brazilian myth, haunted my imagination for a long time. I started my career as an artist with the desire to rejuvenate it into a work of art. I chose a most appropriate metaphor: the whirlwind.

This little *daimon* with a single leg, dressed only in a red cap—the source of his strength—and holding a lighted pipe in his hand, lived in the imagination of old black slaves. His mischief includes braiding a horse's hair and sucking the horse's blood to make it run like the wind, which he then transforms into whirlwinds. To catch a Saci, one must use a bamboo screen with a cross in the middle and throw it in the whirlwind.

The intersemiotic interpretation of this legend through computerized 3D animation was accomplished using a paradigm of association: a whirlwind is a place, a space delimited by energy whose main characteristic is its movement around a loose center. Wind blowing strongly enough to create a whirlwind struggles against the earth. In a desire to free itself from the earth and fly again, it embraces everything within its reach. The whirlwind runs over the earth until it vanishes—it exists just during this point of contact—whereas a tornado originates in the air, moves across the earth, and then takes off again. In my imagination, whirlwinds always embrace a Saci, representing this devilish energy.

Virtual space, which allowed me to generate shapes moving outside gravity, was naturally the perfect setting in which to recapture my childhood memory of Saci. From the same shape several variations were created. The funnel shape appeared wider and thinner, shorter and taller, but the one quality that remained the same was a transparency that perfectly superimposed the shape originated by the wind. Animation carefully embodied in bits of light and color indefinite shapes made only of transmuted information.

Translating this place, this whirlwind, to an imaginary space penetrates to another level of experience where the rules of physics bear no significance, and other possibilities evolve to serve the quoted event. Is that not the origin of any law or rule? ■

Sandra Cínto

Endless Night

BY LISETTE LAGNADO

■ Sandra Cinto's line comes from afar, like a non-stop path that embraces obstacles in its way—walls, columns, alleys, windows—skirting borders haphazardly, from mountain to abyss. It is a never-ending line, hungry for support, a trace that stretches and propagates, a process-driven drawing that takes over space and forms a thin layer with a tenuous existence, like the epidermis on architecture, the pentimento of a primitive tattoo, the outburst of automatic writing, or a lucid meander.

Nonetheless, the void continues in Cinto's photographs and installations; internal space is spare, like icy deserts. Throughout, the artist has created various seats for pleasure or rest: a merry-go-round horse, a swing, a bed. Her bed-bridge, for example, is excessive beyond what is needed to shelter a body: whiteness, height, proportion. The work's persistent mottos are the absence of the other and the dream of wholeness, placing Cinto among a generation of artists whose aim is to elaborate on the distance of the sensorial in contemporary society.

But drawing is joy. Her objects' outlines spill out over the surface, commemorating the expressive act, suspended and charged in the drawings' field of action. Candles are transformed into candelabra, candelabra into fireworks—so many stars of the ephemeral, so many vigils illuminated for the endless night. Perhaps Sandra Cinto intends to camouflage the surface of one world. Perhaps that world is no longer a world. ■

Above: *Noite de Esperança*
(Nights of Hope), 2000
Site-specific wall drawing,
Centre Georges Pompidou,
Paris
Courtesy Galeria Casa
Triângulo, São Paulo

Opposite: *A ponte impossivel*
(The Impossible Bridge),
1998
Automotive paint on wood
106¼ × 118⅛ × 19⅝ in.
(270 × 300 × 50 cm)
Collection of Ricardo Trevisan

Oriana Duarte
Noumenon: The Thing-in-Itself

BY MOACIR DOS ANJOS

Opposite:

Sopa do pedra (Stone Soup),
1998
Video (60 min.)
Courtesy of the artist

Above:

Element from *O gabinete de
souvenirs de A coisa em si*
(Souvenir Cabinet of The
Thing-in-Itself), 1998–2001
Embroidered maps, music
sheets, and souvenirs
Dimensions variable
Collection of the artist

■ There are many movements, repeated several times. Gradually they are slightly, almost imperceptibly, changed. Then, at a given moment, the performance comes to an end, although of course that instant could just as well be any other, sooner or later. The trace remains imprinted in the viewer's memory, dimmed by the deliberate monotony of the gestures, of unfolding action.

Seated at the table, Oriana Duarte has a spoon and a plate in front of her. She gets up and, in a few measured strides, moves around the table and the television, on top of which is a cooking pot. She removes the lid to reveal stones boiled in water to make a thin soup. She takes some soup and covers the pot again, returns to the table, and sits down again. With sparse gestures, she eats some soup, leaving the rest in the dish. Then she gets up again and empties the remaining soup into a glass jar on top of some wooden boxes. She returns to the table, sits down, gets up, and proceeds with the same routine all over again. She returns to the table, sits down, and eats the soup. Again and again. . . .

The work's imprecise temporal distention is joined with its indefinite geographical location and its nomadic condition. Presented in different cities and areas, the performance is always the same and always different—repetition and difference. The gestures are conserved, but multiple chances exist for them to develop into others, perhaps the same ones, perhaps not. Like each movement, each performance—although it seems definitive—potentially leads to the next.

In addition to permeating the formal design of Duarte's work, the concepts of permanence and change render, through their tense opposition, part of the performance's complex symbolic configuration into the opaque world of words. And it is in the artist's body, and in the stone soup she feeds on and finds satisfaction in, that the crude negotiation between what remains and what changes mostly takes place and takes on weight. By swallowing the soup, made of stones from the place she comes from, Duarte metaphorically becomes a repository of everything that distinguishes and identifies that area from all others: its soil, the perennial ground on which all the rest is built and sustained.

Inverting the arrangement by the poet João Cabral—for whom going back to the stone is the only way to learn its lesson—the artist poses a different kind of "education through stone."[1] Here the mineral retained in the water she drinks in each venue works itself into her body and makes its home there, so her body is not exclusive to any particular place. On repeating the performance in another area, new stones and new soil find homes within the impure contraries of her body, dissolving the geographical borders of the outside world and building crossings and passageways within her, connecting what was previously distant. Ingesting the thin soup of stones, Duarte incorporates and carries in her the places she has passed through, deterritorializing them and composing within herself a new and contemporary cartography of the fast-moving world she lives in—a world of simultaneous preservation of dissimilarities and incessant exchange between different ways of belonging to life. ■

■ Dispersion seems to have been the major quality of Anna Bella Geiger's work since she began working in the 1950s. The variety of her media, technique, and material (among them drawing, painting, etching, photography, video, photocopy, and wax reliefs), and, above all, the apparent diversity of results preclude reading the work as a unified personal style. Paradoxically, this very fragmentation reveals the basis of the work's unity.

Heralded by Geiger's visceral period (1965–68), during which the titles of her works alluded to human organs severed from the body by the act of cutting on a metal plate, the diaspora of paths and objectives, the autonomy between part and whole, has progressively become an explicit theme. The works exhibit a strategy of aesthetic resistance to being rigidly framed or inserted into established issues worn out by excessive use and crystallized by common sense. Geiger's poetics emerge in the disquieting plurality of her works.

Anna Bella Geiger
A Sense of Constellation

BY FERNANDO COCCHIARALE

As early as 1973, her works began to investigate the function and nature of the work of art—an essential search for many artists at the time but one that posed problems in Brazil. There was always the risk that the artist, torn between criticizing an issue such as Brazilianness, and charged with traditional ideological connotations and its organization into a work of art, would not be able to overcome such issues. The work of art would then become a simplified illustration of the debate. Faced with the thematic and ideological wholeness of Brazilianness, Geiger opted for parody in her work, turning it into deterritorialized and dissonant fragments. To this estrangement is added the cultural exile in which the Brazilian artist finds her or himself, occupying a secondary position in an international art system.

Postcards, videos, atlases, and primers are an elementary cluster of ideas that mock the mechanisms of Brazilian art and cultural networks.[1] They refer not only to the Brazilian artist's compromise

Am. Latina, 1977
Graphite and colored pencil on paper
23 × 37 in. (58.5 × 94 cm)
Collection of the artist

Amuleto   A mulata   A muleta   Am. Latina

Anna Bella Geiger 77

Above:
Orbis descriptio nº 7 da série Fronteiriços (Description of the World #7 from the Borderlines Series), 1995
Iron, lead, copper, encaustic, gold leaf, and cliché
4 × 24 × 16⅞ in.
(10 × 61 × 43 cm)
Collection of the artist

Opposite:
Orbis descriptio nº 10 da série Fronteiriços (Description of the World #10 from the Borderlines Series), 1996
Iron, lead, copper, steel, encaustic, silver leaf, and cliché
4 × 24 × 17⅜ in.
(10 × 61 × 44 cm)
Collection of the artist

with the country's social reality but also to the possibility of joining the Western art circuit. Formalizing this incongruity, these works define their aesthetic boundaries from the standpoint of ideology. Today it is possible to understand to what extent this investigation has borne fruit.

Concurrent with the explicit questioning of these ideological assumptions, Geiger resumed her etching. In 1978 she began her important series *Local da ação* (Place of Action), whose enigmatic title, which is printed on some of these works, is not easy to decode. In these works, concealed by camouflage (clouds), the world maps of Latin America and Brazil are silent icons. Emptied of its conceptual load, the world becomes an index for Geiger's gradual return to the field of art, to the artist's place of action par excellence. Emblems of a transitory order, her maps allude to nothing but a specific field of production in art. These pictorial works recapture the illusions discarded by modernity in the name of the pictorial plane, but they do not resume the traditional concept of space constructed by linear perspective.

During the last sixteen years Geiger has been producing territories—fields of occurrence—more than spaces: a dislodgment of landscapes into the topography of art. In this locus of production, incomplete illusions are created, images that suggest diverse historic times—a combination whose actualized meaning, however, is possible only in our time.

Geiger's recent works in wax and metal, the *Fronteiriços* (Borderlines), qualify her wandering. They are on the borderline: quasi-objects, quasi-prints, quasi-paintings, surface against stuffing, a kind of constellation-like synthesis of her myriad times and territories. Just as the contiguity of stars suggests the constellations they draw, the meaning of Anna Bella Geiger's works is inseparable from their apparent dispersion, from the contamination between the means and language she uses, just as they are inseparable from the territories she establishes. ▦

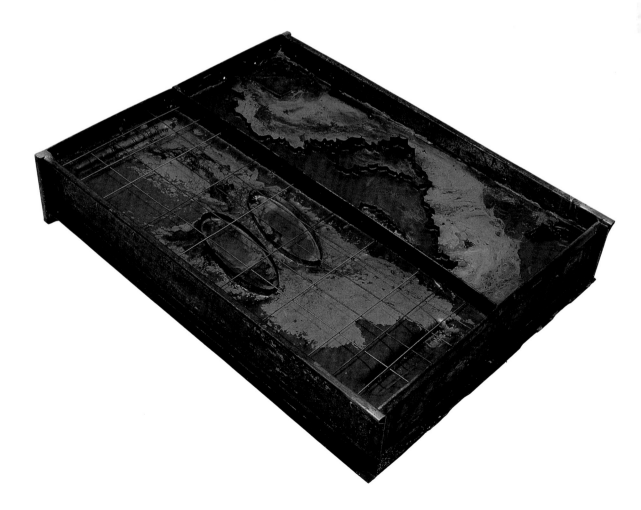

■ Based on the language of video and its devices, the work of the video artist Sandra Kogut represents a multi- and transcultural search that relies on hybrid, fluid video language. Her work—in video art, television, installation, performance, and documentary—crosses different languages and formats, blurring the borders between the experimental and the commercial and playing with the barriers between languages and cultures.

Using video to interfere with and simultaneously blend into the urban scene, Kogut became famous for her "video-booths" project, which resulted in the series *Videocabines São Caixas Pretas* (Video Booths Are Black Boxes) (1990) and *Parabolic People* (1991/1996). Kogut set up an electronic "confessional booth" on the streets of Tokyo, New York, Rio

the image, reworked with graphics, duplications—filmic windows that open, saturating the screen with competing information. In *Parabolic People*, the video maker works with a maximum of saturations and fragmentation, creating an image that goes from maximum information to annulment of meaning.

This saturation of meaning by excess is also present in the video *En Français* (1993), in which Kogut plays with the foreignness of the French language, hyperfragmenting it into the raw material of a texture-like sound. Writing about that video, Kogut said that it was the result of a work on a series of daily recordings done with a small personal camera: "I had the impression that facts from daily living seemed like movie scenes and conversations seemed like dialogue." As in *Parabolic People*, the result

Sandra Kogut
Vídeo Confessíons

BY IVANA BENTES

de Janeiro, Moscow, and Dakar, in which people came to talk, confess, make faces and gestures, or remain silent in front of a video camera.

Starting from these varied performances before the camera, Kogut carried out a second, much more radical operation. She created on the images (records of the camera's mechanical eye) a second skin: a series of specifically videographic interventions, a careful editing of these images and speeches, reorganized in layers and windows.

What is said by the video-booth users (tourists, curiosity seekers, passersby) matters little. Most of the time they are clichés, gestures, banalities. What is interesting is how Kogut works with the material in editing. This is where she creates a new place, or "no-place," where what is important is the surface of

contains little that is familiar; instead, it creates an alienation and poetic distancing from nearby elements while rediscovering the aesthetic potential of everyday speech.

In the short film *Lá e Cá* (There and Here) (1995), featured in this exhibition, Kogut turns to Brazilian iconography, filming around Rio de Janeiro a chronicle with typical "Carioca" gestures and situations. This film has as its base the strong personality and spirituality of the popular Brazilian actress Regina Casé, whom Kogut directed in the TV Globo *Brasil Legal* (Cool Brazil) (1997). *Lá e Cá* shows the daily life of a young lower-class suburban resident as a camera follows her through the streets, recording situations that range from fictional to documentary, without distinction. The dilemma the character

Lá e Cá (There and Here), 1995
Video (25 min.)
Courtesy of the artist

faces is whether to stay in the neighborhood or leave, to go or stay. That quandary is echoed throughout the film, which explores elements of "there"—the other, abroad, distance—and "here"—Brazilian and American music, drama and comedy, fiction and documentary, consumer culture and tradition. *Lá e Cá* further plays with the stereotypes of sincere, happy, and vital Brazilianness embodied by Casé, always criss-crossing the narrow line that separates the banal images and clichés from truly fresh possibilities.

Kogut had already explored a similar subject in the video *What Do You Think People Think Brazil Is?* (1989), which Arlindo Machado defined as "a kind of an antiportrait of Brazil, made up of clichéd images of Brazilianness and delirious speeches by foreign tourists about this exotic country in the Southern Hemisphere." Immersed in both pop and traditional cultures in which discourse flows quickly and fragmentedly, the images of Brazil—and especially about the Brazilian way of being—appear in comic fashion. Again, what is said matters little, but the clichés are repeated and collected in such number that their effect is saturation and irony.

Time is one of the pervasive themes that also cuts across much of Kogut's work. She faces the issue by speeding it up and adding more and more images and information to provoke an aesthetic experience. That experience is like a visual chronicle and a moment of consciousness combined, distanced from saturation, which in her work is both poison and cure. ■

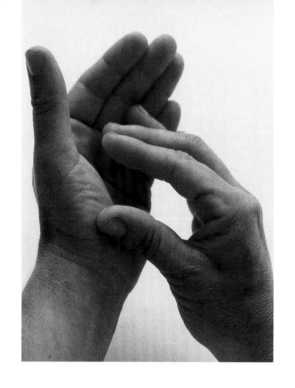

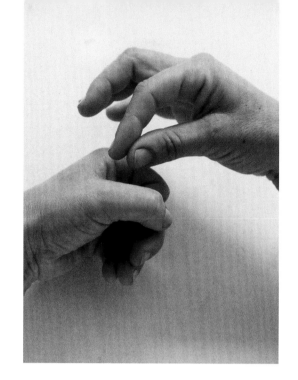

Sonía Labouríau
From Without to Within/
From Within to Without

BY RICARDO BASBAUM

"Migratory Birds *is beautiful; the migration of materials from one state to another. I like the aspect of the performed sculpture. The immediacy of the hand,
and the implication of distance of the bird's migration. Instance and shadow.*"

Guy Brett, London, September 20, 1994

Pássaros Migratórios
(Migratory Birds), 1992–2001
Site-specific installation
Urucum, seeds, binder, water,
glass, and nine C-prints
Courtesy of the artist

■ The proposition *Pássaros Migratórios* (Migratory Birds) (1992–2001) by Sonia Labouriau attempts to deal with a set of issues interrelated with experience, process, flux, and memory. Combining *coloral* (an edible mixture of urucum[1] extract and cornmeal) and a methylcellulose binder, the artist obtains an organic orange-red moldable mass. Labouriau then follows a procedure for producing small "birds" based on four hand movements, the result of which is meant to issue from formal determinations rather than from an operational method: "I seek to create procedures that can, like a musical score, be performed incorporating the circumstances."[2]

Each of the "birds" is produced by this method and preserved until one of them is chosen and placed in a glass dish filled with water. Then, in a matter of time varying from a few hours to two days, the orange-red "bird" dissolves, "migrating to water,"

undoing its transitory formalization—pure process.

It is the art object's very Becoming that *Pássaros Migratórios* makes visible, as it points to a course of dematerialization that reconducts any crystallization back in the direction of a state of flux. The piece also inevitably takes on new substance when experienced by the viewer, for the encounter itself recognizes and continuously renews the potency of the migration. Leaving traces of fluid memory, each state of this process-oriented flight indicates a stage of metamorphosis. Affinities are affirmed not only between art and transformation, but also between art and transmutation as the objects interconnect in different states and are reformulated in the most diverse and adverse conditions. Setting each "bird" in motion means remaking it, heeding its rhythmic whole, and allowing the restoration of its Becoming—experiencing it, experiencing oneself. ■

The greater the distance in time or space, the greater the risk that a tradition will deteriorate, be diluted, and then be lost. Thus, paintings such as the *Mona Lisa* and the *Last Supper*, musical compositions such as Beethoven's Fifth Symphony—at least its first notes—and Bach's *Tocatta and Fugue in D Minor*, and tragedies from Aeschylus to Shakespeare seem as they cross cultures to succumb to multiplication on posters, carpets, plates, and ties; to the claustrophobia of elevators and waiting rooms; to the disposable drama of movies and soap operas.

For Nelson Leirner, it is precisely by means of distance that traditions are reinvented and melded into the body of culture. That is where they, despite conspicuous opinions to the contrary, feed and are converted into food, grow roots, and are transformed into roots. From this point of view, the foreign logic of outsiders ends up as a peculiar form of incorporation.

when he does not precipitate, a collision between diverse and refined expressive traditions and cultural material produced by various ethnic currents, made dense by their unforeseen crossings and thriving in the vast territory that makes up his country. He scans common points, using visual language to explore cultural subversion and displacement.

Relying on hybridity, Leirner's art sits on that indecisive border separating high culture from common objects and expressions. His artistic trajectory has always been punctuated by what can be called variable comprehension or incomprehension: Once he and fellow artist Flavio Mota displayed flags on an important street in São Paulo. Because they did not have a permit to conduct business outdoors—even though the flags were not for sale—all of their materials were seized, and the two ended up in a precinct house and on the pages of the local daily newspapers.

But the most famous and disconcerting of his

Nelson Leirner
The Miracle of the Multiplication of Images

BY AGNALDO FARIAS

Leirner makes fun of his condition, arguing about whether what he does is art and about its corollary, whether or not he is an artist. This is an argument that has been going on for more than forty years, which in itself shows its seriousness. But he is not alone in this situation. Slightly ahead of him was Marcel Duchamp, someone who decided to separate himself from two centers: cubism and Paris. Duchamp opted instead for the non-artwork—his ready-mades—and for New York.

In his own way, Leirner has been researching what happens to traditions when they come crashing onto the coasts of Brazil, a country once so "distant" that Portuguese navigators—those masters of dead reckoning and cartography—claim to have discovered it by chance five hundred years ago when they were blown off a course that would have led them to "discover" the Indies. And that is where much of the material is found that interests Leirner. From the sublime to the sordid, the artist presents,

incomprehensions occurred in 1966, when Leirner sent an enormous stuffed pig for the jury's consideration at the National Salon of Brasília. This gamesmanship examined some of art's tautologies, such as the one that defines art as something produced by an artist and an artist as one who produces art. Art would similarly be what the critics—or in this case, the jurors of the salon—define as such and vice versa. Because the pig was sent in by Leirner, an artist known for expositions and events, it was accepted. He next went to the newspapers to ask the jurors what criteria led them to accept the pig as a work of art. Leirner entitled the collected responses published in the papers (not everyone responded to the provocation) "Jury Happening."

He does not know whether what he does is art, which is the same as saying that he does not know whether he is an artist. His copious, paradoxical work remains valid as a "work-doubt in progress" that may or may not have artistic value.

O Grande Parada (The Big Parade), 1999 Site-specific installation, XXXXVIII Biennale di Venezia, Italy Courtesy Galeria Brito Cimino, São Paulo

Top:
Santa Ceia (The Last Supper),
1990
Mixed media
19⅝ × 27½ in. (50 × 70 cm)
Courtesy Galeria Luisa
Strina, São Paulo

Above:
Santa Ceia (The Last Supper),
1990
Mixed media
31½ × 47¼ in.
(80 × 120 cm)
Courtesy Galeria Brito
Cimino, São Paulo

Right:
Santa Ceia (The Last Supper),
1990
Mixed media
29⅞ × 37¾ in. (76 × 96 cm)
Collection of Museum
of Contemporary Art,
Niterói, Brazil

The multiplicity of images in Leirner's series *Santa Ceia* (The Last Supper), created in the 1990s, favors the artist's speculations. Detached from the wall where da Vinci painted it in 1498, the image—the greatest icon of Christianity and art history—was multiplied into infinite reproductions, from touched up and bright, printed on heavy art paper, to dull and enlarged on a common poster. In the surprising and entertaining form of a souvenir, the *Last Supper* could be stamped on a plate, cup, chalice, or tie, as well as transmuted onto tile, used in relief on a brooch, or made into a sculpture for families to display on their dining table.

According to Leirner, the miracle of an image's multiplication—its popularization—is far from being its end. The transformation is merely its passage into another state, its metamorphosis into spontaneous parodies full of humor and simplicity. Such varied products only affirm the fertility of the original

image. More than simply appropriating unusual versions of the *Last Supper*, Leirner then alters the work, empowering its internal characteristics. He thus demonstrates that the original is an elastic territory from which other images can be constructed. The vulgarization of the *Last Supper* is proof that it is favorable material for the proliferation of new meanings; the diverse products coming from it have the stature of new and unforeseen readings.

For Leirner the *Last Supper* represents the miraculous multiplication of bread and wine, whether sublime or banal. Thanks to another, partially explainable miracle, it will multiply through time, impregnating our entire civilization. It will continue ever more indifferent to the original image and its author until it stabilizes like those sayings we preserve as true, like the pantheon of gestures and expressions that belong to us and at the same time belong to no one. ■

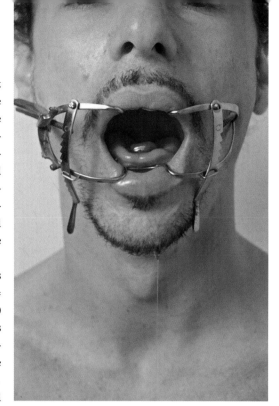

■ To come into contact with Laura Lima, one must go through her answering machine. It's always the machine that picks up the phone, whether someone is home or not. The impression one gets upon initial acquaintance with her work is that this answering machine—specially programmed to record unanswered messages—ends up becoming yet another "entity" in her universe. Despite its mechanical nature, it constitutes another individualized body orbiting around the artist, another creature under her influence and command.

It is not easy to understand the interconnections among the four main series of her work, *Homem=carne/mulher=carne* (Man=Flesh/Woman=Flesh) (her best-known pieces, already shown at various exhibitions and events); *Dimensional Tattoos* (dealing with body projects impossible to realize because they go beyond the limits of the physical body); *RhR* (a collective body involved in rituals and

Laura Líma

The Artíst as Predator

BY RICARDO BASBAUM

secrets); and *Vivia21* (the most pragmatic and quotidian of entities). Lima has developed a strategy of fluidity as well as a personal idiom to experiment with the simultaneous construction and execution of multiple incarnations—in her own body or other female and male bodies (children, adults, and elderly persons). Her four series address both the individual and the collective body, raising questions about how "embodiment" is formed and functions. The artist conceives of mechanisms that regulate the internal and external economy of "embodiment" and the process of "incorporation."[1] The notion of "body" is severed from its ideal and is required to undergo various physical operations and dynamic rituals that yield a different sense of its capacities.

The body and performance art are central currents of Lima's work that embrace these "embodiment/incorporation" operations, but she also approaches the body in terms of other forces. The *Homem=carne/mulher=carne* series (1999) touches on this concern while placing the issue outside the artist's own body. She is not interested in being the focus of the art herself, instead preferring to look for possible alterities (embodiments of the Other) by experiencing something through someone else's flesh. In her own words, "the artist is a predator, the Flesh=Person her prey." But more than for nourishment, the artist as predator is in search of human material for experiences that test the limits of the flesh: building, shaping, and problematizing the body.

The series *RhR* (an acronym practically impossible to pronounce in Portuguese) (1999) stands for "Representative-hyphen-Representative." It is an exercise in producing a collective body that constantly reinvents itself, maintaining a strong pattern of cohesion and protecting itself from outsiders. The group is made up of countless members from all walks of life, among whom Lima herself assumes

Above:

Caramelo (Candy), 1997
Managed Action
Courtesy of the artist

Opposite:

RhR Integrants
(RhR Participants), 1999
Managed Action
Courtesy of the artist

the role of administrator. The headquarters are in her apartment, and she is responsible for a series of meticulous tasks and internal protocols (such as rituals of initiation and farewell, distribution of correspondence, and video recording sessions). Group performances are always discreet—not publicized, almost imperceptible, not characterized by any particular action. Some members of the group attend public events such as military parades, parties, and show openings, all activities where the ritual element is particularly strong. They remain in silence, dressed in "drawing uniforms," which cover their entire body except for the face in such a way that they cannot be singled out.

Viewed in relation to other Lima series, *RhR* repeats her experimentation with various modes of bodily construction and individuation. This double representative drive (*RhR*=Representative-hyphen-Representative) shows the important recurrence in her work of layers of different embodiments,

making it seem perfectly possible for two or more bodies to occupy the same space at the same time. The artist is simultaneously Lima and *RhR*, in addition to overseeing the transformations of others in *RhR*, Flesh and Person. Her work stresses this multiplicity—where each of us is several at the same time, under the guise of a fragmented subjectivity, and its density is focused on sites of passage in ways that problematize and denature them.

Whenever I exchanged e-mail messages with Lima, I communicated with her through another individualized organism: *Vivia21*. This incarnation is more pragmatic, is subject to the exigencies of the material world, and has performed curatorial as well as photography and production services. Managed in conjunction with the artist Marssares, *Vivia21* is, in terms of gender, both male and female.

We are not simply in a dual universe; plots and webs are getting more complex, and art is getting interesting again. ■

■ The last time the installation *Arroz & Feijão* (Rice and Beans) was seen was in 1980, a year after it was created, in the exhibition space of the Federal University of Paraíba, a small state in the northeast of Brazil—not exactly a venue for artgoers. Until now, therefore, most people have known this work only through small images published in a few catalogues. According to the artist's detailed description and instructions on how to re-create the piece (as was done for *Virgin Territory*), the centerpiece of the installation *Arroz & Feijão* consists of a table with a black cloth and six sets of plates and assorted tableware. Each plate contains soil planted with rice and beans. Germination takes approximately twenty-five days, and the plates are replaced within the same time span. The green stems should be bending when they are placed on the table, and they have to be watered every day. Surrounding this centerpiece are four smaller tables, also set with tableware, although the plates are empty.

Anna María Maiolíno
Rice and Beans

BY BERTA SICHEL

Apparently straightforward, this installation-experiment is, as the artist says, saturated with layers of meanings connecting the personal, the social, and the political. Maiolino's unusual hit scores on several sides at once. For one, she mocks a historic Brazilian mythology about the richness of its land, "where anything you plant grows"—a promise never really fulfilled by the country's social ideology. Her work declares that natural fruitfulness does not rule out hunger. *Arroz & Feijão* also provokes the question of whether we are looking at life (the germinated sprouts) or being confronted with the daily scarcities suffered in households worldwide. To add a bit more complexity, the installation has a ritualistic quality: to sit at a table, to share. In the ambit of many religions, ritual is a critical component in grasping a culture and a society.[1] There is also the cosmological reference of the black-draped table, on whose surface life, death, and transformation are experienced together.

Aqui estão (Here They Are),
1999
Permanent installation
550 lathe-turned wood rollers
Collection of Castro Maya
Museums, Rio de Janeiro

The use of food as an artistic device is not the main concern here, although it is important. Food has been widely used as subject matter at different moments throughout the history of art. In the Latin American contemporary and conceptual art universe, *Arroz & Feijão* is related to the Argentinean Victor Grippo's many installations using potatoes from the 1970s onward. Appropriating a television term, Grippo's message broadcasts the idea that, for him, potatoes are the quintessential food of the poor in the Americas.[2] In comparison, although Brazil is part of the Americas, rice and beans are its basic staples as they are in Cuba and other countries where the African presence made an indelible mark on the local diet. Maiolino's work repositioned the rice and beans of such everyday meals while infusing them with a beautiful sense of locality, as well as with a cultivated economy of means. The alchemy is there as these basic food-stuffs are converted into a source of art.

Using a living sign—popular food items of Brazilians generally and the core meal of the poor—the artist "writes" her protest and perhaps her hope. At the time the work was created, Brazilian society was flirting with the possibility that the tunnel indeed had an end and that there was light there. After more than fifteen years of a repressive military dictatorship that seized power in 1964, artists (not to mention the whole of society) were desperately looking for a way out. As people took to the streets, artists also took over unusual spaces such as a vacant lot on São Paulo's rua Augusta, a street where the action was at the time. (An impossible comparison would be the cultural vibrancy of Broadway and Prince in New York a couple of decades ago.)

Maiolino was one of the participating artists in the performance event *Mitos Vacios*, organized by Hélio Oiticica in 1978. On that occasion, she presented a restaurant table for four, covered by a black cloth. It was an extremely simple, *arte povera*–style

Above:

Arroz & Feijão

(Rice and Beans), 1980

Site-specific installation,

Federal University of Paraíba

Opposite:

Arroz & Feijão

(Rice and Beans), 1979

Site-specific installation,

Artists Space: Alliance

Française, Rio de Janeiro

piece that included at the center of the table only two medium-size bags of transparent plastic: one full of black beans and the other full of white rice. Both were tied together by a black ribbon, and she titled the work *Monument to Hunger.* In some cultures, including the Brazilian, wearing a piece of black ribbon is a sign of death in the family.

The following year *Arroz & Feijão* was reconceived as a vehicle of expression for a real situation. In Rio de Janeiro, where she was living, the artist was a member of a group that organized the event Artists Space in the facilities of the Alliance Française. While not exactly an artists' collective, the group's main goal was to recognize and engage with issues affecting the production and exhibition of their art within their current political and social context while facing the possibility of change. The sociopolitical aspects of art production had been vividly present in Maiolino's mind and work since she had become actively involved with the Brazil-

ian art scene in the 1960s. For her, as for feminist artists in the United States and Europe, sculpture and painting were associated with masculine expression. She abandoned representation and started to experiment with different media, from poetry to film. Like many women artists at the time, Maiolino also eschewed conceptual art as primarily language based, and she proceeded to incorporate into her work tendencies borrowed from minimalism, *arte povera*, performance, and body art. On many occasions, her "female condition" was the source of subject matter as well as a way of bridging worlds: her studio, home, country, continent, and the globe.

What is the reaction of a present-day viewer of *Arroz & Feijão*, more than twenty years after its first showing? While there may be no way to answer this question, it is enough to read the newspapers and watch the news to believe that *Arroz & Feijão* remains undestroyed by time. It has surely been empowered by it. ■

■ The film *O descobrimento do Brasil* (The Discovery of Brazil) was released in December 1937, but the project goes back at least to 1935. Despite recent favorable attention to this work and the motivations behind it, many facts about its production and rationale remain obscure. Countless elements marking its creation have been masked by the obvious yet circumstantial association with the authoritarianism of Gétulio Vargas's Estado Novo (1937–45) and its government financing, as well as the involvement of certain leading figures and institutions.

At its inception, the film was financed by the Bahia Cacao Institute under the direction of Alberto Campiglia. Humberto Mauro, the most famous director of early Brazilian film, was not originally associated with it, but it would eventually come to bear his directorial stamp.

Mauro's inclusion in the project probably determined subsequent modifications made to *O descobrimento do Brasil*. He must have perceived the possibilities of the short film initiated by Campiglia. In the early 1930s Mauro had placed himself within the sphere of influence of the anthropologist Edgar Roquette-Pinto and was taken by the anthropologist's admiration for his talent, especially in the field of scientific and educational film. (Roquette-Pinto had been particularly impressed by *Ameba* [Amoeba], which Mauro directed for Cinédia in 1932.) The two of them must have spoken about the creation of an institution to produce educational films, for in 1936 Roquette-Pinto established the National Institute of Educational Film. In 1935, when the institute was still just a dream, the possibility of demonstrating its need with a great historical film celebrating Brazil's discovery very likely seduced them to the cause.

Mauro was meticulous and faithful in adapting Pero Vaz de Caminha's letter to Dom Manuel I (1500) to his epic account of Pedro Álvarez Cabral's

Humberto Mauro
O descobrímento do Brasíl

BY HERNANI HEFFNER

O descobrimento do Brasil
(The Discovery of Brazil),
1937
Video version of 16mm film
(62 min.)
Courtesy Estate
of Humberto Mauro

discovery. He also surrounded himself with the brightest talents, such as the composer Heitor Villa-Lobos, then in charge of music for the Ministry of Education and Health. Recognized for his famous choral presentations and his knowledge of Brazilian folk music, Villa-Lobos provided the film's musical score. Nonetheless, the soundtrack was entirely redone twice, and that and other technical setbacks extended production throughout 1937, making it the most expensive film of its time. Today analysis of the film is somewhat difficult, as approximately one-half hour of the final version is lost.

Although the official tone and the complete reliance on Pero Vaz's account displeased some critics and intellectuals such as Graciliano Ramos, *O descobrimento do Brasil* represented an original and, to a certain extent, successful cinemagraphic effort. By converting a specific historical text and its iconography to film, it remains an important statement in the early life of Brazilian cinema. ■

Beth Moysés

Memory of Affection

BY KATIA CANTON

Above and opposite:
Memória do Afeto
(Memory of Affection), 2000
Video (7 min.)
Courtesy of the artist

Right:
Luta (Battle), 1998
Boxing gloves and
wedding lace
$14\frac{1}{8} \times 13 \times 11\frac{3}{4}$ in.
($36 \times 33 \times 30$ cm)
Courtesy Galeria Thomas
Cohn, São Paulo

■ Since 1994 Beth Moysés has taken up the bridal gown as a symbolic articulation of love relationships and all that concerns them. At first, she lined a chapel ceiling with an arsenal of bridal gowns. Raised to the heights, they spoke of pledges, exposed failed expectations, and attested to the literal absence of a firm footing. Hanging by their fabric-stuffed skirts, the anonymous "bodyless" dresses exuded loneliness and disenchantment; they suggested a field mined with tears.

This disenchanted criticism has since been replaced by a vigorous performance-manifesto. The gowns are finally being (re)occupied. Having descended to the ground, they are now reinhabited by the women to whom they once belonged. No matter how old, tight or loose, short or long these gowns may be now, in putting them on the women (re)claim memories of love or affection that the mere presence of the gown once ritualized. Wearing these bridal gowns, the women parade down city streets and thoroughfares, along an itinerary in which past promises come together to claim future fulfillment:

may every dream contained in the symbol of the white gown come true as a banner of peace, love, and solidarity that mirrors and permeates the forevermore. While plucking and dropping rose petals to the ground, the women seek to trace memories and permeate both the urban space and its inhabitants with feelings of peace and affection. Finally, at the end of the parade, the thorny and bare rose stems are placed in a deep hole that the women dig with their own hands. All distress is then buried in a symbolic act combining bravery and resignation.

The performance-manifesto thus transcends all artistic borders and achieves a meaning of amorous urgency within a universe of daily violence, which starts from family relationships and contaminates the rest of city life. May the women in white conclude their journey, influencing other people along their way. May these women ultimately bury all their thorns. And may their path replace a resigned attitude of consolation, while claiming a status of generous and contagious affection. May this path be taken up—and followed. ■

■ Unlike most of her Brazilian colleagues, who seek to enter or consolidate a position in the restricted market for local art, in 1999 Mônica Nador broke with submissiveness to dealers, collectors, and the other elements of the art circuit and chose to proceed with her painterly poetics among the marginalized sectors of society. In truth, her opposition can be seen as a natural outcome of a problematic relationship she always had with art and the Brazilian artistic milieu.

In the early 1980s, when Nador began to show her work, she was prominent in developing an approach to painting that ran contrary to the spontaneity and personal narratives typical of what many called postmodernism. Instead, Nador insisted on exploring the nature of the pictorial plane by means of exhaustive analysis of the elements that make up painting. Such work, claiming a certain orthodoxy that was still modernist in flavor, by modernism. The tense dialogue that Nador's painting maintained with the best painting being produced in São Paulo and elsewhere in the country, however, did not hold her interest. She put aside formal research in favor of a more ideological approach.

The need to establish a more direct relationship with the public—no longer restricted to museums and galleries—became an ever-greater concern, one manifested in two quite visible strategies. First, taking a formal point of view, Nador tried to achieve a repertoire displaying the form and color of powerful working-class extraction, letting her interest in synthetic images, even archetypes, flow. Second, taking a more strategic view, she began to search for alternative ways of introducing her work into places that, in her words, were not consecrated as "art spaces."

In 1995 and 1996 Nador created ephemeral works—paintings on the walls of a library and a

Mônica Nador
Transformations of Place

BY TADEU CHIARELLI

served as an antidote to the expressive extremes reached by the era's most popular painting style.

In the course of that decade, Nador's output nevertheless became impregnated with the need to re-evaluate; it was no longer constituted solely of pictorial language but also incorporated visible traces of its history. In this period and up to 1990, she produced her so-called landscapes and, immediately thereafter, the mandalas—in which her prior focus gave way to a curious search for the ornamental—and an equilibrium between form and color very close to more working-class tastes.

That work, which aimed for contact with a larger public, again headed against the grain of the painting then in style, especially in São Paulo, where she was living. The "return to painting" vogue having passed, artistic debate in the city again took up matters of pictorial language—flatness, material, and so forth—in an approach basically influenced

hospital in Uberlândia—at the invitation of the local university. In 1996 she inaugurated the *Projeto Parede* (Wall Project) at the Museum of Modern Art in São Paulo, creating a mural approximately four meters high and twenty-three meters long, which was on exhibit for six months. In spite of the success of these projects, especially the last one, Nador was not satisfied. Although aimed at a broader public, the works occupied places that were, in effect, exceptions within the sad Brazilian reality: a library, a hospital, and a museum—places not much frequented by the majority of Brazilians.

Conscious of these limitations, Nador looked for conditions under which to create paintings that were less isolated and sacrosanct. She determined that she should focus on needy communities, creating her walls not *for* individuals who belonged to social groups that were divorced from the so-called learned field of culture and art, but *with* them.

Untitled, 2000
Acrylic on wood
Site-specific wall painting,
Vila Rodhia, São José
dos Campos
Courtesy of the artist

Everywhere she carried out and is carrying out her work—towns in the interior of the Brazilian Amazon, encampments of the landless, slums, for example—Nador uses the same strategy: she captures the interest of one family, then proposes to modify the facade of their residence with a painting of a specific subject, often proposed by a family member. The transformation of the first facade mobilizes other residents to join the work. With the initial help of the artist (or not), they transform their own residences.

Socializing the conception and production of these works, Nador seeks to motivate people to develop an aesthetic concept based on the transformation of the place where they live and of the visual repertoire they already know. In turn, a consciousness that residences and living spaces can be transformed for the better broadens the consciousness of citizenship in those involved in these projects, increasing their self-esteem and ability to demand respect.

Nador's method points to her radicalized attitude about the art circuit. Setting aside the notion of art as a manifestation of a solitary individual predestined to create unexpected forms—the typically bourgeois conception of an artist—Nador appropriates archetypal images, breaking with the persistent myth of the artist as a creator of original forms.

By proposing that community members participate in both the conception and execution of her wall paintings, the former artist Mônica Nador, in theory, dives into the anonymity of working-class art. In that, the artist (now an artisan) is distinguishable from her peers only by being the holder of some knowledge or talent shared with others for the common good, belonging to all.

If the individual artist in this process melts into the collective, trying to reactivate the perceptive capacity of the community, that perception is not limited to aesthetics. Helping aestheticize the day-to-day life of the most diverse social groups, Nador effectively politicizes her action, which ceases to be merely aesthetic or artistic, in order to gain other dimensions unthinkable within the main currents of contemporary Brazilian art. ■

As heirs of the *arte povera* and postminimalist traditions, Nazareth Pacheco's first three-dimensional pieces—filiform objects made of metal or rubber that I call "dependent objects"[1]—seemed to be completely at the mercy of their surrounding stimuli. The viewer could either handle and rearrange them or simply observe them in their inertia. They did not appear to exist in themselves but instead served as counterpoints to the self-sufficiency of conventional art objects.

Her works, however, featured other characteristics that did not affect me with such great intensity as they do now. To rubber objects, the artist added spikes made with the same material, elements that interrupted the smooth rubber-strip surface, conferring on the piece—as I clearly see now—a strange resemblance to torture devices. The same effect occurred with the tin fillets that Pacheco hung on the wall, at the viewer's eye level; here too she added evenly spaced rubber spikes.

artist's physical journey, including various torture-like procedures and objects used to conform her own body to hegemonic standards of feminine beauty. In turn, the work also represented her desire to find a meaning that justified her life as an individual, a woman, and an artist.

Although the 1993 exhibition was cathartic, by this time Pacheco had grown to see herself not just as an isolated individual but as one of millions who had submitted to countless torture procedures designed to shape the female body to conform to an aesthetic dictatorship. She left aside autobiographical documentation and took up the production of objects and installations created with apparatus conceived for the examination or "improvement" of the female figure, regardless of their abusive, invasive, overbearing, and basically authoritarian characteristics.

Pacheco next began to work with medical and surgical instruments, particularly those used for

Nazareth Pacheco
A Lacerating Reality

BY TADEU CHIARELLI

Pacheco next produced a series of latex objects, retaining the same linear characteristics as before. Now she made immense strips of rugged latex interrupted by knots that violently folded and twisted the material, only to proceed along to another knot. Without a doubt, these objects were still "dependent" and resembled the previous rubber and metal strips. However, the aggressiveness of the previous works, spikes, was now manifested in a more "organic" manner—through both the aggressive materiality of the raw latex and the rough knots that structured the filiform pieces.

By the time of her 1993 exhibition at Gabinete Raquel Arnaud in São Paulo, most of Pacheco's work differed formally and conceptually from this previous output. She showed small boxes replete with assorted objects that narrated a long history of reconstruction of her own body from childhood to adulthood. Manifesting a strong cathartic and nearly therapeutic nature, the show traced the

women, such as speculums and myoma screws. In the exhibition *Espelhos e sombras* (Mirrors and Shadows), held at the Museum of Modern Art in São Paulo in 1994, the artist showed a series of acrylic speculums arranged side by side; among these instruments she placed a single metal speculum. While using the minimalist prescription of one module following the other as a metaphor of industrial mass production, Pacheco ironically contrasted the acrylic speculums' apparent lightness and near lack of materiality (both visual and conceptual) with the ascetic roughness of the same instrument made of metal. She seemed to be asking, Is it possible to discern in these devices, so close to other instruments of torture, only the cool beauty of anatomical design—without forgetting the function to which they are destined?

For her next showing, at Galeria de Arte Valú Ória in 1997, Pacheco created essentially sadistic objects: necklaces of crystal and piercing and cutting

Untitled, from the *Jóais* (Jewelry) series, 1997
Cut stones, bugle beads, and needles
15¾ × 7⅞ × 2⅜ in.
(40 × 20 × 6 cm)
Courtesy Galeria Brito Cimino, São Paulo

devices such as hooks, assorted needles, and blades. By and large, necklaces and other such body adornments are part of daily life. Created to offset our substantially imperfect, ephemeral, and human condition, they are alluring objects that always tend to perfection and the eternal. They suggest the secret desire—prompted by any ornament—to wear them on our body so we can absorb their attributes or the attributes they should have. These crystalline and sparkling necklaces seduce us. To touch them, possess them, handle them, and wear them close to the body—this is the desire that stimulates us. Just as dependent as her first works and just as filiform, they are so familiar and seductive yet so perverse in their new proposition that they introduce a real capacity to wound.

Pacheco's necklaces belong in a very small jewel box of twentieth-century art. Like Duchamp's ready-mades, the box doubles as the receptacle that art history has created for constructed objects. It contains precisely those objects that, despite preserving the appearance of innocuous everyday objects, aggregate new elements to either deny or subvert, or even prevent, their original functions. Man Ray's *Gift* (1921) is perhaps the most emblematic of constructed objects: a prosaic clothes iron, onto the face of which the artist attached fourteen metal spikes. Sadistic, both in terms of its final configuration and in its own title, *Gift* transcends the limits of reality through a cool and calculated perverseness. Its abrupt self-sufficiency derives from the hazard it presents: physically it can jeopardize the integrity of other objects or a potential user's body, and emotionally it does away with our certainties about everyday reality.

Pacheco's necklaces cause these same sensations. As adornments (objects that depend on our will), onto which piercing elements are introduced and mixed with stones, they acquire a self-sufficiency derived precisely from the artist's interference with the concept of the necklace itself. Originally conceived to ornament, to offset the limits of our existence, now they pose a threat to that same existence. Pacheco has always worked with filiform objects that depend on the spectator. Today, however, her objects are more beautiful, and the potential hazard they posed in the early 1990s now has turned into a lacerating reality. ■

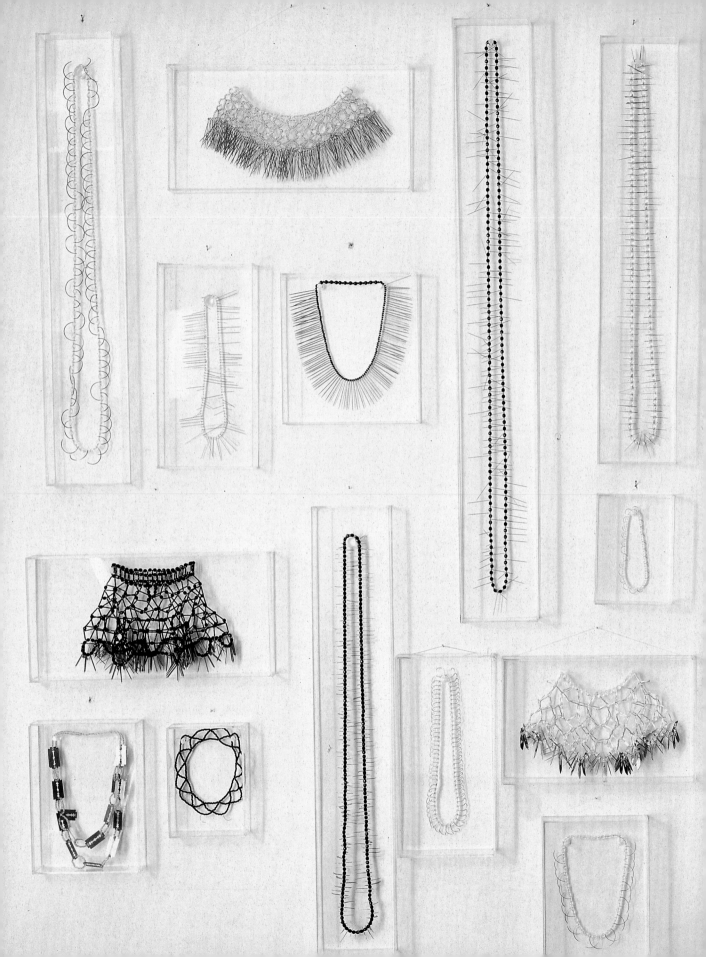

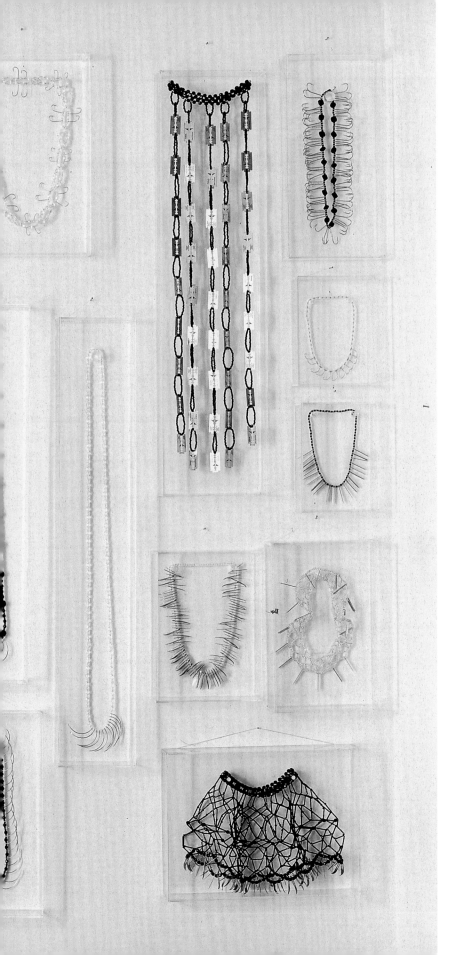

Installation view of *Jóais*
(Jewelry) series, 1997
Plexiglas wall boxes; crystal
beads, cut stones, surgical
needles, razor blades,
scalpel blades, fish hooks,
lancets, and X-Acto blades
Dimensions variable
Courtesy Galeria
Brito Cimino, São Paulo

The idea of marginality—living on the margin of society—is a durable bourgeois notion. But this is not the sense in which the sort of films I made and still make are marginal. What is marginal is the revolutionary act of invention: a new reality, the world as change, the mistake as adventure, and discovery of freedom—films that are ten or twenty seconds long, anticinema.

I had taken part in radical movements, such as the neo-concrete group, which proposed an unadorned and nondiscursive language—"Less is more." Pure minimalism. This clearly stated aesthetic implied a position worlds apart from movies with predetermined scripts, nearly always telling pat stories with a beginning, a middle, and an end; an Aristotelian concept. To interpret a script was precisely what I did *not* want—that would produce nothing new, no risk, only the predictable sort of traditional movies that are the staple of film festivals, exhibitors, and inattentive audiences. My friend Glauber Rocha was bold enough to work with a script that was con-

To us, Georges Méliès was always more important as a pioneer of early cinema than the Lumière brothers. While the brothers were and still are the original source and driving force of a literary, narrative cinema, Méliès stood for the power of pure image as expression. It is seductive cinema, but it cannot hope for box-office success because the public is addicted to what is facile, to clichés. This is an overwhelming fact for all filmmakers. Dalí with Buñuel; Carl Dryer and his mysterious vampire, created without special effects; the constructivist Ozu, whom people insist on seeing as a social analyst; and particularly René Clair's *Entréacte*—these are the heirs of Méliès, my idol.

The Cinema Novo, or new realist films, made from 1960 to 1970 presented image pure and simple—free, brilliant images with which my imagination built chiaroscuro structures, as if they were paintings. I worked for the Cinema Novo as a professional designer, making credits, posters, and displays for Nelson Pereira dos Santos's landmark film

Lygia Pape
My Work in Marginal Cinema

BY LYGIA PAPE

cocted as the movie—a feature film—was being shot.

I opted for short subjects so that I would not be involved in major productions, bureaucratic hassles, and, most of all, financial problems. It was to be the sheer joy of creation. The production team was a close-knit group consisting of one director-editor, one friendly photographer (I always work with 35mm film), and one electrician; that was it. The director is the real sovereign. Nothing can be done without him or her.

In the 1960s there was an intense dialogue between artists in Rio de Janeiro and filmmakers interested in the visual arts, such as Rocha and Paulo Cesar Sarraceni, who screened the first version of *Arraial do Cabo* at my house, the Patio, as Rocha had his first movie. With Gilberto Macedo and Luis Carlos Soares I set up a small film society, and we watched movies of all kinds. Another source of information was the film festivals: José Sanz and the British, French, Japanese, Spanish, and most of all, the Russian movies.

Mandacuru vermelho (Red Mandacuru) (1961), the most elaborate project. For it, I made alphabets with wood and printed every subtitle, letter by letter, on precious Japanese paper so that the grain of the wood would show through, imitating the look of traditional northeastern *cordel* poetry. At the same time, I was working on my own projects, making quite a few "visual poems" with movie images—the images built themselves as Brasília was being built.

In 1963 Cosme Alves Neto asked me to create a film vignette for all the films in the Cinematheque (Film Library) at Rio's Museum of Modern Art (MAM). Because people used to say, "I'm going to MAM" (pronounced *mohm*), I used a cow from *Vidas secas* mooing over the image of the MAM logo, which faded in and out several times. Then came the syllables of the word *ci–ne–ma–te–ca* hidden under stills from old movies that had a sound or visual relation to the word. This short film was well received but was suppressed by order of Niomar Muniz Sodré, who did not grasp its humor.

I entered a contest at Expo 67 in Montreal for a fifty-second film, the theme of which was Saint-Exupéry's *Terre des hommes*. This was when the great interplanetary journeys were beginning, so I thought of man not on earth but in space. I used NASA footage showing an astronaut emerging from the mother ship like a child from a womb and floating in space as if he were a fetus connected to his mother by an umbilical cord. The film begins in black and white, but suddenly the screen goes red, and a crying child is heard. The new man is born—*La nouvelle création* (The New Creation), as the film is called—not only on earth but also in outer space.

Soon afterward, I started a film about movie kisses. It remained unfinished. I made three feature films in Super 8, all of them in 1974. In *Wampirou* (suggesting "the vampire went nuts"), in addition to

The film is edited mathematically, divided first into two parts, then the second half broken in two, and so on, building a pulse that increases to the very end. The voice heard shouting or singing at a certain moment is Yoko Ono's. This experimental film—an attack on the mass media—was read as pornography by the censors. It was finally cleared three years later; only then could it be shown in movie theaters.

In 1978 I made *Catiti–Catiti*, a black-and-white 16mm film (my only one in this format) with an explicit sense of deconstruction. In it I speak of anthropophagy (the concept of devouring other cultures and making new things out of them), spiritual or otherwise. Images of Rio are shown with the text of Pero Vaz de Caminha's 1500 letter as background. Forests are seen while the sound of chain saws is heard, and girls

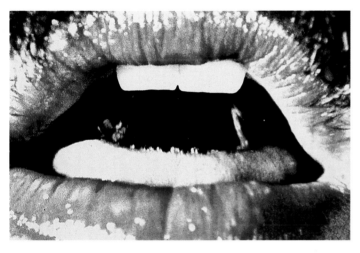

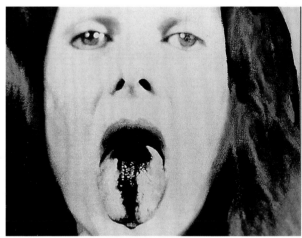

Above left:

Eat Me, 1975

Video (9 min.)

Courtesy of the artist

Above right:

Poemas Visuais:

Língua Apunhalada

(Visual Poem: Blood Tongue), 1968

Photograph and light box

70⅞ × 47¼ in.

(180 × 120 cm)

Courtesy Galeria Camargo Vilaça, São Paulo

actors there are artists including Lygia Clark and poets Waly Salomão in walk-on roles. *Carnival in Rio* is about people who go out in the streets and celebrate Carnival alone; it was shot in downtown Rio around the area from Praça Mauá to the Obelisk. *Arenas calientes* (Hot Sands) was the most interesting film, in which my characters had all sorts of adventures in a desert with huge dunes, at the present site of the Nova Ipanema residential complex in Rio. When the characters were thirsty they drank gasoline at the service stations in the area.

In 1975 I shot *Eat Me*, a film that creates an erotic atmosphere using only close shots of a mouth that sometimes looks like an eye, sometimes like a vagina, sometimes simply like a mouth. Voices speaking in different languages rhythmically repeat the phrase, "Gluttony or lust."

on Ipanema Beach are shown as if they were early-sixteenth-century Indians. At the end a politician's voice is heard, making campaign promises. *Sedução 111¹¹* (2000) is a video of groups of people coming and going that is repeated infinitely, like a wave. Similar to *Eat Me*, it was edited on the basis of a mathematically determined rhythm. *Maiakovski, A Viagem* (2000) is a video made to be shown in the street. It uses an image of Vladimir Maiakovsky's head made by the Russian painter Alexandre Rodchenko, and out of the character's mouth come two phrases that are actually titles of poems by Maiakovsky—"From street to street" and "In the automobile"—while little green cars move around all over the screen.

Right now I'm working on a video about shadows. Let's see how it comes out. ■

Women approached as bodies, intensive expression and gestures, lines frozen in the air. Expression approached as a wound. Feminine body, space for generating nuclei, repository of life. At a time when artists are refraining from representing the human figure because they want to avoid fatigue or are restrained by shyness, discrimination, or the difficulty of creating anew, Rosana Paulino makes the feminine body her own subject. It is a theme much focused and worked on, retrieved and refocused in faces, bellies, a sequence of gestures that remind us of a diary. Even in drawings clearly inspired by Anita Malfatti in her best period (around 1917) or by the visceral transparencies of Ismael Nery's late period (1929–34), Paulino does not shy away from retrieving artistic history.

She emerged and became known in São Paulo's art milieu with her installations and objects triggered by family pictures. The artist sees them as that generously traverses the paper's surface in a nearly random motion. Her line can also be tortuous, leading to a graphic universe like Philip Guston's, where they nearly always border the edges of the rectangular page like restrained convulsions.

Paulino is a daring artist for her generation. She has crafted a visual diary in exercise-book albums, using crayon or graphite; sometimes she chooses to be just linear or makes watercolors with a crayon wash or china ink. Her color is always precisely apportioned and applied at crucial points. One detects a diversification in her approach to the feminine body: distinctive forms, with an emphasis on stained, marked, nearly half-open genital organs. Sex is projected as a painful attribute of the body, withholding the pleasure derived from appeased desire. She also shows the feminine body in movement, as an expressive ges-

Rosana Paulíno
Women and Their Bodies

BY ARACY AMARAL

"prisons in which the 'soul' of the photographed person seems suspended," frozen in time. Her own contributions, stemming from an affectionate and singular painterliness, immediately drew attention for their delicate expressiveness. Her works incorporated embroideries and wrinkled pieces of fabric with different textures and embroidery hoops; in them the image of faces, "mirrors of the soul," are attacked and silenced by the subtle violence of sewn stitches. Although sewing is considered domestic work, Paulino overcomes feminine nostalgia.

In addition to these works, the artist draws with intensity, showing a painful imaginary syntax that also seems to project a veiled "secret," such as can be seen in the manipulated photos displayed in her *Parede da Memória* (Walls of Memory) (1994). Her recent drawings have been informal, closely linked to gesture, with an abstract, calligraphic line ture, with belly and buttocks highlighted as points of reference.

Paulino frequently uses monotypes as an exercise in freedom. As a starting point for new series, as a triggering drive that overcomes the restricting control of drawing, the monotype as a medium retrieves the rigidity of the created image, thus achieving her drawings' sense of randomness. This process comes as close to surrealistic procedures as frottage (rubbings that record textures such as wood grain, relief carvings, and so forth), freeing the connection between hand and subconscious and enabling an expression free from rational limitations.

Among other series of Paulino drawings, the body is seen as a shelter for the heart, uterus, spinal column, and skeletal structure. Women contain growing embryos; the fetus, linear or nebulous, lacks definition, just like the profile of the woman's face, whose expression is unimportant. In

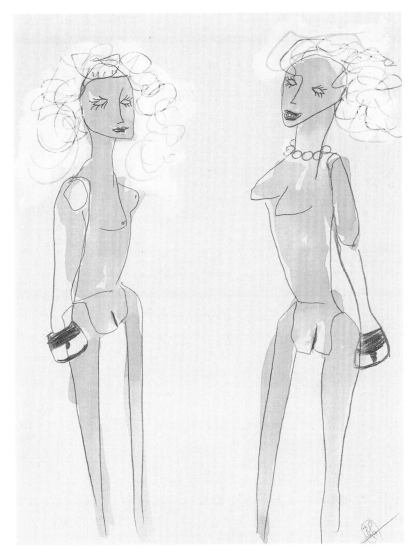

Drawing from *Models* series,
1996–98
Ink, pastel, charcoal,
graphite, and acrylic on paper
Dimensions various
Collection of the artist

still another series, the cruelty of the woman-doll emerges, reduced to a profusion of eyelashes, hard lips, and vaginas the color of blood. Broken graphite lines cross the paper as if in a trance, a medium-like message suddenly revealing a face on which the smile becomes spasmodic, a mortuary grimace rather than the representation of a *figée* (set expression of happiness); the squalid doll-dummy can be playfully dressed, undressed, and combed as if it were alive. The renewed overlapping line stresses the dramatic quality of the lifeless bodies, on which their attributes—vagina, necklace, handbag, ornamented shoes—are projected. They are appropriate toys for a childish curiosity, a kind of non-sense entertainment conveying perplexity immersed in frightening black humor.

Paulino's figures in the air remind us of Di Cavalcanti's early expressionism, as seen in his *Fantoches da Meia-noite* (Midnight Dummies), painted before the *Modernist Art Exhibition* of 1922. In her devotion to Brazilian art history—a rare stance among young Brazilian artists—she shows her fascination with the dramatic, emotional lines in Flavio de Carvalho's drawings *Minha mãe Morrendo* (My Mother Dying) (1947). Paulino also knows equally well Egon Schiele's Viennese contortions from the period 1910–18. Although she may not have seen them, her dolls also remind us of the erotic dolls portrayed in the strange photographic images created by Hans Bellmer in the 1930s.

Focusing on the many paths and images opened up by the female body as a counterpoint to the implicit anorexia of the body-dummy, Paulino resumes her incursion in art history in search of the attributes of the feminine figure as a reproducer, fat in her abundance, seductive in her fertility. Thus was the definition of woman through the centuries: a round nucleus, generous, with up to eight breasts. The multibreasted figure and the apparently pregnant woman on all fours are rooted in woman's procreation ability, the very source of life.

These figures created, re-created, and elaborated on by Rosana Paulino have a ghostly quality; they are like gestures frozen in midair, conveyed in graphite, crayon, and watercolor. They craft a difficult graphic vocabulary of intimate sensibility. ■

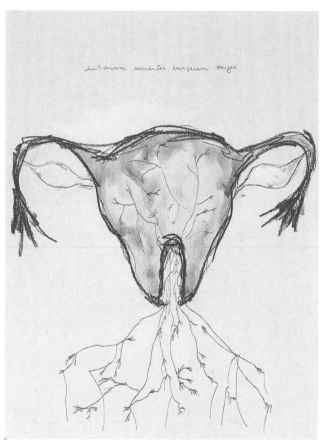

Drawings from untitled series
(Diário de uma doença)
(Illness Diary), 1999
Graphite, ink, watercolor,
and pastel on green
gessoed paper
15⅛ × 11⅜ in.
(38.3 × 29 cm) each
Private collection

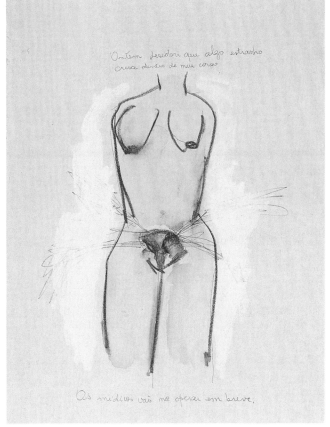

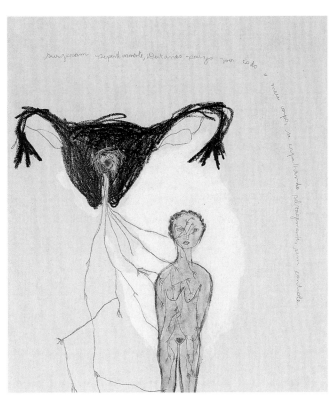

Rosângela Rennó

Vera Cruz

BY ROSÂNGELA RENNÓ

■ The only documentation possible for the moment of the discovery of Brazil in 1500 would have been a drawing or a written account. If some pictorial document ever existed, it did not survive. There are, however, three text accounts, the most complete in the form of a letter signed by Pero Vaz de Caminha and addressed to Dom Manuel I of Portugal, informing him of the discovery of a new "Eden."

The document is frustrating because, in spite of its rich details about the ten days its author spent on the coast of the "Ilha de Vera Cruz" (Island of the True Cross), it rests on the perceptions only of the discoverer. We are missing the reply as well as the reaction of the indigenous people—those Edenic creatures so different from the European conqueror. In any case, dialogue between the Portuguese and the Amerindian natives was impossible for obvious reasons. The absence of any recorded conversation creates in the letter's modern reader a desire to imagine the real discussion, an action that would have been difficult to transcribe, no matter how detailed.

Impossibilities like these can only engender a work that is based on similar impossibilities. The impossibility of dialogue between the Portuguese and the natives finds its double in the impossibility of the existence of an image and a sound constituting a documentary. Nevertheless, if in fiction everything is possible, you have to see it and hear it to believe it.

Vera Cruz (True Cross), 2000
Video with English subtitles
(44 min.)
Courtesy of the artist

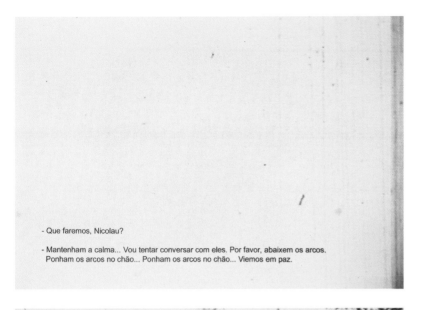

- Que faremos, Nicolau?

- Mantenham a calma... Vou tentar conversar com eles. Por favor, abaixem os arcos.
  Ponham os arcos no chão... Ponham os arcos no chão... Viemos em paz.

- O colar... ele gostou do colar.

- É de ouro. Ouro... Ou... ro... O quê? Em terra? Eles apontam para a terra.
  Há ouro em terra? Então deve haver ouro em terra.

Vera Cruz (True Cross) (2000) reproduces on video an impossible film that fluctuates between documentary and fiction genres. The image was removed, leaving only an old, scratchy "movie image," seemingly worn by time and excessive use. The sound of the words was also removed, as the dialogue between the discoverer and the natives did not, properly speaking, occur. What remained was just the sound of the sea and the wind—witnesses. Nevertheless, the account remained, which in the case of this video took the form of a text with subtitles.

Vera Cruz is thus a documentary-fiction about the moment of Brazil's discovery, in a version with Portuguese subtitles. Also available in English. ∎

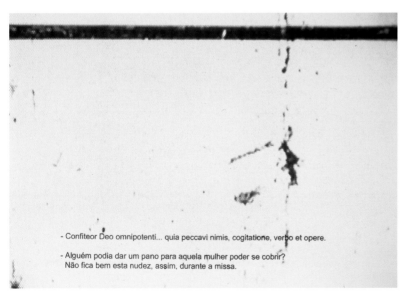

- Confiteor Deo omnipotenti... quia peccavi nimis, cogitatione, verbo et opere.

- Alguém podia dar um pano para aquela mulher poder se cobrir?
  Não fica bem esta nudez, assim, durante a missa.

Photographing Poetry

Looking, seeing, stealing, and collecting life moments and then choosing, using montage, collage, sawing, or mainly putting together a patchwork—these are some of the things involved in the construction of my feelings. This is not about using photographs and film as documents of something other than an inner self. The theme is something that after a while disappears. It is not really necessary and is something that we forget very fast. When you use photography the outside is only an unavoidable element, and even if you do not immediately recognize what is shown, there is still a document.

Míguel Río Branco
Door ínto Darkness

BY MIGUEL RIO BRANCO AND LIGIA CANONGIA

But when we begin the construction of a discourse and the deconstruction of the documented, when the patchwork is finished, or unfinished, we get into poetry. And when we get into poetry it is like making music. The work is not something about some subject, some specific time; it goes deeper inside and leaves your mind open to itself. If we really need to say something about it, *Door into Darkness*, as the title itself suggests, talks about fear. But somewhere in the darkroom, there are some images, some noise; it looks as if there is something electronic, not very clear but definitely cold, definitely electronic, and possibly sexual.

—Miguel Rio Branco

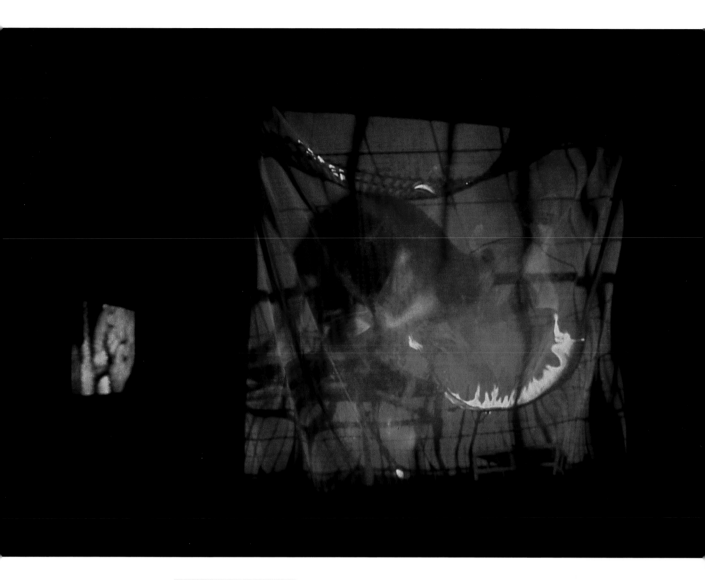

Door into Darkness, 1995
Projection of seventeen slides
Dimensions variable
Courtesy of the artist

*Nada levarei quando
morrer aqueles que mim
deve cobrarei no inferno*
(I Won't Take Nothing When
I Die Those Who Owe Me
Something Will Pay in Hell),
1979–81
DVD version of 16mm film
(20 min.)
Courtesy of the artist

The Question of the "Theme"

The photographs of Miguel Rio Branco frustrate the expectations of the usual observer of photography who, despite the value of the image, rushes to find meaning in the theme. The subject, the factual reality, in fact the thematic, merely "survive" in Rio Branco's work to the extent that the focal point of its real and primary significance is transferred to another fictional one.

The "theme," however, is a question of an almost dissolved residual character, even rendered characterless in this process of transfer from fact to image, from reality to fiction. The artist's images belong to a sphere of enigma and drama that extrapolate the definition of a precise factual field and transform it into another more sensitive universe, redimensioned by its subjective poetry. The theme is obscured, secondary and soluble, and its function is merely indicatory because the alterations produced by the incisions of the cuts, of light and color, always end up revealing an "other" reading, a new route of access to that reality. The theme has a fluctuating and transformable presence. The images themselves manifest bordering states: between real and unreal, physical and metaphysical, sacred and profane, whole and fragment, and human and beast. The work fluctuates on the border itself, constituting a register of an empirical and objective fact while demarcating an authorial field, declaring a singular conscience and point of view.

But stubborn focal points exist: violence, transgression, corrosion, time, sex, and wounds—signs of the violation of life or the throbbing of death. The theme is not a "thing" but rather a concept; not restricted to objects, people, scenes or events, physical elements or observed concrete reality. On the contrary, the interest is in the abstraction, the immaterial, a deeper spectrum of chance that can go beyond the circumstance and contingency of things to turn them into poetic signs. With his emotional and dramatic vision, Rio Branco seeks to restore an ontological dignity to more immediate and common situations, raising them up from the stigma of banality.

The emotion in color, the loss of contours, the juxtaposition of planes, the dissolution of images, the play of mirrors—in short, the very experience of the work itself—configures "that which we see" in such a way that the theme does not preexist the work. Rather, it emerges in its own way through the work itself.

—Ligia Canongia

Regína Sílveíra

Recapturing History

BY SUSANA TORRUELLA LEVAL

■ Latin Americans find a profound sense of themselves by looking at their past. This sense of history is inextricably bound up with their identity as Latin Americans. It elucidates the present and projects the future in an unbroken continuum. Contemporary artists of Latin American descent often embody this historical consciousness in their work. In widely varied forms and strategies, they recapture their past from distortion or oblivion. For them, historical memory—the act of remembering, of salvaging the past—is equivalent to collective survival. Some recapture the past indirectly, through poetic visions or imaginary journeys into time. For others, the excursions into history have required actual physical pilgrimages. Still others have found that their perspective of the past must be translated into direct, political terms that reflect current events.

Regina Silveira has chosen to question an accepted viewpoint of historic events by reinterpreting a key public monument in her native city of São Paulo. The Bandeiras Monument rises in Ibirapuera Park as a proud metaphor of São Paulo's progressive spirit. It celebrates the brave forays of the *bandeirantes* (seventeenth-century Portuguese, Indian, and black explorers) who set out from São Paulo into Brazil's rugged interior to look for gold. Each political administration has claimed identification with the heroes of the monument, which was commissioned by the modernists in 1922 from the French-born artist Victor Brecheret but not built until 1953 by de Salles Oliveira. During the 1950s the modernists identified the energetic forward momentum of the monument's band of "men setting off in conquest of a new world" with their dreams of progress, to be achieved through the "civilizing" effects of industrialization and technology.[1]

Silveira questions that "progress" and its consequences in her overwhelming *Monudentro* (Inside the Monument), a 130-foot-tall painted silhouette in a hexagonal space, created for the 1987 São Paulo

Opposite top:

Natural Beauties
(from *Brazil Today),* 1977
Book of six altered postcards
Paper
4¼ × 6⅛ ×⅛ in.
(10.2 × 15.6 × .5 cm) closed
Collection of the artist

Left:
Monudentro
(Inside the Monument),
1986–87
Paint and carpeting
Site-specific installation,
XIX Bienal Internacional
de São Paulo

Bienal. The piece is paradigmatic of her installation work since 1980, which, as described by the artist, uses "projective" images of "silhouettes, viewpoints, and distortions" to create a complex changing play of visual images, illusions, and perceptions. With characteristic irony, *Monudentro* uses the monument's sharply defined silhouette to generate ambiguity by means of a multiplicity of views. Through a series of distortions in the projected image, Silveira's version arrests the original monument's forward thrust—in fact, reversing its movement. She chose "to reverse the meaning through the distortion,"[2] a strategy characteristic of her projective work. As the pun in the title implies (*dentro* means "inside"), Silveira's version places viewers at the vortex of the giant projection, which surrounds them on three sides. From its center they can question politicians' promises as well as the city's historical "progress" and their own role in it. ■

Opposite top and above:
Computer model for
Monudentro
(Inside the Monument), 2001
Developed by Claudio Bueno,
Architect
Collection of the artist

Opposite bottom:
Model for *Monudentro*
(Inside the Monument), 1987
Wood, paint, and fabric
Height: 8⅞ in. (22.5 cm)
Circumference: 31½ in.
(80 cm)
Collection of the artist

■ For more than a decade, Valeska Soares has consistently transformed neutral environments into works of art, but unlike most installation art to date Valeska's work focuses on what happens beyond the space and time of the exhibition itself. In a way, her installations work as life-size models, oddly scaled metaphors for events that could have happened long before the exhibition ever takes place. In these installations, the spectator-participant seems to experience a split between real and representational time; one becomes aware of the immensity of one's own daydream. Through a seemingly inexhaustible range of techniques, themes, and strategies, Soares's work oscillates between materiality and memory, desire and decay, sensation and intoxication.

vs: I am really interested in that faint line between being seduced by something and being completely

Valeska Soares

Intoxication

BY VIK MUNIZ

intoxicated by it. In my work, perfume has become a metaphor for possibilities of intoxication. It's a substance that crosses that border between being pleasurable and being overintoxicating.

vm: In other words, you're asking the question, What if lethal gas smelled good?

vs: What is desire if it's not this faint line between being intoxicated by something or sickened? You can be intoxicated by many things: hate, desire, love. Our societies have become so normalized that one of the only transgressive points we have is this very faint line of intoxication.

vm: When one thing becomes another.

vs: Yes, when you cross the line, even if it's only for a minute or so, you abandon yourself to something. You've lost control.

vm: I love your piece with the hummingbird feeders. What do you call that?

Opposite:
Detail of Untitled
(from *Strangelove),* 1996
Lead, blown glass, wine, and poison
Site-specific installation, Laumeier Sculpture Park, St. Louis, Missouri
$14\frac{1}{8} \times 9 \times 3$ in.
($36 \times 23 \times 7.5$ cm) each

Overleaf:
Strangelove, 1996
Installation view, Laumeier Sculpture Park

vs: Oh, *Strangelove*. It's inspired not only by hummingbird feeders but also by IV bags and medical tubing. The color of the liquid is red, because that is the color that attracts hummingbirds. But the liquid in the piece contains poisoned wine, and on the outside are lead flowers. The piece functions like a minefield—it's placed inside where the birds can never get to it, but human beings can. The feeders are sealed, but if anyone were to actually complete the action and ingest the fluid, he or she would die.

vm: There's the paradox of Zeuxis and his contender, Parrhasius. Zeuxis painted fruit that could attract birds. When Zeuxis went to see what Parrhasius was doing, he stood in front of Parrhasius's painting and said, "Okay, unveil it." And Parrhasius said, "It is already unveiled; it is a painting of a veil." The question being, Which image is the strongest—the one that fools a man or the one that fools a bird? I believe Parrhasius wasn't as good because for man, art is primal experience. We're always trying to retrieve our primitive, more animal-like senses. We're trying to go to the limit. That's my view, that we're always trying to retrieve a bit of this trance and sensation and sensibility that we had before.

vs: I'm thinking of a text where the author talks about the development of human beings. He said that in the beginning there was only imagination. We understood the world through images. But then imagination became so dense that we had to conceptualize because we couldn't deal with such a huge amount of images. That's how language was created. We have come to a point where language and concepts are so dense that we are moving back to the imagination, but it's not the original imagination anymore.

vm: It's an image of an image.

vs: It's contaminated, intoxicated by the conceptualization of the two processes. We can't isolate ourselves and go back to this primitive place where we understand only through images or mythological icons. It's nonsense to try to separate mind from body. ∎

■ I was in front of the television set when Carmen Miranda fell. I was a boy living in Florida. It was Jimmy Durante's show. Many years later I watched the scene again in Helena Solberg and David Meyer's movie *Bananas Is My Business*. I heard the dialogue between Carmen and Jimmy Durante. She falls: "Oh. . . . I cannot breathe. . . ." Jimmy: "Don't worry, I'll say your lines." Carmen, looking pale, recovers her composure and leaves through the stage door, dancing. Smiling, with her hands flying in circles and whirling her shiny skirt, she slowly disappears through the door, which Jimmy closes with a tense look on his face. And she leaves life.

The film is precious to those who want to join the First World. Solberg and Meyer, in a work of research and lyricism, took a step beyond the mere documentary and redesigned the rise and downfall of Carmen Miranda while they painted a portrait of Brazil's eternal fragility. Brazilians must watch *Bananas Is My Business* to see who we are. In the

We see in the American movies that they, even in the past, were in a "present." Refrigerators were white, telephones were black, they wore hats, but it was the same America as today. Americans always lived according to their time. Brazilians did not. In the images of long-gone Brazil, we always seemed to be late for progress, always a mock image of something that was not us. Old movies give us the feeling that everyone died without knowing better days. Even fictional movies are documentaries of our needs, seen right there in the actors' faces. Poor Copacabana, poor Cariocas (Rio de Janeiro inhabitants), unprotected before the world's eyes.

Then came Carmen Miranda with her smile, her style. She was a future. Her gestures were a parody of the world around her, and no one realized it. She was smarter than all the rest. She intuited mass culture, as tropicalism's most famous singer-songwriter Caetano Veloso would say many years later;

Helena Solberg
Bananas Is My Business

BY ARNALDO JABOR

1930s and 1940s, Brazil as we now know it was under development. Our meagerness becomes so clear in those old movies. Brazil was so fragile, so unprotected in the face of foreign desires, so poorly filmed in the past, so badly preserved. Only eight minutes of scenes with Carmen were shot in Brazil.

Not only the movies were poorly preserved. The fact is that reality was also tremulous and badly preserved; everything was naive and poor, and we were actors "short of" our time. We realize that we were not yet in the "present" but that in the past we were in the "past." In the past we were already "old." I look at the fragments of old images desperately trying to understand the mystery of our fate. Copacabana, the Bando da Lua, the striped shirts of the samba school, rascally bon vivants, the Art Deco microphones, the radio days, the feeble reproduction of sound and image, the cartoons by J. Carlos, mustaches á la Clark Gable, hats, Getúlio Vargas—everything through the three dimensions of an empty academic picture. What was wrong with us?

it was she who already pointed to what would eventually become tropicalism. Carmen lights up her time, and with her light we can also see the track of something that was part of our destiny and that was lost later on; we can see the footprints of the steps we were still to take. There lay the mystery of a classic Brazilianness that faded away and disappeared in the 1970s.

Today we see *Bananas Is My Business* as a lost bond. (How will we be seen in fifty years? Will we be shaky like those weak men in hats?) It's all there. "Today" is there. The Americans and French don't feel the same. In fact, the only color images we have of Brazil in the 1940s were shot by Orson Welles. It is our only color Carnival, while *The Wizard of Oz* and *Gone with the Wind* were shot in color in 1939. We see ourselves through other people's eyes.

Only American movies recorded Carmen's talent, and in them Brazil is portrayed indirectly, in the perfect Technicolor of the 1940s. Carmen triumphantly arrives on Broadway, with the beauty of

Carmen Miranda:
Bananas Is My Business,
1995
Video version of 35mm film
with English subtitles
(92 min.)
Courtesy Women Make
Movies

her perfect gestures, her voice drawing a calculated joy. Carmen used her body as if she were another person who sang. Appearing as an exaggeration was her idea: fantasying herself, being another person, an "I" without a center. Carmen invented the modern live allegory, which prefigures the indeterminacy of today's constructed identities. From that came the immense current fascination with her. That is why transvestites adore her.

Solberg and Meyer's movie becomes a great documentary about our colonial situation, an anthropophagy (cannibalism) of Carmen committed by the American people from down to up. It is Hollywood sucking the light out of the tropics as an antidote to the 1930s depression. Newspapers said literally: "Carmen Miranda has announced the end of the Depression!"

But from our darkrooms the movie seems a cruel picture of her face changing. Right after her initial success, when she becomes fascinated by the dazzling perfection of her joy, the intercultural conflict

begins between Latin fragility and practical Yankee market sense. Carmen arrives (and we along with her) with the naive belief that she was conquering America. The Office of Coordination of Inter-American Affairs had recently been created. The only purpose of that "friendly relations" policy was to keep Latins from becoming allied with Hitler and to find a market for American products in case something happened to Europe.

Subsequently organizations such as the Pan-American Operations and the Alliance for Progress were established, and today we have the great and charming casino of neoliberalism. And as usual, we are attracted by the sweet hope that we will be accepted for our "beautiful eyes." We always think that we will belong to the First World ball, but at the eleventh hour we play the role of the maid, the waiter, or the prostitute. Sonia Braga was dubbed a Puerto Rican by the Americans who bought her movie *I Love You*. In her last work, Rita Moreno gave Jack Nicholson a blow job in *Carnal Knowledge*. Carmen left dreaming that she would become a cordial utopia and was slowly smashed between two nationalisms: ours, racist and envious, and theirs, racial and exclusionary.

When Carmen came home in the late 1940s, she was received with terrible silence and hatred by the aristocratic audience of Urca Cassino. ("She is a hatter," my aunts used to say, "from the Travessa do Comercio," a street in Rio.) She never recovered. In Brazil, samba belonged to the "hill"—the *favelas*, the poorer neighborhoods. She was rejected, in anticipation of WASP racism that would come up later when Bing Crosby grotesquely mocked her (as did Mickey Rooney and Jerry Lewis), singing, "Take back your samba." The need for Latin markets was guaranteed; they could let her go. The United States is the most nationalistic country in the world, do not delude yourselves. Carmen Miranda, the perfect sexy joy, was slowly transformed by producers into a unisex virago, a sinister caricature of herself. She was rejected in Brazil for being Americanized and deformed in the north into a vulgar, comical "Chicana."

This film could not have been more timely. We are living in the "friendly relations" days of the global market. We must be careful not to be spit out after lunch. After all, bananas are still our "business." Will we die from this trauma? ■

"Draw near, illustrious Odysseus, flower of Achaean chivalry, and bring your ship to rest so that you may hear our voices. No seaman ever sailed his black ship past this spot without listening to the sweet tones that flow from our lips, and none that listened has not been delighted and gone on a wiser man. For we know all that the Argives and Trojans suffered on the broad plain of Troy by the will of the gods, and we have foreknowledge of all that is going to happen on this fruitful earth."

"The lovely voices came to me across the water, and my heart was filled with such a longing to listen that with nod and frown I signed to my men to set me free. But they swung forward to their oars and rowed ahead, while Parimedes and Eurylochus jumped up, tightened my bonds and added more. However, when they had rowed past the Sirens and we could no longer hear their voices and the burden of their song, my good companions were quick to clear their ears of the wax I had used to stop them, and to free me from my shackles."

Homer, *Odyssey*, Book 12

Janaína Tschäpe
Fables for a Body in Pieces

BY CELSO FIORAVANTE

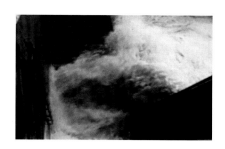

■ The work of the young Brazilian artist Janaína Tschäpe moves between antitheses, between opposites that are so close as to be indistinguishable. In her art the programmed and the unexpected cohabit, as do beauty and horror, fact and fiction, solid and liquid, parts and the whole.

Tschäpe has recently produced a series of photographs using fragments of her own body. These images represent hands, arms, legs, and ankles wrapped in transparent latex, water-filled balloons (in fact, condoms), whose presence deforms the vision of the body parts. She has also produced a video, displayed in an endless loop that shows her face also submerged and deformed as if she were the victim of imminent drowning. In both works the observer sees a body that is distant from the ideal norms and situations of beauty. In both, Tschäpe uses references tied to a well-known mythological character, the mermaid.

The relationship could not be more natural. The artist was born already linked to that ancestral myth of female beauty and mystery. Her mother, who was living in Germany at the time, named her daughter after Iemanjá (in Yoruba, the queen of the sea) as a way of placating her own nostalgia for Brazil: the name Janaína reminded her of the ocean and the country's mysticism.

Brazilian culture has incorporated the mermaid myth in a variety of ways. Indians have a cult to Iara, the mother of water, a mermaid who inhabits the country's rivers and lakes. They also believe in the *boiúna*, a mythological figure that sinks vessels and takes the shipwrecked to the bottom of the river. Afro-Brazilians venerate Iemanjá, Janaína's namesake. Western culture contributed as well by enriching the popular imagination with representations of the sirens going back to Homer.

In the *Odyssey*, Homer described two encounters by Odysseus (Ulysses) with these beings. In the first of these, when his ship was sailing from Ithaca to Troy, he was saved by the song of Orpheus, whose beauty overcame the sirens' song. On the way back, all the crew stopped up their ears with wax; Ulysses, however, was tied to the ship's mast and thus could hear them with impunity. In Homer's description, the sirens lived on high rocks, and the upper part of their bodies was represented by that of a woman while the lower had the body of a bird. In the course of history, sirens came to be portrayed as women with a fishtail.

Mermaids are one of those rare myths that populate a great part of Western and Eastern cultures. Examples or derivations can be found in Phoenician, Etruscan, Celtic, Scandinavian, Hindu, German, African, and Japanese cultures, among others. "What fascinates me about the image of the mermaid," says Tschäpe, "is the idea generated around woman and the discovery of new lands, travels by sea, the unknown. The mermaid is always a being who was in all the places that man had not discovered yet."

Created on the basis of her own body, Tschäpe's mermaids are fragmented and anonymous. They are demystified self-portraits, turned around and unglamourous, in which beauty gives way to drama. But she grants them some privileges, ideal situations—such as birth, relationships, and death—to which mermaids would not have access, for they are prisoners of their cruel and tragic eternity. "The need to work with my own body came about unexpectedly," she explains. "I always traveled alone, taking my memories with me, and at the same time tried to introduce myself into the new space. My interest is not in making a portrait of myself but in creating a character that I can manipulate to create situations and stories that I might want to record."

It is also possible to perceive in Tschäpe's work a certain political bias: the rejection of female predestination to a tragic condition or a submission to the stereotypes of beauty. It is not by chance that mermaids were one of the myths of pagan cultures (such as the Greco-Roman civilization) that survived the advance of Christianity. That, however, does not mean that they were liked by the Church. In fact, those who profess the existence of a single true God saw in the mermaid a symbol of beauty, vanity, and sin and thus a means by which virtuous men became disoriented.

Woman, meanwhile, earned her independence and no longer lives as a prisoner high on isolated rocks in the middle of the sea, appearing only to deceive careless sailors who let themselves be fooled by their extreme beauty and melodious song, taking them to the depths of the unknown. "What interests me," explains Tschäpe, "is to enter this mythological being from the female point of view, imagining what her role is, what her physical representation is, demystifying and reviewing the female role in contemporary daily circumstances."

A good part of the vigor of her oeuvre originates in her own day-to-day life. Tschäpe incorporates facts and situations from her daily living and transforms them into performances, photographs, films, videos, and sculptures. "I like the domesticity and simplicity with which stories happen, how encounters can occur and personal moments that exist in the life of each of us. They are moments that I transform into fiction by means of a simple physical modification, such as a mask or a transformation of the body."

Tschäpe intends to awaken in us the type of reaction that the ancestral mermaids gave rise to in careless sailors who, deceived by the siren songs and melodious notes, forgot their oars, sails, and tillers and let their vessels be dashed to pieces against immovable rocks. The artist wants to disorient spectators in order to take them toward the unknown. ∎

Opposite top three:
*He Drowned in Her Eyes
as She Called Him to Follow:
Medusa*, 2000
Video version of DVD (5 min.)
Courtesy of the artist

Opposite bottom:
*He Drowned in Her Eyes
as She Called Him to Follow:
Moss*, 2001
Video version of DVD (5 min.)
Courtesy of the artist

■ Adriana Varejão's work continuously evokes a sense of passage, a journey among divergent images, cultures, times, and spaces. Alluding to the notion of a universe in constant expansion and transformation, she uses diverse imagery, infinitely projecting one onto "the other." Following an intricate and paradoxical path toward the baroque, the artist's empowering poetic strategy addresses the complexities of cultural constructions, influences, and exchanges. Varejão appropriates and remaps a vast body of images, forms, and ideas disseminated by the Europeans during their colonization of Brazil: a history of violence and domination; of resistance, displacements, and syncretisms, one in continuous reformulation, always revealing its own dense layers of representation. The artist states,

Adriana Varejão
Travel Chronicles

BY RINA CARVAJAL

I am interested in verifying in my work dialectical processes of power and persuasion. I subvert those processes and try to gain control over them in order to become an agent of history rather than remaining an anonymous, passive spectator. I not only appropriate historic images—I also attempt to bring back to life processes which created them and use them to construct new versions.[1]

The baroque is more than a theme or an iconographic source for Varejão—it is a linguistic strategy, a mode of analysis that permits her to critically reexplore past legacies and, at the same time, elucidate the paradoxes of the present. The work is always open, mobile, placing itself among interstices and fissures, in spaces occupied by contradictory realities. Following the processes of baroque construction, Varejão sets up an infinite assemblage of images, an elusive hall of mirrors intended to defuse the power of the intended to gaze. In an unending rhythm that moves from one plane to another, one

Opposite:
Testemunhas Oculares
X, Y e Z (Eye Witnesses X, Y and Z), 1997
Oil on canvas, porcelain, photography, silver, crystal, and iron
Three paintings: 33½ × 27½ in. (85 × 70 cm) each
Three objects: 34⅝ × 6¼ × 9⅞ in. (88 × 16 × 25 cm) each
Collection Frances Marinho, Rio de Janeiro

Right:
Detail of *Testemunhas Oculares X, Y e Z*
(Eye Witnesses X, Y and Z), 1997

571

perception to another, one narration to another, the work establishes a kind of *mise en abîme* of images, layers, and folds that continuously condense, juxtapose, and transform the representations created by the colonizer. Varejão's documentation allows her to confront distinct narratives, contaminating one discourse with another, thus provoking multiple layers of meaning, always resisting and subverting a reductive or totalizing effort.

In *Filho Bastardo* (Bastard Son) (1992), Varejão transplants and recontextualizes Brazilian figures and landscapes from the watercolor paintings by the nineteenth-century French Mission painter Jean Baptiste Debret (1768–1848), using them to create a disturbing *tableau* that reveals the violence exercised by the colonizers, a violence silenced by "official" history. In this oval-shaped work, whose form derives from a series of decorated panels painted by the Brazilian colonial artist Leandro Joaquim (1738–92), a priest rapes a slave while two armed soldiers with similar intentions approach an indigenous woman tied to a tree. A deep gash cuts through the center of the piece—the bloody mark of a wound, a raped vagina—materializing in and rising out of the surface of the painting itself.

The notion of painting as body-flesh saturated with memory—testifying and substantiating history—is fundamental to Varejão's language. Tactile, corporal, always unfolding and expanding through their own physicality, her paintings bring scars and wounds to the canvas surface. Thus emulating the violent strategies of the colonizer, the artist reapppropriates them to transgress their original purpose. Adopting the conspicuous language of church iconography and using explicit theatrical strategies of indoctrination methods of colonial catechizing, Varejão is able to surreptitiously desecularize and display the content of the images.

She documents the images as a way of testifying to the "historical existence" of her version. She first examines engravings, travel chronicles, chinaware, theater, ornaments, architecture, relics, maps, and a vast list of other references and then voraciously appropriates and transforms them, leaving them cannibalized, contaminated, different. Her strategy is related to the context of Brazil's modernist movement in the late 1920s, when the poet Oswaldo de Andrade resurreced the term *anthropophagy* (the practice of cannibalism) to suggest the critical absorption of foreign influences, of the discourse of the Other and its remaking in Brazilian terms through a hybridization process. *Antropofagia*, which emerged as a cultural allegory for Brazilian art in the twentieth century, represented a strategy of emancipation from hierarchical relationships with other cultures, as well as a particular attitude toward history and the European legacy. Through metaphors of selective digestion and metabolization, the movement sought to affirm a Brazilian culture open to the world but decolonized.

Anthropophagic ritual is embodied in all of Varejão's work, in her recontextualizations of cannibal scenes in travel narratives, in her use of relics and votive offerings, her incorporation of images of dismembered organs on Portuguese baroque kitchen tiles, as well as in the injuries and mutilations she inflicts on her own paintings. In the diptych series *Proposta para uma catequese: Parte I e II* (Proposal for a Catechesis: Part I and II) (1993), Varejão refers to anthropophagy and its notions of the absorption of the Other, evoking parallels between the alleged cannibalistic practices of Brazil's natives and the Eucharist ritual as a symbolic swallowing of the body of Christ. In part I, *Morte e Esquartejamento* (Death and Dismemberment), she uses images from engravings narrating anthropophagic practices published by Theodore de Bry in 1591, meant to accentuate "barbaric" and "demonic" practices. Varejão interchanged de Bry's images with others depicting the martyrdom of Christ, whose body, cut into pieces and devoured, reappears in the following diptych, *Aparicao e Reliquias* (Apparition and Relics) (1993), in the form of a relic and a china plate of the West Indies Trading Company. Like Portuguese religious tile panels and travel chronicles, the work weaves simultaneous threads of narrations and obliterations to convey its history of fissures, opaqueness, and destabilizations. By exaggeration, parody, and the transgressing syncretism of a baroque rhetoric, Varejão proposes narratives of an Odyssean voyage through history, reinterpreting the past through a vision of history and identity as open, continuously reformulating processes. ■

SOURCEBOOK

ESSAYS

Tordesillas, 1494

In 1494 the geographic space of the New World had not yet been revealed in its totality. Much of it was still imagined space. Nevertheless, it was already being divided between Spain and Portugal and delimited by Tordesillas, the treaty that consolidated a series of papal bulls and recorded Catholicism's interest in following the spread of mercantilism on the new continent. The *mare clausum*[1] that made up the maritime and terrestrial spaces soon to be discovered through Spanish and Portuguese navigation consecrated a markedly Catholic America that extended from Mexico to the southern tip of the continent.

Tordesillas can be understood as "a symbol of the frontier/limit tension that constitutes one of the components of Brazilian historico-geographic formation. The frontier is the future that is present. It is a space not fully incorporated into structured systems and, for that reason, potentially generating new realities. It represents undifferentiation,

with its verdant forests, abundant water, and naked humans—suggested an oneiric, tropical Eden. The deep, unknown interior, however, was imagined as being inhabited by monsters or fierce female warriors—Amazons. Among the Europeans, prejudices formed against the new continent: "Do Indians have souls? If the wild animals are smaller (for there are no lions, tigers, or elephants), is that not an indication of inferiority?"[4]

Prejudice against the Americas, which has its origin in the fact that they began as mere overseas territories of the European powers, has been recorded to the present day, although it has not hindered a constant influx of population and capital to the new continent. In 1776, the year the British colonists in North America signed their Declaration of Independence, even Immanuel Kant, who was impressed by the new nation's racial composition, commented that the Americans "constitute a subrace (somewhat degenerate) still not properly formed." For the sophisticated English of

Geographic Contingencies.
Space and Memory

BY PEDRO P. GEIGER

transgression, and conflict. The limit, on the other hand, represents differentiation, contention, and consensus, but recognition of the other and therefore, its own identity."[2]

Virgin Territory, 1500

The cry "Land ho!" was raised by Cabral's squadron in 1500. Seeing the space—to the Europeans, virgin territory—anticipated penetration. To give a name to a place is to found it. A name offers consistency to an extended entity; "it establishes, between the space and the man, an order of life and connection."[3] The name of the territory came to be Brazil, an allusion to the dyewood that was its first natural resource to be exploited. This replaced the original name, Vera Cruz, and thus mercantilism won out over Catholicism. Researching its contours, interrogating its format, was the first step in appropriating the space and transforming it into territory.

Life on the coastal strip of the new continent—

the Victorian era, Americans were barbarians without culture. Peter Conrad, in *Imagining America*, writes that the English felt insulted because in America a society was being created in which people assigned their own value to themselves. In Europe a person was circumscribed by the circumstances of his or her birth. One did not invent one's position; one inherited it.[5] Nevertheless, there were also writers and philosophers—de Tocqueville, Humboldt, and Goethe, among them—who were enthusiastic about the New World.

Maps of the Discovery, 1631

In 1631 João Teixeira Albernaz II the Elder, the Portuguese court cartographer in Lisbon, prepared an important series of new maps of Brazil. When pieced together Albernaz's maps, charting the territory in the form of diagram blocks, depicted Brazil's entire Atlantic coastline. On each map the strip of land between the coast and the highland plain is colored in sepia. The locations of

Lopo Homem
(Pedro and Jorge Reinel)
Detail of *Terra Brasilis*,
1515–19
Illuminated manuscript
on parchment
16½ × 23¼ in.
(41.5 × 59 cm)
Bibliothèque Nationale
de France, Paris

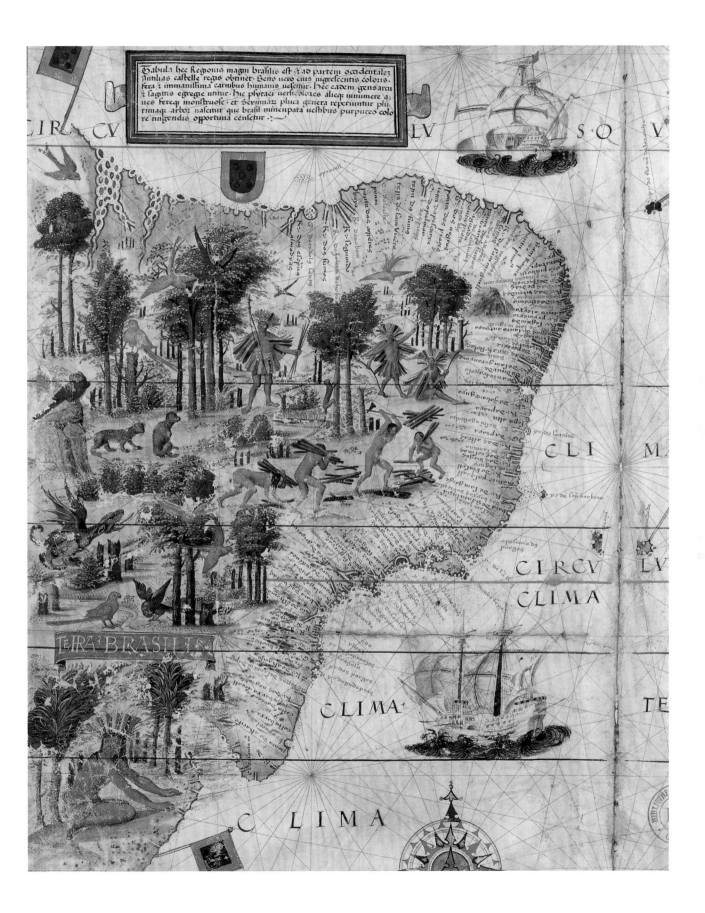

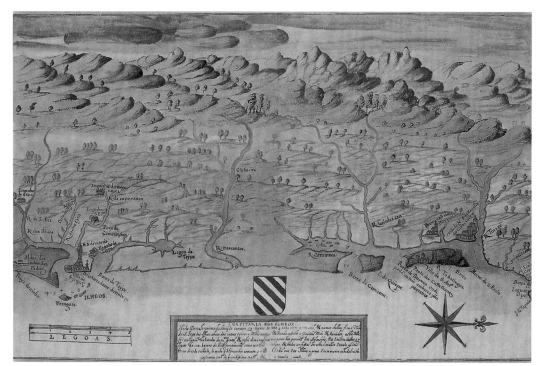

Portuguese settlements, Indian villages, and watercourses are indicated. The area from the edge of the highland plain inland is colored blue; this space appears to be deserted, without any references except for *hachures* representing an irregular and undifferentiated topography.

The cartographer seems to have been reproducing the color codes of European painting, in which warm colors such as sepia were used for the foreground, closest to the observer, and cool colors such as blue were used for the more distant background. This color code is evident as well in the beautiful work of the Dutchman Frans Post, who visualized Brazil for European eyes (see page 127). Nevertheless, the idea of near and far on Albernaz's maps is apparently not limited to physical distances. It takes on a political significance, with nearness being what is consolidated by Portuguese power and distance being what will come to be: territory that is for all intents and purposes virgin. By using the diagram block format, Albernaz stressed the comparison of the map to the landscape, thereby establishing "the relationship between the modeling of human action and esthetic enjoyment.... The way in which people come to see their world is a vital key for the way in which they understand and relate to it."[6] On the other hand, the separation of the coastal strip from the interior complies with the platonic dialectic of rivalry

(*amphibetesis*) or the postmodern philosopher Gilles Deleuzes's concept of the pretender,[7] for Albernaz intended his maps to be well-founded copies, as evidenced by their resemblance to an idea.

Bandeirantism, 1600s–1800s

Beginning in the seventeenth century, as Candice Vidal e Souza has noted, "Going beyond the limits imposed by the treaties between the Portuguese and Spanish Crowns, bandeirantism would indicate the beginning of the development of a sentiment of autonomy ... in search of another Brazil."[8] Marching into and conquering virgin territories, the explorers of Brazil's interior known as *bandeirantes* created a new way of appropriating and occupying land, living in society, and reproducing (crossbreeding with the native peoples).

Passing deep into Brazilian territory, far distant from the coast and even farther from Lisbon's social control, the *bandeirantes* were guided by their own independent behavior and social standards. On the coast, the Portuguese Crown granted land concessions; in the interior (*sertão*), the *bandeirantes* took possession of the land themselves. Under the exigencies posed by the newly occupied space, they developed new cultural and social practices, growing from within a true Brazilian identity. On the coast, where the agricultural export economy continually attracted European immigrants, who brought in African slaves to work the land, the population was mainly foreign. In the interior, the proportion of full-born "Brazilians" increased and a sense of Brazilianness developed. Later, in the 1800s, when Brazil was no longer a colony—a Portuguese coastal strip connected mainly to Europe—bandeirantism created another idea: that Brazil was a nation "made up of space."

This new construct, created by the *bandeirantes'* move to the interior, can be interpreted as what Deleuze calls "surface effects," which correspond to what the ancient Stoic philosophers called events or happenings. The Stoics distinguished between two types of things and consequently two planes of being, according to Deleuze: ". . . on the one hand, the deep being, the real, the force; on the other hand the plane of facts that occur on the surface of the being . . . disembodied events on the surface that result from mixtures of bodies in depth. . . ."9 They singled out bodies with their tensions, physical qualities, relationships, actions, and passions, and then their corresponding "states of things," made up of surface events, actions, and effects. By developing this totally new relationship, the Stoics referred causes to causes, effects to effects, and made certain ties between effects in themselves. "The disembodied events are never causes, some in relation to the others, but only 'almost causes,' according to laws that express, perhaps, in each case, relative unity, or, the mixture of bodies on which they depend, as of their real causes."10 The geographic contingencies of the history of bandeirantism can be understood as "quasi causes" and the events of that history as "surface effects," when the *bandeirantes*, by setting off into virgin territory, showed themselves to be a different people.

In Brazil the Portuguese Crown, the greatest landholder in the entire kingdom, was the main colonial manager and the source of state patrimony, which played the most significant role in forging Brazil's national development. In the seventeenth and eighteenth centuries, offical expeditions known as *entradas* were sponsored by the Crown. In contrast, the *bandeiras* were grassroots movements that inspired the people's imagination. As a result, the term *bandeirante* came in the popular mind to designate a person from the civil sector who was enterprising, innovative, and not limited by what had gone before.

Expansion and Independence, 1822

If Brazilians were to achieve direct relations with the world at large, then independence was another territorial line that ultimately had to be crossed. In laying the groundwork for that eventuality, the coast-interior (coast-*sertão*) opposition was to play a major role in early Brazilian historiography. For some, the interior was seen as where Brazil's true identity and its higher moral standards were first manifested. These parochial historiographers did not realize, however, that the geographic isolation of the *bandeirantes* and their descendants prevented this true Brazilian identity from becoming a national political identity. In their view the coast had exposed its populations to foreign influences and to vice. For others from these more developed areas of Brazil, the interior was the main source of their country's backwardness. Speeches filled with each contingent's founding memories and sense of territorial entitlement and superiority fueled an extended national debate over how the country's identity was and had to be constructed.

Actually, when the push for independence came, it originated with the people on the coast and the area contiguous with the coastline and was based on the growth of their relationships with the people of the interior. In general, a territory is characterized by the density of its population and activities and by the density of its system of relationships with the exterior world. In the end, events occurred along the coast and its contiguous territories that conflicted with the interests of Portugal's colonial authority and eventually led to independence in 1822.

Rather than characterizing the move toward independence as a linear progression, in the 1940s the historian Caio Prado Júnior presented Brazil's independence as the result of micropolitics, the aggregation of thousands of events that created the social support necessary for the break: for example, the rancher in conflict with the merchant, the consumer in conflict with the retailer, these traders being identified as Portuguese, and so forth. According to Prado, "Each will forge or adopt—this is the more common occurrence—some idea for his or her own use that justifies a position and pretensions . . . the idea of independence is being created in the minds of individuals, in each case, in its own way organizing into an aggregation of interests."11 The process was nourished by the congruence of economic and cultural interests and by ideologies from abroad: the interests of coffee plantation owners, desirous of freer access to world markets and supported by England,[12] the cultural influence of the French and American Revolutions, the influence of Freemasonry, which included the Andradas—the founding fathers of Brazil's independence—among its members. "The role of Masonry is wide and deep, as it also is the oldest, and more than anything, it is organic, articulated inside and outside the colony, systematically and consciously, Masons acting as 'Brazilians.'"[13] Perhaps the most astonishing fact of the country's independence is that it finally came at the hands of King João IV of Portugal's second son, Pedro, who in 1822 broke with his forebears by declaring an end to Portuguese rule in Brazil. Crowning himself Pedro I, the first emperor of Brazil, he established the only constitutional monarchy in South America.

Copies and Simulacra

The earlier discussion of Albernaz's maps and his use of two colors to differentiate Brazil's coast and its interior alluded to the platonic method of division, the dialectic of rivalry or Deleuze's notion of pretenders. On one side were the Portuguese, members of the "central civilization"[14] or the "world-system."[15] On the other side were primitive, indigenous populations that did not participate in world relationships. The intention of the Portuguese, who saw themselves as a hegemonic world power, was the establishment of a Brazilian territory.[16]

In the coast-interior (coast-*sertão*) model of Brazil's settlement and expansion, however, the dialectic was not a division like that observed by Albernaz. Rather, the new model began with the premise that at one time the two parts were components of the same unit: the "pretender" that is the Brazilian nation. The two parts—coast and interior—were similar and unequal, "contraries" of a single unit. Even before independence, the growing interactions between the coast and the *sertão* led to the relative decrease of Portuguese cultural influence. In this case, was the coast-interior model a simulacrum of Albernaz's model and therefore, in the platonic view, false?

Not according to Deleuze, who calls into question this platonic vision. As he sees it, the concept of copying, of building on the basis of resemblance, is valid only in the world of representation, where "only what is similar differs."[17] In a portrait photograph,

for example, the photograph and the photographed resemble each other, but they are different: the photograph is made of paper, while the subject is made of flesh and blood. The simulacrum—the representation—causes unlike or heterogeneous elements to communicate. It is constructed of convergences and continuities, as well as interiorizing dissimilarities and divergences.

To the simulacra, "only the differences are alike."[18] The disparity will be judged in itself; it will not be prejudged by a preliminary identity. Additionally, resemblance cannot be thought of as other than a product of internal difference. The simulacrum, unlike the factual or the factious, comes to the surface with the capacity to provoke actions and realize potential.[19] As such, the affective charge present in the coast-interior model is as strong as that found in Albernaz because, although it is different from his platonic model, it contains the internal resonance—the capacity to provoke actions—of all simulacra.

Territory as the Place of Memory, 1960

Many reasons can be found to explain the transfer of Brazil's capital in 1960 from Rio de Janeiro to Brasília, which was constructed in a relatively empty space. The memory of the interior's Brazilianness—the internalized territory—however, provided the necessary legitimacy for this move.

For the geographer Jean-Luc Piveteau, memory models, or suggests, a different, singular space, whereas space makes memory lasting. Memory semioticizes space, and space stabilizes memory; the moving synthesis of the two interpenetrated times is territory.[20]

In order for time (which is understood to exist for an individual or a collective being) to express itself, it must become personified in space. It becomes a place or a symbolic place, a landscape or a territory. Inversely, for space to gain substance, to make sense, it must become inscribed in time. Thus, as Piveteau notes, the "topic of place of memory furnishes additional signifieds to the representations included in the notion of territory, the same as for the representations included in the relations connected to place, symbolic site and landscape."[21]

Events that occur on the surface of a territory make up its history and differentiate it from other territories, even in the eyes of those outside it, the Others. Through time each locality—a city, a region, or a nation—undergoes an evolution that is

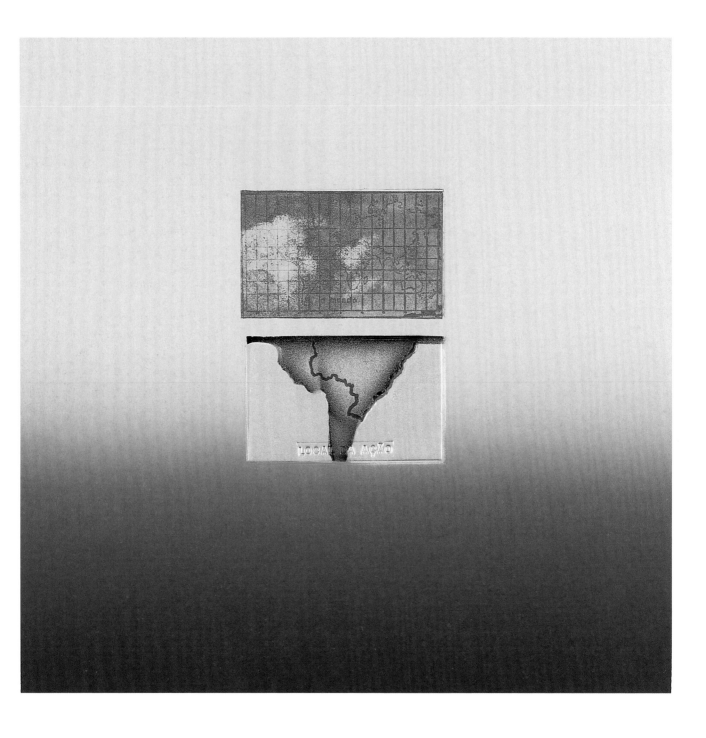

peculiar to itself and that maintains, insofar as possible, its own identity. The fact that each place has its own history makes it a territory of memory. What does it mean that each territory is the depository of a simple memory group? The group of memories depends on the plurality of scales contained in the territory—local territory, regional territory, national, and supranational, such as the European Union—the plurality of actors that acted or are still acting. The space in which we all live juxtaposes or superimposes elements from the past, elements that are reinterpreted and reintegrated in a contemporary context, in rhythms that can be associated with long, medium, or short time cycles. In this manner space appropriates, rises as a concrete project, and comes to be the memory of the future, of becoming.[22]

In these processes of territorialization and the formation of memories, deconstructions and reconstructions also occur. One example well known to settlers and immigrants to the Americas is to be found in Johann Wolfgang von Goethe's song to the new continent:

America, you're better off
Than our continent, the old.
You have no castles which are fallen,
No basalt to behold.
You are not disturbed in your inmost being,
In the very pulsation of life
By useless remembering
And unrewarding strife.
Use well the present—and good luck to you!
And when your children begin writing poetry,
Let them guard well, in all they do,
Against knight-, robber-, and ghost-story.[23]

Piveteau points to the current aspects of deconstruction and reconstruction of geographic space—for example, the deconstructions caused by the spread of the automobile, mirrored in a profusion of traffic signs. Similarly, civil society's increased participation in various nations' plans for land use and global environmental concerns are an expression of the rediscovery of memory of the planet as a whole.

For Piveteau, space is identified as the place of memory to the extent that it takes on the character of a place (an emerging spatial being), of a symbolic place (transcendent space), of a landscape (collec-

tive property off the market), or of a territory (the whole greater than the sum of its parts). To territory belongs the greatest possible symbolic load with regard to humankind's relationship with the environment. It is territory that identifies more with the idea of human action in general.

The word *territory* is used in this context to treat Brazil as a whole that is greater than the sum of its parts. Brazilian territory includes both its locations and its landscapes.

Making a Clean Copy, 2000

"Making a clean copy" is a Brazilian expression that suggests deconstructing and reconstructing: rewriting. This expression was probably never used by Brazilians as often as it is now being used to refer to the needed review of Brazil's historical inheritances, current social structure, income distribution, cultural portrait, and stewardship of its physical territory.

Brazil began its accelerated drive to urbanize and industrialize in the 1930s, led by an authoritarian regime. Since then, economic growth has been subject to greater and lesser degrees of authoritarian control, dominated by state management. Growth has not significantly altered Brazil's social composition, however, particularly the distribution of wealth. Nevertheless, Brazil's urban population has increased from 30 percent in 1930 to 70 percent in 1980 to 80 percent in 2000. The state encouraged the city, and the city amplified the market and civil society. Beginning in 1984, Brazil became a democracy and during this period of free expression advanced as it never had before. But deep social inequalities persist. New borders have to be crossed.

Today it is not a matter of topographic or political lines nor a question, as Tordesillas was, of expressing a border-limit tension. "The lines are others, varied, real or virtual,"[24] established within institutions and in people's minds. In this regard, Brazil is undergoing great transformations. In the "rediscovery" of the country—by Brazilians and by the world—growing importance is attached to the first word of the term *nation-state:* that is, "nation . . . stressing its cultural and ethnic diversity, as well as its historic creativity in search of solutions to the conflicts that have become naked."[25] At the heart of this movement is the empowering of Brazilian culture. ∎

Anna Bella Geiger
Local da ação nº 2
(Place of Action #2), 1979
Engraving, etching, and
silkscreen
15⅜ × 15⅜ in.
(39 × 39 cm)
Collection of the artist

In a 1951 essay about European immigration,[1] Emílio Willems noted that the concept of "minority" was not accepted in public debates about the problems of assimilation in Brazil because Brazilian society never admitted that minority groups existed within its territory. Willems does not mention the nationalization campaign during the Estado Novo (1937–45), the effects of which were still present for those groups—primarily the descendants of German and Japanese immigrants—most affected by its repressive measures. Nevertheless, the reference to the "assimilation problem" goes back to the existence of more or less organized ethnic groups in some regions of Brazil that, in spite of their high profile, were not recognized as legitimate.

The Process of Colonization

Brazil's first immigrants arrived shortly before independence in 1822, but it was not until 1824—the year the São Leopoldo colony was founded in Rio Grande do Sul by a group of Germans—that a his-

Sul, Santa Catarina, and Paraná. Simultaneously, the colony system appeared in the province of São Paulo, with the more explicit purpose of replacing slave labor with immigrant labor. Here the system did not allow immigrant land ownership, and families labored under contracts that were not always favorable to workers. The first experiment in the colony system, carried out by Senator Vergueiro at the Ibicaba Ranch in the 1850s, ended in a mass protest by foreign settlers brought about by the poor contract and work conditions. But this did not make the system less viable, because large-scale farming needed workers and the landowners were determined to implement an immigration policy supported by the São Paulo state government. Thousands of immigrants came to Brazil through colonization projects in the south or as workers in the colony system in São Paulo.

In addition to rural immigration, which was given priority by the state, countless immigrants settled in the cities, primarily in the south and southeast, either leaving the countryside or set-

Ethnic Identities in Brazil

BY GIRALDA SEYFERTH

torical process of colonization began. It was based on small, family-owned plots and was an undertaking of the imperial government, which aimed to populate unoccupied lands with farmers from European countries. Colonization in the three southern states was interrupted by civil war (the Revolução Farroupilha) between 1835 and 1845, but it started up again with greater vigor in 1850.

That was an emblematic year, in which the slave trade from Africa to Brazil was finally formally prohibited and Law 601 (the Land Act) was promulgated. Among its other stipulations, Law 601 established the rules for access to land ownership. Those regulations facilitated the settlement of immigrants in colonial areas, a process taken on by provincial governments in a broad program whose main assumption was the replacement of slave workers by free workers. For that reason, colonization plans, driven by the flow of immigrants from the German states and, beginning in the 1870s, also from Italy, Poland, and other European countries, were taken up again in Rio Grande do

tling directly. During the period of so-called mass immigration to Brazil, which encompassed the last decade of the empire (1870–80) and the First Republic (1880–1930), close to four million immigrants arrived.[2] Of these, more than 1.2 million came during the 1890s, immediately following the abolition of slavery and the proclamation of the republic. Portuguese and Italians were the largest contingents (almost 60 percent of the total), followed by Spaniards, Germans, and Japanese. The last group came primarily to the state of São Paulo beginning in 1908, when Italian immigration began to decline. Smaller contingents of Russians, Austrians, Syrians, Lebanese, Polish, and other nationalities also entered. São Paulo received the greatest numbers, followed by the southern states (Paraná, Santa Catarina, and Rio Grande do Sul), Rio de Janeiro, and Minas Gerais. With a total of 5,536,035 newcomers during the 1819–1959 period, Brazil's immigration is considered "significant" compared to countries that offered better conditions for migratory movement.[3]

Jean Baptiste Debret
(1768–1848)
Interior de uma Casa de Ciganos (Inside a Gypsy Home), 1823
Watercolor on paper
6⅞ × 9 in. (17.6 × 23 cm)
Museus Castro Maya – IPHAN/MinC, Rio de Janeiro

Immigration and Assimilation

Brazil's different immigrant groups, concentrated in the regions considered the most developed, formed ethnic identities based on criteria of national origin and the preservation of national cultures. In this way, they confronted the assimilationist ideal of Brazilian nationalism, expressed by the word *forging* (which denotes miscegenation). Ethnic discourse by the immigrants and their descendants

identity systems, resulting in the formation of ethnic collectivities.[4]

The formulation of ethnicities obeys privileged cultural codes, although the belief in the affinity of origin, having a racial connotation even when it merely evokes the idea of a people, is common to all. The ethnocentric rhetoric that accompanied construction of these immigrant identities also led to an inevitable contrast with Brazilians, who

was based on the cultural diversity that resulted not only from immigration and but also by the creation of community institutions—recreational, assistance, cultural, educational, and so on—that reinforced group boundaries. Immigrant settlements were also relatively isolated from national society, and ethnic neighborhoods appeared in cities. Each group developed habits and lifestyles based on its cultural distinctions and symbolic

were considered inferior in the universe of work. Representations about the "pioneerism" of the predominantly Polish, German, and Italian immigrants who settled agricultural areas on uninhabited lands in the south, for example, mark out such ethnic differences. They are couched in an ethos of farm work in which productive diligence and the settlers' civilizing capacity are contrasted with the laziness and indolence attributed to

Brazilians. The same type of opposition—work taken as an ethnic value or virtue—appears among urban immigrants. Many groups are further identified through professional activities. "Ethnic specialization" became an economic strategy for many groups, such as the Armenians in footwear manufacture and sales in São Paulo, who set up a mutual aid network involving established immigrants and recent arrivals.[5] Ethnicity demarcated by a supposed vocation, although almost always bearing racial overtones, was less uncomfortable to the Brazilian assimilationist ideal than social practices that created racial and cultural limits between groups.

The Example of German Immigration
German immigrants played a significant role in the colonization of the south beginning in 1824, contributing to the development of a peasantry whose economic base and small family farms became especially important in Brazil. In new colonial regions where the Germans predominated—the Vale do Rio dos Sinos and other tributaries of the Jacuí River (Rio Grande do Sul), the Vale do Itajaí and northeast Santa Catarina state, and urban areas such as Porto Alegre and Curitiba—there were manifestations of an ethnic discourse starting at the time of the empire. The first German-language newspapers appeared in the 1850s and 1860s, emphasizing the *Deutschtum* (Germanness) of the immigrants and their descendants. The press and other institutions, such as recreational and cultural societies and private schools that taught in German, developed gradually, gaining visibility as they defended a Teuto-Brazilian perspective of belonging. Community institutions such as German schools appeared to fill a need or even a lack of basic public services, among them education and health. Later on, they assumed ethnic characteristics that stressed the pertinence of a German nation imagined as a cultural and racial entity.

Teuto-Brazilian identity established a double link to both Germany and Brazil, assuming that these immigrants were ethnically different from other Brazilian citizens. The ethnic component of this identification alluded to elements of daily life, such as the use of the German language and typical ethnic customs and behaviors. The list of "ethnic attributes" was long, extending from *Wohnkultur* (a kind of perfect home and a model quality of life) to forms of sociability, eating habits, and social organization. More than any other group, the Germans used and abused the image of the pioneer as a corollary for the superiority of "German work," because in the south they were the first to found colonies.

Examples of how ethnicity was shaped can be found in countless periodicals: newspapers, almanacs, specialized lay and religious magazines, magazines aimed at specific segments of the population (German school teachers, for example), and even Teuto-Brazilian literature that circulated until 1939. *Deutschtum* represents the belief in a shared racial or national origin that supposes a link with a primordial fatherland, the German nation. The category of identification assumes this ethnic belonging through *jus sanguinis* (a criterion of ancestry) and also signals the condition of the Brazilian citizen, ensured by the *jus soli* (naturalization).[6]

The emergence of Teuto-Brazilian identity at the end of the nineteenth century occurred at the same time that the sociological process of assimilation was beginning in Brazil.[7] It was a time of interethnic contact and claims to rights of citizenship without abdication of Germanness. Teuto-Brazilian discourse was one of the most radicalized, perhaps because it was influenced by pan-Germanism before World War I and Nazism in the 1930s. But similar processes of constructing ethnicities, with equivalent labels—Italianness and Polishness, for example—gave rise to a heterogeneous reality repudiated by Brazilian nationalism and by politicians and technicians who proposed and debated immigration policies.

"Whitening" the Brazilian Race
In the period of mass immigration, the predominant tendency in Brazilian nationalist thought focused on the idea of three races—Portuguese, Indians, and blacks—plus the *mestiço* population of mixed ancestry. Such an ideology, which externalized the belief in a racially democratic society, was one response to a homogenizing concept of nationhood and pointed to the possibility of a future "historic Brazilian race," based on the proposition of a mixture that had been operational since the sixteenth century.

To overcome the ethnic diversity produced by

immigration, a race was to be formed through a broad process of assimilation and *mestiço* formation. It was imagined in explicitly racist terms because the movement started with assumptions about the inferiority of blacks, Indians, and their crossbreeds. The thesis that the population should be "whitened" backed nationalist speculation about Brazil's future after 1888. The racist implications of this concept were well known but never officially recognized by its founders.

As a scientific theory, whitening assumed that Brazil could have a population with a white phenotype as developed through a process of selective miscegenation that began in colonial times and could be accelerated by European immigration. Its idealizers in the field of science and Brazilian social theory believed in the progressive elimination of blacks and their crossbreeds, whom they considered incapable of adapting to a civilized, capitalist society.

The expectations surrounding whitening lay in the assimilation of the immigrants into the Brazilian nation, a process variously called *forging, dilution, mixture, merger, fusion,* or *miscegenation,* all terms that denoted racial crossbreeding. In fact, this homogenizing concept resulted from the confusion between race and people that is contained in almost all nationalist discourse. Race imposes the idea of common characteristics, phenotype, and people; according to the canons of whitening, a "historic race" could not be heterogeneous. The idea of racial and cultural fusion imposed, therefore, a single-voiced Brazilian identity, one based on the *jus sofi*; a Brazilian should have a white phenotype, be a representative of Latinity, and speak Portuguese. Immigrants were not regarded merely as the solution to economic problems or as occupiers of land considered demographically empty; to many, mass immigration's ethnic differentiation also seemed a menace to national unity.

The debate about the assimilation of the Japanese—the largest contingent of immigrants to enter the country in the 1930s—shows how this concern with whitening persisted even after scientific racism was discredited.[8] The pro-immigration elite that favored the admission of Japanese spoke of their penchant for farm work and assimilation. The faction against Asian immigration opposed it in the name of miscegenation, regarding the Japanese as a race that could compromise the path of national formation, that is, of whitening and westernizing.

The debate is evidence that the immigration question was still discussed in the 1930s and 1940s as a "racial question."[9] The period saw a marked decrease in the entry of Europeans and an increase in Japanese immigration, along with pressure for the country to receive refugees fleeing persecution, mainly Jews. Quotas set in 1934 and maintained throughout the Estado Novo were now aimed at blocking undesirable immigration.

In addition, Brazil's great miscegenated melting pot, idealized since the end of the nineteenth century, seemed to be menaced by the incipient black movement of the 1930s. It was carried out mainly by militants of the Frente Negra Brasileira (Brazilian Black Front), who denounced the discrimination against the colored population and the racism imposed on them for being insufficiently whitened.

Nationalizing Brazilianness

In this scene, in which the immigrants, their descendants, and blacks, not to mention the indigenous population, appeared as obstacles on the path to national unity, a nationalization campaign was conceived to force assimilation of all those who could not exhibit enough Brazilianness to become nationals. The campaign began in 1937 with the closing of all schools teaching in a foreign language (the largest number of which were Teuto-Brazilian). During World War II all institutions with some ethnic character were banned, as was the daily use of foreign languages. The military had a fundamental role in the conception and imposition of these nationalizing measures. The Nazi presence, widely denounced by institutions of repression during the Estado Novo, was one more element in determining the campaign's direction. So was the declaration of war against the Axis powers in 1943, which resulted in greater repression of communities of German and Japanese origin and the suppression of individual rights until 1945.

This forced assimilation was inspired by the idea of a melting pot, an amalgamation of ethnicities assimilated and integrated into society without racial prejudices. In the United States the expression referred to Americanization of European immigrants. In Brazil, the term became synonymous with fusion or miscegenation and the possibility of incorporating immigrants and their descendants into a

Brazilian culture with Portuguese roots, colored by elements of indigenous and African cultures. Implicit in this formulation was the difficulty in accepting differences of an ethnic nature, pluralism, or even official cultural heterogeneity. More than not recognizing the existence of minorities, as Willems pointed out in 1951, nationalism had difficulty recognizing ethnic identities as legitimate, even in exemplary citizens. "Other" cultures are almost always reduced to the uncomfortable position of being anachronisms condemned by Brazilian modernity.

The assimilation ideal did not disappear at the end of the repressive period initiated in 1937. The end of the war and of the Estado Novo itself, in 1945, did not produce a recovery of formal ethnic institutions (with their communitarian nature). Nevertheless, the expected assimilation process did not occur, demonstrating the impossibility of eliminating ethnicities by means of decree or repression. Furthermore, the inclusion of elements from indigenous and African cultures in the canons of national culture did not eliminate barriers for those whose skin color was not white.

An Immense Melting Pot?

Assimilation was thought of as producing a single hybrid model of Brazilian being. Equivalent to an immense melting pot, the idea of racial democracy was anchored in part on a theoretical model of assimilation and acculturation developed in Brazilian academia from 1930 to 1950. The model, which emphasized cultural and social change, sought to demonstrate the progressive disappearance of ethnic cultures and groups in a dominant society.

Thus, the descendants of Brazilian immigrants went through a process of assimilation, as shown in studies by Willems, Diegues Júnior, and other social scientists.[10] They were subjected to constraints during the nationalization campaign to speed up their "Brazilianization," but the cultural systems constructed in the course of the immigration flux—"hybrid" cultures, in the words of Willems—and modified by interethnic contact in subsequent generations still furnished distinctive symbols of identity.[11] The daily use of a native language, for example, did not disappear. It declined in urban areas, mainly beginning with the third generation, even among the descendants of groups considered the most circumscribed in 1939: Germans,

Japanese, and Polish. Yet even today, a representative portion of these groups, especially those who stayed in rural areas, remains bilingual, using their ethnic language at home, with friends and neighbors, and in collective social situations, such as in clubs and marriage ceremonies. The native tongue is for many an ethnic qualifier, although as a criterion of ethnicity it is surpassed by belief in a common origin, an ancestry that is an indicator of race and that evokes a corresponding ethnicity.

Contrasting identities are formalized and point out Brazilians as others, especially when the representations involve colonization. In this case, "Brazilian" is synonymous with *mestiço*, *caboclo* (mixed Indian and Portuguese), or other stigmatizing categories, especially when issues of work ethic or intermarriage are concerned. For example, the descendants of German, Italian, and Polish colonists in the south still regularly represent themselves as pioneers and cultivators of forests, builders of progress and economic power. In contrast, the Brazilians are described by the words *lazy, unskilled, unrooted*, and other stereotypical terms that evoke racial distinctions. The capacity to work is thought of as an ethnic quality and as an inherited quality.

In the second case, differences in social and economic organization are used as the principal argument against marriages between ethnic colonists and Brazilians. There is a clear emphasis on the farmer's virtues as a colonist "of origin" (an expression indicating European ancestry through immigration); these are not considered attributable to Brazilians. Disorder is a stigma used to condemn marriage to Brazilians, who are characterized as lacking a tie to the land, not valuing property, not giving dowries to their daughters and sons, being unkempt and disorganized, permitting many couples to live in the same house, eating manioc flour and drinking *cachaça*, and so on. The list of negative attributes used to insinuate that such a marriage would mean descending the social ladder is endless. It also points to differences in ways of transmitting patrimony, house rules, organization and division of labor, eating habits, and ultimately to the colonial tradition that, under certain circumstances, is transformed into an ethnic symbol.

In spite of assimilation attempts that culminated in direct government interference between 1937 and 1945, the integration of Brazilian society did

Marc Ferrez (1843–1923)
Negresse da Bahia, Brazil, 1870–99
Courtesy Fundaçao Biblioteca Nacional

not annul the processes of updating identities. Today other motivations derive, on one hand, from globalization, mainly among descendants of immigrants originating in countries that recognize dual citizenship, and, on the other, from the acceptance of differences, assuming that a modern society should be receptive to contrasts. In one case, descendants search for proof of original nationality and promote formal teaching of the mother tongue, a path for children and grandchildren of immigrants to obtain a German or an Italian passport, for example. Such a search can bring the realization that immigration is a rupture without return, one that transforms immigrants into Others, into foreigners, or simply into Brazilians. For others, recognizing one's ancestry enables immigrants to obtain work permits in their country of origin and escape Brazil's continual economic and social difficulties. The best-known example of this is the *sansei* (grandchildren of Japanese immigrants), who are transformed into *dekasseguis* (Brazilian descendants of Japanese) who work in Japan.

Recognition of Differences

The Brazilian assimilationist ideal now seems to have been superseded by a recognition of ethnic and cultural differences—but only apparently, because the conception of a pluralistic Brazilian society does not exist. In fact, it just attests to the assimilationist ideal, imagining an equality and an understanding lacking in everyday life.

What is ethnic can have some place in the general panorama of national culture, but it is a place that allows mainly for differences labeled as "folklore," however popular; these include dances, clothing, foods, and parties that are tourist attractions, such as the reproduction of Munich's Oktoberfest in the German colony of Blumenau. Nevertheless, folklore and its popular significance are forms of ethnic manifestation. Local purists who seek the authenticity of German culture may condemn the beer festivals as tourist attractions, but these festivals are inevitably associated with German colonization and celebrate the ethnic origins of German "pioneerism."

Ethnic differences have also been transformed into exoticism, anachronism, and even affronts to nationality. In the 1980s a judge threatened to nullify the voting cards of a Pomeranian colony in Espírito Santo that uses its dialect on a daily basis. The Pomeranians, descendants of 1870s Prussian immigrants, are frequent subjects of newspaper articles; in June 1994 their customs were reported in the magazine *Veja* under the title "People from Another World," which transformed aspects of Pomeranian daily life into a synonym for backwardness and exoticism.[12] Although Pomeranian identity is not unique, it has persisted with reinforcement by endogamy and distancing of the group from other descendants of German immigrants since the last century.

Another kind of fragmentation of identities has recently occurred, mainly among descendants of Germans and Italians, characterized by a return to regionalisms lost in the course of immigration. Categories such as *badense, hunsruckerücker, trentino,* and *veneto* are used to emphasize minimal differences in which dialects and eating habits are the main identifiers. Subdivisions that refer to regional traditions also appear among Spaniards and Portuguese. They demonstrate that dynamics exist in the appropriation of different identities and that the regionalisms manifested in certain spaces—such as regional Portuguese and Spanish houses, as well as Pomeranian parties—do not cancel a feeling of ethnic belonging.

For the desendants of African slaves, the black movement begun by the Frente Negra Brasileira in the 1930s was taken up again in the 1940s, and it has multiplied since then, always asserting an Afro-Brazilian identity in the fight against racism. Ethnicity appears, then, as an element for articulation of a shared origin, along with the statement of a black Brazilian culture. Culture and race have become positive criteria for self-identification in such manifestations as the *blocos afro* of Bahias Carnival, the samba and other dances, Afro-Brazilian music, and *candomblé* spiritualism, among many African-derived traditions.

Ethnic and racial identities do not, however, always depend only on internal criteria for self-attribution. They are also elaborated by others in stereotypes with negative attributes. In Brazil, the categories of identification associated with race can be stigmatizing and serve as means of objective discrimination. Categories such as *preto, negro, mulatto, crioulo, baiano* (which, outside Bahia, is a synonym for black), among others, denote black skin—all deprecating terms tied to physical appearance and the broadest types of

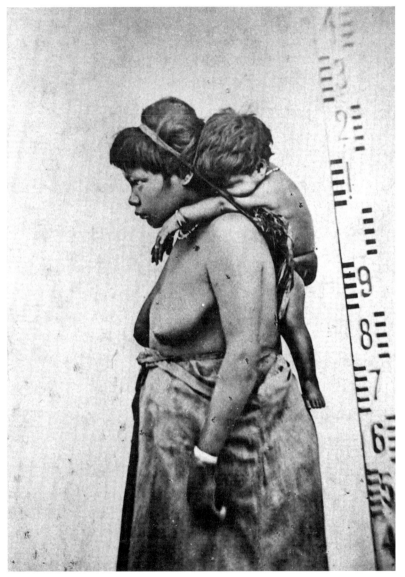

stereotypes indicating such behavioral deviations as laziness, ignorance, and sexual laxity. The so-called deviations are usually attributed to ignorance, but the weight of appearance cannot be left out. It is not limited to skin color but also includes other marks of African heritage, among them hair type and shape of nose. Racism can also be observed in some common expressions derived from the belief in whitening, such as "money whitens" (referring to social climbing by individual enrichment) and "cleaning the blood" (referring to marriage to a lighter person). And in spite of the phenotype as a racial marker, [13] references to a slave past are also evoked as an expression of prejudice. To say that somebody has "a foot in the kitchen," for example, can be assumed to be a joke, but in most social situations it has an accusatory character that refers to the social role attributed to people of color. Thus, in spite of the founding myth of nationality and the assimilationist discourse, racial signs appear as attributes of inferiority, making up one of the dimensions of racism in Brazil.

National Ideal and Ethnic Identity

Assimilation, as a nationalist ideal and a social process, did not annul the various expressions of ethnic belonging, nor did it lead to the longed-for homogeneity assumed in the idea of fusion. The nationalist discourse from the start of the republic, which spoke of whitening the race as a basic process of Brazilian formation and leaned on a policy of incentives to encourage European immigration and condemn any nonwhite immigration, was not very different from the nationalist discourse that spoke of a melting pot and fusion in the 1930s. Nor were they very different from the rhetoric of harmony that today apparently asserts recognition of the country's ethnic and cultural diversity but does not manage to hide the racism that discriminates against a good part of the black and *mestiço* population.

In Brazil, as in other places where ethnic and racial differences are relevant, ethnocentrism and racism persist, for the tolerable differences are, as a rule, those that can be comfortably labeled "folkloric" or that are regarded as part of national culture. Together with cultural elements and the ideology of common origin, ethnocentrism and racism make up systems of symbols that demarcate ethnic and social borders. ■

■ Today's world: an infinite ocean churned up by swirling waves—variable flows with no possible totality, no stable borders, in constant rearrangements. In the opinion of some, a second flood—except that this time the waters will never recede, never more will there be land in sight, the arks are many, and they will drift forever, captained by myriads of Noahs of all shapes and sizes.[1] Never again will we walk the stable landscape of solid land: we must get used to the idea that "sailing is necessary,"[2] with no fixed direction, no general point of view on this tumultuous and moving surface. No longer is there just one form of reality with its own map of possibilities.[3] Possibilities are now reinvented and redistributed all the time, at the mercy of the waves of flows that undo the forms of reality and generate others, which also end up dispersing themselves in the ocean, carried along by the movement of new waves.

Today's subjectivities: grabbed from the soil, they have the gift of ubiquity—they fluctuate at the

some meaning? How to conquer free zones of serenity? And this transnational chorus oscillates in variations on the theme, variations composed by affective positions that range from wonder to the apocalyptic. Hope or hopelessness—it's all the same: poles of a moralistic position that naturalizes a value system and uses it to interpret, judge, and predict what is going on—a happy ending or the end of everything.

However, another kind of voice is clearly dissonant from this teleological tone. Its timbre expresses neither judgment nor drama but the vibration of the movements of the world where it is intoned, transmitting the sensation that this world of today is neither better nor worse than others. Like any other, it is unique, with its own problems, its own ways of affirming life and also ruining it, with territories in the process of disappearing and others in the process of becoming, which require cartographies of meaning to make them intelligible and strengthen their gain of consistency. In tune

Beyond the Identity Principle:
The Anthropophagy Formula

BY SUELY ROLNIK

mercy of the mutable connections of desire with flows from all places and times that all pass simultaneously through electronic waves. A singular and fluid filter of this immense and also fluid ocean. With no name or permanent address, without identity: metamorphosing modulations in an endless process managed tirelessly day after day.

Voices in all languages and from all corners of the earth, the voices of experts and also those who are not experts, are shuffled together in an infinite conversation, somewhere between afflicted and excited, about the same question: Have we all become homeless? Did the subjective house dissolve, collapse, disappear? Where is identity? How can we construct an identity in this world where national, cultural, ethnic, religious, social, and sexual territories have lost their aura of truth, irreversibly denaturalized themselves, got mixed up in all possible ways, fluctuated, or ceased to exist? How can we rebuild a territory in this shifting world? How to get along with this disorientation? How to reorganize

with this, a voice from Brazil can be heard, a voice very old in the tradition of this country, a voice that at a given moment received the name "anthropophagist."

The inspiration for the idea of anthropophagy came from the Tupi Indians: it consisted of eating their enemies—but not just any enemy, only brave warriors. A certain relationship with alterity thus ritualized itself: a choosing of their others with respect to the vital power that their proximity would intensify; allowing themselves to be affected by those desired others to the point of absorbing them into their own bodies, so that particles of their virtue would integrate into the chemistry of the anthropophagists' souls and promote their refinement.

During the 1930s anthropophagy acquired a meaning that extrapolates from the literalness of the act of devouring practiced by the Indians. The so-called Anthropophagist Movement extracted and reaffirmed the ethical formula of the relationship with the Other that governs this ritual in order to

Regina Silveira

Intro (Re: Fresh Window, R.S.), 1997

Wall painting

Dimensions variable

Galeria Casa Triângulo,

São Paulo

allow it to migrate to the sphere of culture. This movement disclosed the active presence of this formula in a mode of cultural production that has been practiced in Brazil since its foundation.

Brazilian culture is born under the sign of a variable multiplicity of references and their mixture. However, also since Brazil's birth, there have been many strategies of desire vis-à-vis this mixture, different grades of exposure to alterity, which this situation intensifies.

Brazil's founding elite, unlike those of some other New World nations—the United States, for example—is oriented toward Europe and does not invest in the construction of an "at home" in Brazilian territory. The body is as if it were separated from experience, anesthetized to the effects of living together in heterogeneous groups and therefore deaf to the demands the creation of meaning for the singular problems delineated in this exposure. The tendency that has maintained its hegemony since that time

is that to consume European culture and more recently the American one, which beyond the fact of having constituted itself in its origin as the cartography of an experience of nonmixing is removed from the context that led to its production and is not, moreover, problematized in its consumption in the new context. Mere games of erudition and intelligence resulting in sterile repetitions and an "at home" lacking in elegance and devoid of meaning. It is just this "professor side, quotations side, well-known authors side" with their "speculative boredom"[4] that Oswald de Andrade tells us about—a kind of academic superego acting against thought.

Popular culture is traditionally produced from the exposure to this varied Other, out of the necessity to construct a territory of existence here, an "at home" made of the consistency of that everyday life—a matter of psychic survival. The result is an exuberant, irreverent, and inventive aesthetics. All this production is carried out on the margin of local, official culture, which disqualifies it or, in the best of hypotheses, folklorizes it, thus avoiding any danger of disruptive contamination.

A third tradition, however, insinuates itself between these two sides, one in which the discriminatory border that separates them is erased, promoting a general contamination not only between the erudite and the popular and between the national and the international but also between the archaic and the modern, the rural and the urban, the handcrafted and the technological. An "at home" takes a shape that incarnates all the dynamic heterogeneity of the consistency of sensibility from which is made the subjectivity of any Brazilian, a subjectivity that is created and re-created as the effect of an infinite miscegenation—and has nothing to do with identity. The Anthropophagist Movement makes this position explicit, giving it retrospective visibility but above all the dignity to affirm it in the present. The creators who take up this position take on the right to construct their own problems. Therefore they incorporate the banal in their own way and affirm the exuberance of this irreverent aesthetic that impregnates the everyday life of Brazil within the official system of culture, mixing it with the most current and sophisticated erudite repertoires from the so-called hegemonic centers, which up to then reigned supreme in Brazilian official culture, disconnected from any labor of thought.

The anthropophagist strategy allows at least three operations worthy of attention. The first is the bastardization of the elites' culture and, indirectly, of European culture as a standard. Neither submissive and sterile repositioning nor opposition that maintains that culture as a reference: there is a radical dislocation of the idea of "center." The supposed power of generalization of this or of any other model is overlooked, since all are understood to be provisional coagulations of language, selected in an experimental and unique process of the cultivation of meaning, in, by the way, the same form as that of the indigenous or African world.

Thus the Indian and the black are presented not as good humanity, bearers of a truth to be ingested, but as, in contrast to the European, bad humanity, distant from truth, to be vomited up. As Darcy Ribeiro writes, we are "as much de-Europeans, as we are de-Indians and de-Afro."[5] This is because the criteria for selection for the anthropophagist ritual in culture is not the content of a value system per se but whether it functions, with what it functions, how it allows intensities to pass and meaning to be produced. And this never works for a system as a whole but only for some of its elements, which are articulated with elements of other systems, losing in that way any connotations of identity.

The second operation that the anthropophagy strategy makes viable is that the exercise of creating culture has nothing to do with meaning, explaining, or interpreting to reveal truths. The truth, according to the "Anthropophagist Manifesto" (1928), is "a lie many times repeated."[6] To make culture in the anthropophagic style is related to cartography: to trace a map that participates in the construction of the territory it represents, in the taking shape of a new figure of one's self, a new "at home," a new world. "Routes. Routes. Routes. Routes. Routes. Routes. Routes"[7]—the manifesto insists seven times in a row. It is from the paradoxical closeness among heterogeneous elements, made of unsolved agreements and not referred to a totality, that meaning emanates: route, cartography of real social movements, critical effect. Any pragmatic experimentation, if it is well carried out, is worth more than the sterile imitation of models.

A third operation derives from the first two: the breaking down, already during the 1920s, of the

Rosana Paulino
Auto retrato com máscara africana II – Volpi
(Self-Portrait with an African Mask II – Volpi), 1998
Linocut
15 × 11 in. (38 × 28 cm)
Collection of the artist

Auto retrato el museu Africam II - VOLPI"

division of the world into the "colonized" and the "colonizers." If at that time the breaking down of the division had barely begun, today, in the era of globalized neoliberalism, such figures have definitively no place any longer. The axis of power relationships has changed position and altered its figures. The pairs that defined political conflict in the modern period have entangled. It is no longer a matter of the sovereignty of a colonial type: the hegemonic power no longer confronts its Other, there is no more exteriority, because hegemonic power has progressively extended its frontiers until it covers most of the planet.

This strategy of desire defined by the irreverent juxtaposition that creates a tension between worlds that do not touch each other on the official map of existence, that demystifies every and all value a priori, that decentralizes and renders everything equally bastardized, sets into motion a mode of subjectivization that I will call "anthropophagist."

In a first approximation, restricted to the visible, the anthropophagist subjectivity defines itself as never adhering completely to any system of reference, a plasticity to mix at will all kinds of repertoire and a freedom to improvise language based on such mixtures. However, to the sharper eye, one that catches the invisible, anthropophagy is actualized according to different strategies of desire, moved by different vectors of power, that range from a greater or lesser affirmation of life to almost its complete negation. They are basically distinguished by the way in which the subjectivity knows and explores the world, in what motivates its search for meaning and the criterion used to choose what will be absorbed in order to produce that meaning. Actualized in its most active vector, the anthropophagist mode of subjectivization in its invisible facet functions according to some essential characteristics.

Above all, this mode depends to a significant degree on the exposure to alterity: to discover and desire the singularity of the Other, without feeling shame in discovering and desiring, without feeling shame about expressing that desire, without fear of contaminating oneself, because it is through this contamination that the vital powers expand, that the batteries of desire are charged, that a series of becomings of subjectivity incarnates—the Tupi formula. This kind of relationship with alterity produces a joy in the body—"the litmus test,"[8] as the

"Anthropophagist Manifesto" asserts twice, the test of a pulsating vitality.

This capacity depends on a second characteristic of the anthropophagist mode of subjectivization actualized in its most active vector: a certain state of the body, in which its nerve fibers vibrate to the music of the universes connected by desire; a certain tuning with affective modulations provoked by this vibration; a tolerance to the pressure that such unfamiliar affects exercise on the subjectivity so it will incarnate them, reinventing itself, becoming another. It is probably what Lygia Clark called the "state of art without art"[9] and what Hélio Oiticica refers to as the "state of invention."[10]

A third characteristic of the anthropophagist mode exercised in its most active vector is which joins together to form an "at home"—that is, which functions as an operator of the subjective consistency, which is the nomadism of desire that goes its way making its connections, guided predominantly by the point of view of the vibratility of the body and its will to power. An ethical criterion for making choices—again, the Tupi formula.

A fourth characteristic is the kind of subjectivity that is constituted thus: an impersonal singularity, completely open, dispersed in the multiple connections of desire in the social field and which merges among the negotiated worlds. While the subjectivity controlled by an identity-figurative principle consists in a personal "I," it is an immured individuality, imprisoned in its psychic living space and commanded by the fear of losing itself.

A fifth characteristic is the way this kind of subjectivity emerges: its genesis is created through alliances and contagion, an infinite rhizome that changes nature and direction at the mercy of the racial mixtures that take place in the great factory of our cultural anthropophagy. Different from the genesis of an identity-figurative subjectivity that is constructed through filiation, promoting the fantasy of a linear evolution and the imprisoning compromise with a system of values adopted as the essence to be perpetuated and reverenced.

However, the same absolute nonadhesion to any system of references, the same plasticity in mixing them together at will, the same freedom to improvise language as a result of the mixtures, which define the anthropophagist mode of subjectivization in its visible dimension, might constitute a kind of subjectivity in which in invisibility none of

the previously mentioned characteristics is present. When this occurs, we face an actualized anthropophagy in its most reactive vector. This differentiates itself fundamentally through the absence of an ethical criterion commanding the connections of desire and the creation of meaning, replaced here by a narcissistic criterion. It is the formula that falsifies itself, overflowing the carcass of certain procedures without the stuffing of the body as a compass needle, a body that knows through vibration and contamination and not only through representation and that has life as a criterion to make its selections. Is this not the vector that one of the manifestos refers to as "low anthropophagy," declaring that it is against this "plague of the so-called cultured and Christianized nations . . . that we, anthropophagists, are acting?"[11]

There are many examples of this kind of actualization of the anthropophagist mode, this everything goes in function of the ego's interests, so common on the national scene. A recent example is the construction in Rio de Janeiro of buildings with sea sand: as might have been foreseen, the buildings collapsed with their inhabitants.[12]

Actually, between the most active pole of anthropophagy (in its ethical actualization) and its most reactive pole (in its narcissistic actualization), there are many shades in which these positions combine in different proportions. This is not a matter of an ontological or axiological—and much less psychological—dualism. What occurs is a diversity of modes in the affirmation of anthropophagy: from the most ethical to the least ethical, from the everything goes in function of the life interests to the everything goes in function of the ego interests. These modes are never definitive because they depend on the dominant force in each context of individual and collective existence.

The voice of Brazil that is heard in contemporary discussions that swirl around the identity crisis is that of anthropophagist subjectivity in its most active vector. As if we were forever this "mixed and bastard blood people that is now constituting itself all over the Earth,"[13] as if we brought to this globalized conversation a know-how with regard to navigating this infinite ocean churned up by swirling waves of a variable profusion of flows which is what makes up today's world. Basically, what the anthropophagist voice brings to this impasse that is unique is that it shows not only theoretically but, above all, pragmatically that the problem being posited is not the reconstitution of an identity, hallucinated horizon that divides mankind into hopeful and hopeless. The issue is to detach the sensation of subjective consistency from the model of identity; displace oneself from the identity-figurative principle in the construction of an "at home."

If living without a concrete house is difficult, there is no human life possible without a mode of being in which one can feel oneself "at home." Therefore we are not all becoming homeless: it is not true that the subjective house has disappeared. It is only suffering a radical transformation in the principle of its construction—which is nonetheless disturbing. To build an "at home" today depends on operations that are rather inactive in modern Western subjectivity but familiar to the anthropophagist mode in its most active actualization: to be in tune with the transfigurations within the body, resulting from the new connections of flows; to surf with the events that such transfigurations trigger; to experience concrete arrangements of existence that incarnate these palpable mutations; to invent new life possibilities. Such operations depend, of course, on the exercise of powers of the body equally inactive in contemporary subjectivity: to expand beyond representation, to conquer an intimacy with the body as a vibratile surface that detects the waves even before they arise, to learn how to surf, establish zones of familiarity within the movement itself—that is, "sailing is necessary," because if we do not, our destiny will probably be shipwreck. An "at home" made of partial, unique, provisional, fluctuating totalities, in a constant becoming, that each one (individual or group) build up from the flows that touch its body and its selective filtration operated by desire.

Freeing ourselves from the identity-figurative principle is an urgent need all over the planet. We are the bearers of a vaccine that allows people to resist this addiction: the "anthropophagy vaccine," as one of the manifestos calls it, indicated for "the spirit that refuses to conceive of the spirit without the body."[14] Oswald de Andrade ultimately defended the thesis that anthropophagy would constitute a "social therapy for the contemporary world."[15] The fact is, the anthropophagy vaccine would seem to be indispensable for an ecology of the soul (or of desire?). ■

154. Convento
Cena da aparição de

■ As a vast New World country, similar to the United States in both historical formation and ethnic diversity, Brazil constitutes a kind of southern twin whose strong affinities with the United States have been obscured by ethnocentric assumptions and media stereotypes. While in no way identical, the two countries are eminently comparable. Indeed, their histories run on parallel tracks.

After millennia of indigenous habitation and culture, both Brazil and the United States were "discovered" during Europe's search for a trade route to India. Each country began its official history as a European colony, one of Portugal, the other of Great Britain. In both nations, colonization led to the occupation of vast territories and the dispossession of indigenous peoples. In the United States the occupiers were called pioneers; in Brazil they were *bandeirantes* and *mamelucos*. After colonization, both countries imported Africans in massive numbers, forming the two largest slave societies of modern times. Slavery was abolished in the United States

pluralism of the present day. This most recent period has been marked by Oscar nominations for such films as *O Quatrilho* and *Central Station* and a resurgence of cinema within Brazil itself.

Brazilian cinema both stages and represents a multicultural society. But to what extent have Afro-Brazilians and indigenous Brazilians, for example, been able to represent themselves? How does Brazilian cinema stage its racial representations? How useful are such notions as stereotypes, positive images, realism? What is the role of cultural difference in reading films? What voices have not been heard in Brazilian cinema?

Brazilian films inevitably reflect—or, more precisely, reflect on—ambient realities as filtered through competing ideologies and social discourses. The lack of rigid racial segregation, the existence of a *mestiço* population, and the ubiquity of Afro-Brazilian cultural expression, combined with the equally undeniable reality of the powerlessness of people of color, all leave traces in films. The

Brazilian Cinema:
Race and Representation

BY ROBERT STAM

with the Emancipation Proclamation of 1863. Twenty-five years later, the "Golden Law" ended slavery in Brazil. Over the next century, both countries received waves of immigrants from the world over, ultimately forming multicultural societies. The complex national culture of Brazil, representing substantial indigenous, African, Italian, German, Japanese, Slavic, Arab, and Jewish (Ashkenazi and Sephardi) populations and influences, is richly expressed in what a 1998 commemoration describes as the century of Brazilian cinema.

The Cinema Century
This history takes us from the earliest cinematic "views," in the 1890s, through the *bela epoca* of 1908–11, during which Brazilian cinema dominated its own market. It continues to the studio musical comedies (*chancadas*) of the 1930s and 1940s, through the just-like-Hollywood ambitions of Vera Cruz (1949–54), to the various phases of Cinema Novo, beginning in the late 1950s, to the stylistic

challenge is to discern the patterns within these traces, for films do not merely reflect social reality in an unmediated way; they inflect, stylize, caricature, allegorize. Poststructuralist theory reminds us that we live within language and representation, that we have no direct access to the "real." Nevertheless, the constructed, coded nature of artistic discourse hardly precludes reference to a common social life. Human consciousness and artistic practice, Mikhail Bakhtin argues, do not come into contact with the "real" directly but rather through the medium of the surrounding ideological world. Literature and, by extension, cinema do not so much refer to or call up the world as represent its languages and discourses. Artistic discourse thus constitutes a refraction of a refraction—a mediated version of an already textualized and "discursivized" socioideological world.[1] The issue is less one of fidelity to a preexisting truth or reality than of a specific orchestration of ideological discourses and communitarian perspectives.

Avaeté–Semente da Viganca
Directed by Zelito Viana
Brazil, 1985
(100 min.)
Courtesy Funarte–
DECINE/CTAv

Celluloid Stereotypes

One important socioideological grid through which films "see" and are "seen" is that of the stereotype. As a kind of mental shorthand, a stereotype constitutes a device whereby people characterize, in a schematic manner, another group with which they are only partially familiar. Within a situation of racial domination, however, stereotypes have a clear function of social control. They indirectly rationalize and justify the advantages of the socially empowered. Much

The art of both features the indigenous "noble savage," although there is no Brazilian counterpart of the war-whooping savage of the Hollywood frontier western. There is in fact no Brazilian conquest narrative in which the Indian is the explicit or implicit enemy. In its place are innumerable adaptations of romantic Indianist novels, a few comedies about urban white Brazilians going to live happily with largely female Indians (for example, *Casei-me com um Xavante* (I Married a Xavante) (1957), alongside many

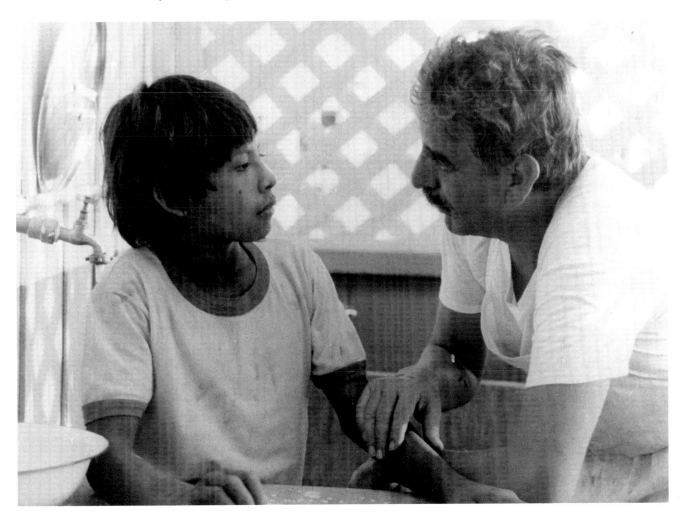

of the literature on blacks and Native Americans in North American cinema revolves around the issue of specific stereotypes, classically summarized, at least as far as blacks are concerned, in Donald Bogle's *Toms, Coons, Mulattoes, Mammies and Bucks* (New York: Continuum, 1989).

To what extent, we might ask, are stereotypes congruent in the United States and Brazil? Given the countries' status as two white-dominated New World societies, certain similarities are virtually inevitable.

politically engaged features such as *How Tasty Was My Frenchman* (1971), *Avaeté* (1985), *Capitalismo Selvagem* (1993), and documentaries including *Mato Eles?* (1983) and *Terra dos Índios* (1987). At times Indians have been forced to carry a heavy burden of allegory. For the romantic poets, the Indian symbolized Brazil, yet that same Brazil was subjugating real Indians. And within Brazilian cinema, blacks too have sometimes been used as allegorical shorthand for the poor or the oppressed, a conflation that mim-

ics the class-over-race discourse typical of a certain Brazilian sociology.

Both Brazil and American film history also offer the noble, faithful slave, the honest, devoted subaltern. In the United States that figure is Uncle Tom or Uncle Remus. In Brazil it is *pai joao*. As products of the narcissistic projections of whites, these emblems of happy servility represent slaves as the masters desired them to be. Both societies also display Tom's female counterpart, the devoted woman slave or servant: in the United States the mammy and in Brazil the *mae preta* (black mother), both products of slave societies where the master's children were nursed at the black woman's breast. The *mae preta* was celebrated in sentimental poetry as patient and self-sacrificing for the good of the whites in her care. Aunt Nastácia, in Monteiro Lobato's children's tale *Viagem ao Céu* (1934), represents the type: obese, with thick lips, large eyes, and a kerchiefed head, reminiscent of Aunt Jemima.[2]

Both societies similarly generated a split between the "good black" and the "bad nigger," a split superficially about virtue but really about the question of black refusal or acceptance of white domination. The black who accepts domination, within white racist discourse, is by definition good. The black who refuses is by definition bad. In Brazil the question of the "bad nigger" becomes linked to the history of black revolt and resistance. In most cases, in the cinema at least, this figure is positively valenced.

The mulatto is often seen as pretentious and vaguely ridiculous in Brazil, a constellation of associations not entirely foreign to the United States. D. W. Griffith's *Birth of a Nation* (1915), for example, constantly portrays mulattoes as the most "uppity," the most treacherous and dangerous to the system. The Brazilian constellation of stereotypes also features the "sexy mulatta," the presumably lascivious, sensuous product of racial mixing. According to the reigning mythologies, the adoration of the mulatta can be traced back to Portuguese idolatry of dark-skinned Moorish princesses. While white North American society also projected blacks as lascivious, this quality was not so exclusively focused on the mulatta as in Brazil. The sexy Brazilian mulatta figure is found not only in literature— for instance, Vidinha in *Memórias de um Sargento de Milicias* (1854) and Rita Baiana in *O Cortiço* (1890)—but also in many sambas, in theatrical reviews (*Oba Oba* in Rio), in advertising, and in film.[3] The mulatta was especially popular in the *pornochanchadas* of the 1970s, as reflected in the titles of such films as *Uma Mulata para Todos* (A Mulatta for Everyone) and A *Mulata que Queria Pecar* (The Mulatta Who Wanted to Sin). She is seen more as mistress than as wife, as in the well-known

Above:

Ganga Zumba

Directed by Cacá Diegues

Brazil, 1963

(92 min.)

Courtesy Funarte— DECINE/CTAv

Opposite:

Chico Rei

Directed by Walter Lima Jr.

Brazil, 1986

(115 min.)

Courtesy Funarte— DECINE/CTAv

rhyme *"branca para casar, mulata para fornicar, e negra para trabalhar"* (white woman to marry, mulatta to fornicate, and black woman to work). The black woman can choose, in other words, between sexual and economic exploitation. White men draw the line of their desire at marriage, so as not to compromise the family prestige and inheritance. Literary mulattas such as Rita Baiana in *O Cortiço* (1890) and Ana Mercedes in *Tent of Miracles* (1977), moreover, tend not to be constructed as mothers.[4] For Leilia Gonzales, the mulatta is a "sophisticated form of reification, an export product to be consumed by tourists and the Brazilian bourgeoisie."[5] While apparently providing symbolic compensation for quotidian oppression, the adoration of the mulatta as cultural icon in fact forms part of that very oppression.

Preto Velho and Other Black Stereotypes

Whereas Donald Bogle posits five stereotypes in relation to blacks in American cinema, João Carlos Rodrigues, in *O negro brasileiro e o cinema* (Rio de Janeiro: Globo/Fundação do Cinema Brasileiro, 1988), the sole book-length study devoted to blacks in Brazilian cinema, posits twelve stereotypes about black Brazilians:

1. The *preto velho* (old black man) is the humble subaltern, reminiscent of Uncle Tom or Uncle Remus in the United States, whom Rodrigues finds more typical of São Paulo films such as *Caiçara, Sinhá Moça* (1953), and *O Saci*. In *umbanda* folk religion, the *preto velho* smokes a pipe, walks with a cane, and speaks incorrect Portuguese, but he is also the repository of deep wisdom.

2. A counterpart of the North American mammy, the *mae preta* is found in theater (José de Alencar's *Mae)* and cinema, for example, in *Joao Negrinho.*

3. The martyr, a classic literary figure, was adapted for the screen by Augusto da Silva Fagundes in *O Negrinho do Pastoreio* (1973), the story of an innocent black shepherd cruelly abused by his master and devoured alive by ants before his miraculous resurrection.

4. The black with a white soul represents, in its "positive" version, the good-hearted Negro who knows his place. In its negative variant it represents the uppity mulatto who thinks he's white. Rodrigues cites as positive examples the protagonists Joao Negrinho in the eponymous film and Repo in *Aleluia, Gretchen* (1975).

5. The noble savage stereotype also has literary origins—for example, in Lope de Vega's *El Santo Negro*—and is more typically associated with the Indian.

6. A variant, the black rebel, is capable of resistance. Rodrigues finds traces of this figure in the *quilombeiros* of *Ganga Zumba* (1963) and *Quilombo* (1984). The most positive example for Rodrigues is the title character of *Chico Rei* (1985), the Afro-Brazilian who buys his own freedom and that of his family. Literature includes black rebels such as Victor Hugo's *Bugh-Jargal* (1883), which was inspired partially by the black Jacobins of Haiti, the first black country to claim its independence. The black rebel appears in Vera Cruz costume dramas, such as *Sinhá Moçá*; in commercial super-productions, such as *A Marcha*, and in more politicized films, such as *Barravento* (1962), *Ganga Zumba*, and *Quilombo* (1983).

Compasso de Espera features two kinds of black rebel: American-style militants who say in English, "Burn, baby, burn," and their pacifist brothers who respond, "Build, baby, build."

7. *O Negao* (big black) is more or less like the North American "buck": a black man notable for brute strength and hyperbolic sexuality. The novel *O Bom crioulo* (1895) features a gay *negao*. At times the *negao* is bracketed as part of a dream or fantasy sequence, as for example in the sexual fantasies of the white woman protagonist of the film adaptation of Nelson Rodrigues's play *Bonita mas Ordinaria*. In the *pornochanchada A Viagem ao Céu da Boca* (1981), similarly, a perverted black man cruelly violates two women and a transvestite, yet the whole episode is subsequently revealed to be merely the dream of a sleeping burglar. In *A Menina e O Estuprador* (The Girl and the Rapist) (1983), a black man is accused of sexual crimes but is proven innocent.

8. The *malandro* (street-smart hustler) is a trickster figure who gets by on his wits. The *malandro* has perhaps more positive connotations in Brazil than a hustler would in North America (Sammy Davis Jr.'s Sportin' Life in *Porgy and Bess* would be a *malandro*, and Blaxploitation films played to some extent on the ambivalence of the *malandro* figure). In literature, the *malandro* is seen in Chico Juca of *Memórias de um Sargento de Milicias* and in Firmino of *O Cortiço* and was crystallized in popular music in the sambas of Wilson Batista and Zé Keti. In film we encounter the *malandro* as early as 1908, in Antônio Leal's *Os Capadócios da Cidade Nova*, which, according to the marketing brochures, included "*capoeiras e malandros.*" Grande Otelo often played the role of the naive *malandro*, as in *O Cacula do Barulho* and *Amei um Bicheiro*. The adolescents of *Bahia de Todos os Santos*, as Rodriques points out, also qualify as *malandros* in that they survive through small-time theft, gigolo-like activities, and contraband. A number of 1960s plays, such as Antônio Callado's *Pedro Mico*, Gianfrancesco Guarnieri's *Gimba*, and Nelson Rodrigues's *Boca de Ouro*, revolved around the *malandro* figure. All three, as it happens, were adopted for the cinema, but in only one, *Pedro Mico*, was the part played by a black actor (Pelé). The juvenile delinquents of *Pixote* are distant cousins of the *malandro* as well as drug-dealer Bira in *Rio Babilônia* (1982).

9. The *favelado* (shantytown dweller) was first portrayed cinematically in Humberto Mauro's *Favela dos Meus Amores* (1935) as well as in dos Santos's socially conscious 1950s films about Rio.

10. The *crioulo doido* (crazy black) combines comedy with childish naivete. The figure can be traced back to such folkloric figures as Saci, the one-legged black man who smokes a pipe and performs devilish tricks, and to specifically white traditions such as the Harlequin of Commedia dell' Arte. Its feminine equivalent is the *nega maluca* (crazy black woman) figure from the Rio Carnival. The *crioulo doido* conveys an infantilizing impression of blacks as mischievous "eternal children," a portrayal that indirectly justifies control by the more "mature" elements of the population. Some Grande Otelo roles have aspects of the *crioulo doido*, as does the black character Mussum in the comic quartet called the *trapaloes*, a kind of Brazilian *Three Stooges*. The most sustained treatment of this archetype is found in Carlos Prates Correia's *O Cioulo Doido* (1971).

11. The *mulatta* is defined largely in sexual terms. She is adored during Carnival but exploited (as maid or prostitute) during the rest of the year. Although the "sexy mulatta" is typically Brazilian, one detects a kind of convergence of sexual and racial images in the erotic valorization of the mulatta in present-day American music videos, including rap music videos.

12. The *musa* is encountered in the work of black poets such as Luis Gama (who speaks of his "*musa de Guiné*") and the symbolist poet Cruz e Sousa, and in the prose of the mulatto novelist Lima Barreto. The figure is more or less absent, as Rodrigues points out, in Brazilian films.

Rodrigues's typology is enormously informative, useful, and suggestive. He traces stereotypes back to literary antecedents and imaginatively links the diverse figures with the attributes of the *orixás* in Afro-Brazilian religion. Some of his categories, such as *crioulo doido*, had not been noted before. The typology suffers, however, from blurring and redundancy. In practice, it is often difficult to distinguish the "noble savage" from the "black with a white soul," while the *malandro*, the *favelado*, and the *crioulo doido* often blend together. Furthermore, the typology is strikingly heterogenous; some of the categories (*negao*, *pai joao*) constitute stereotypes in the classical sense, others (such as the

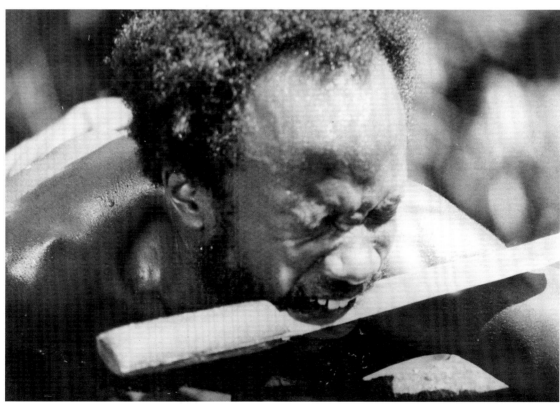

muse) are literary archetypes, some (*favelado*) have to do with place of social origin, while still others (the martyr) have to do with narrative function. Some of the types are not race specific. The *malandro*, for example, can be either white or black. And while the schema has a place for the female mulatta, it does not include the male mulatto.

Positive and Negative Images

Apart from these concerns, Rodrigues's analysis of stereotypes is immensely useful, allowing detection of structural patterns of prejudice in what had formerly seemed random phenomena. Still, it seems necessary to go beyond the concept of stereotypes and the corollary notions of positive and negative images. An exclusive preoccupation with images can lead to a kind of essentialism, as the critic reduces a complex diversity of portrayals to a limited set of stereotypes. When seen reductively, stereotypes run the risk of reproducing the very racism they were initially designed to combat.

The notion of a positive image, for example, is fraught with pitfalls. The nature of what is positive is relative; one must ask, Positive for whom? Black incarnations of patience and gradualism, for instance, have always been more attractive to whites than to blacks. Even among blacks, one needs to know, Positive for middle-class blacks, or for the black dispossessed, the wretched of the earth? Oppressed people might have a vision of morality that is not only different but even opposite. (The black slang use of *bad* to mean *good* merely dramatizes this social relativity of moral evaluations.) In slavery, as Zumaba implies, it might have been admirable and therefore "good" to deceive, manipulate, and even murder a slave driver. Because the slave's status as property was itself the result of theft, the normal definitions of crime were necessarily open to revision. The emphasis on moral character rather than social structure places the burden on oppressed people to be "good," rather than on the privileged to change the system. The oppressed, in order to be equal, are asked to be better.

As Frantz Fanon initially and Homi K. Bhabha later have pointed out, stereotypes also can be ambivalent, hiding guilty attraction under a mask of rejection. Many apparently positive compliments to blacks historically contained hidden insults. The exaltation of Indian "innocence" had as its corollary their powerlessness. The lauding of the "natural" ability of blacks in sports or music or theater had as its tacit corollary the suggestion that their achievements have nothing to do with work or intelligence. A cinema dominated by positive images, in which filmmakers refused to allow the slightest hint of negativity to enter into a racial portrait, would be as suspect as one conveying only negative images. It would betray a neurotic lack of confidence in the group portrayed, which usually entertains few illusions concerning its own perfection. More important than that characters be heroes is that they be subjects.

Primitivism, exoticism, and folklorization meanwhile use the colonized other as an erotic fiction to reenchant the world. In Brazil it is largely the Indian who is exoticized in this way. But Afro-Brazilian culture has also been "folklorized," rendered as charmingly picturesque but ultimately premodern, allochronic, inconsequential. Folklorization characterizes texts as diverse as Varig Airlines promotional films, television news visual logos, and such films as *Pagador de Promessas* (The Given Word) (1962). When black culture is reduced to "a generating source of sensuality, a plethora of genital tricks, and an eternal fountain of recipes," as Muniz Sodré puts it, "then prejudice and ethnocentrism persist."[6] Such "affectionate" tributes depoliticize the black contribution, recapitulating a certain romantic or essentialist strain to be found in the works of such writers as Jorge Amado but also in the negritude movement la Senghor, which posited Greco-Europe as Reason and Africa as Emotion. Thus, "boomerang" compliments concerning creativity and energy become minuscule compensations for powerlessness. Folklorization also works against domestication—portrayals of people in their routine, daily lives. Thus, scores of Brazilian films show black people participating in *candomblé* and Carnival and *quilombos*, yet few films show the everyday struggles of ordinary black Brazilians. While many films depict racism under slavery, few depict contemporary racism. If some cinemas are guilty of a flight from history, Brazilian cinema has occasionally been guilty of a flight for history, opting for gloriously remote triumphs while shying away from contemporary struggles.

As Ella Shohat and I have argued elsewhere, the positive-negative image approach entails more general methodological-theoretical problems, which could be summed up as essentialism (a complex

Dona Flor e seus dois maridos (Dona Flor and Her Two Husbands)
Directed by Bruno Barreto
Brazil, 1976
(158 min.)
Courtesy Funarte–DECINE/CTAv

diversity of portrayals is reduced to a limited set of reified stereotypes); verism (fictional characters are discussed as if they were real); ahistoricism (a static analysis ignores mutations, metamorphoses, altered contexts, changes of valence); moralism (social and political issues are treated as if they were matters of individual ethics); and individualism (the individual character, rather than larger social categories, is the point of reference).[7]

For example, as a portrait of a gay black mafioso transvestite, *Rainha Diaba* (1973) completely scrambles any notion of positive and negative image. Is it positive that a talented black actor gets to play title roles? Milton Gonçalves's acting is an artistic tour de force, and that is important for other black performers. Moreover, his character is portrayed as a powerful leader, in a country where blacks are treated affectionately even as they are shorn of power. *Rainha Diaba* indirectly poses the question of power by posting a black leader of indisputable energy and charisma, playing provocatively with a whole series of spectatorial stereotypes. With a drag

queen black mafioso as hero, one can hardly accuse the film of being either merely positive or merely stereotypical. Although the *Rainha Diaba* character was based on a real-life historical prototype, a literal-minded sociological approach would point out the demographic improbability of such a character; only a tiny percentage of black Brazilians are actually transvestite mafiosos. But in fact the film's truth transcends demographics. Anyone who thinks that blacks cannot be homosexual, or that homosexuals cannot be macho, or that blacks cannot be Mafia godfathers is being prodded to think again. By mixing gayness with tongue-in-cheek machismo, the film suggests that the macho world might have unconfused and subterranean feminine and homoerotic tendencies (expressed, for example, in the "homosociality" of the biracial male buddy films). In this sense, the film elaborates an insight into the repressed gay underside of exaggeratedly masculine behavior.

That films on some level reflect ambient social life and ideologies should not lead us to expect a

naive mimicry. Brazilian films, taken as a whole, do not reflect the majority status of the country's black, mulatto, and *mestiço* citizens. Although the majority population of Rio de Janeiro, the center of film production in the silent era, was black and *mestiço*, this demographic fact is not reflected in the films of the period; Afro-Brazilians constituted a "structuring absence." On another level, this very absence reflected, if not the demographic reality, at least the real power situation in Brazil. As Abdiaas de Nascimento puts it in discussing Brazilian theater, "The white monopoly on the Brazilian stage reflects the white monopoly on land, on the means of production, on political and economic power, on cultural institutions."[8] In demographic terms, *Dona Flor and Her Two Husbands* (1978) portrays a Bahia considerably less black than the real one. Disney's *The Three Caballeros* portrays a Bahia without any blacks at all. Antunes Filho's *Compasso de Espera*, to take a different example, reflects on racial repression in Brazil, yet the film's protagonist, a black poet and advertising agent closely allied with the São Paulo elite, is sociologically a highly atypical figure. The point is not to demand point-for-point demographic equation but to be aware of the extent to which the films reflect social stratification.

The cinema forms part of a larger spectrum of media representations. Blacks are vastly underrepresented in the Brazilian mass media, certainly in the cinema, but also in television and in advertising. As the film *Mulheres Negras* (Black Women of Brazil) (1986) points out, television commercials, news programs, and advertisements are more evocative of Europe than of a *mestiço* country. Although African-Americans, a demographic minority, are highly visible in U.S. media, Afro-Brazilians, a demographic majority, are virtually invisible in Brazil. A 1988 analysis found that blacks appeared in only nine of 203 ads from Brazilian television and weekly newsmagazines. The television star Xuxa, with her fair skin, blond hair, and blue eyes, seems to incarnate a certain ego ideal for the country. Even in Salvador, the most Africanized city in Brazil, the news anchors tend to be light skinned. Most prime-time television soap operas and miniseries similarly have white protagonists and relegate black characters to the margins. Recently, however, some miniseries—*Zumbi, Sinhá Moza, Xica da Silva*— have Afro-Brazilian themes, often presenting costume dramas set in the times of slavery.

Missing in Action

The most striking absence in Brazilian cinema is that of the black woman. The *chanchads* feature Afro-Brazilian male performers but very few black women. The romantic involvements of black men in Brazilian films (for example, Jorge in *Compasso de Espera*) tend to be with white women, a portrayal consistent with a tendency in real life for upwardly mobile blacks to link up with lighter-skinned partners. Cinema Novo features a number of roles for black women (Cota in *Barravento*, the mistress in *A Grande Feira*), but they are rarely the political or social equal of the male characters. Adaptations of novels often cast white actresses for mulatta roles: Bete Faria as Rita Bahiana in *O Cortizo*, for instance, and Sônia Braga as Gabriela in *Gabriela*. A few films feature prestigious white men in love with black women, notably Diegues's

Xixa da Silva and Senna's *Diamante Bruto* (Rough Diamond) (1977), a film about a television star who returns to his native Mínas to find his long-lost love. Even the films by male Afro-Brazilian directors tend to neglect the black woman. The black poet Saul, in Onofre's *Aventuras Amorosas de um Padeiro*, falls in love with white Riat, not with a black woman. The posited alliance between black men and white women ends up leaving black women without male allies while ignoring solidarity among black women themselves. Documentaries such as *Mulheres Negras*, not surprisingly, try to make up for the lack of black women on screen.

The other group strikingly absent is black gays and lesbians, one of the few exceptions being the transvestite mafioso protagonist of *Rainha Diaba*. Black gays appear briefly in a number of films, among them *Toda Nudez Sera Punida* (All Nudity Will Be Punished) (1978), but usually in caricatured or ephemeral roles. Moreover, gay characters die off with suspect rapidity and regularity. Here too the documentary and fiction shorts by such directors as Eunice Guttman and Karim Ainouz take up the representational slack.

A privileging of social portrayal, plot, and character often leads to a slighting of the specifically cinematic mediations: narrative structure, genre conventions, cinematic style. Eurocentric discourse in film may be relayed not by characters or plot but by lighting, framing, mise-en-scene, music. Some basic issues of mediation have to do with the *rapports de force*, the balance of power as it were, between foreground and background. In the visual arts, space has traditionally been deployed to express the dynamics of authority and prestige. The cinema translates such correlations of social power into registers of foreground and background, on-screen and off-screen, silence and speech.

The Lessons of Anthropophagy

The comparative approach used here, I would argue, works both broadly and in relation to specific films. The film *Macunaíma* (1969), for example, can be seen as part of a broader Pan-American genre—the racial transformation film—that ultimately is a product of a Pan-American magic realism that thrives on real-life cultural disjunctions coexisting in the same time and space. In this the film is comparable to Woody Allen's *Zelig* (1983), in which a character duplicates himself in miraculous feats of ethnic doubling. Born white and Jewish, Allen's chameleon-man protagonist subsequently becomes Native American, African-American, Irish, Italian, Mexican, and Chinese, just as Macunaíma is born black and Indian yet becomes white and Portuguese. Macunaíma and Zelig personify the heteroglossia, or "many-languagedness," of the cultures from which they emerge. They resemble their cities (New York and São Paulo), which are the sites of constant metamorphosis, disintegration, assimilation, and renewal. Both cities received parallel waves of immigrants, often from the same countries (Germans, Italians, Jews from Eastern Europe, Arabs from the Middle East, Chinese, Japanese), just as both received internal immigrants, such as blacks from the South in the case of New York and blacks from Bahia and Mínas in the case of São Paulo. Both cities have their Italian neighborhoods (Little Italy in New York, Bras and Bexiga in São Paulo), their turn-of-the-century Jewish communities (the Lower East Side and Bom Retiro), and their Asiatic communities (Chinatown and Liberdade). As chameleon men who literally become their ethnic neighbors, both Zelig and Macunaíma illustrate the opportunistic appropriations typical of a mobile, multilanguage culture. Both characters exemplify the process by which diverse ethnicities meet, clash, and interact; their metamorphoses simply render palpable the constant process of synchresis that occurs when ethnicities brush against and rub off on one another in a context of cultural "many-languagedness."[12]

Brazilian popular culture draws on the contradictory processes of the diverse and complicated communities that make up Brazil. At times the cultural juxtapositions and counterpoints within Brazilian cinema are surprising, even disconcerting. Arthur Omar's *Triste Tropico* (1977) superimposes recordings of Hitler's speeches on slowed-down images of blacks celebrating Carnival, a counterpoint that disturbs precisely because the relation between sound and image cannot be clearly interpreted as one either of total opposition or of total alliance. A similar counterpointing of blackness and Nazi discourse occurs in Sylvio Back's *Aleluia, Gretchen* (1975), a film about a Nazi-sympathizing German community in the south of Brazil during the 1930s. In one sequence,

Xica da Silva
Directed by Cacá Diegues
Brazil, 1976
(117 min.)
Courtesy Funarte–
DECINE/CTAv

the black servant character Repo dresses up as Santa Claus while regarding himself in the mirror. He tries on a white wig, reminiscent of the aristocratic wigs from the samba pageants, and performs samba steps around the room. He powders his face until he becomes completely white, thus literalizing the ideology of whitening. He repeats German words (*ja, jawohl, fertig, bitte, danke*), all of which have to do with etiquette and submission. His performance of colonial mimicry pays homage to the Aryanization favored by right-wing Germans in Brazil. He becomes, as Flora Sussekind puts it, "the obedient caricature of an alien identity and culture."[13] But as he observes the Kranz family at the dinner table, tears run down his cheeks, disfiguring his makeup and bearing witness to the psychic trauma evoked by Fanon's title: *Black Skin, White Masks*. The cultural counterpoint of the final picnic sequence, in contrast, introduces a note of hope, when German music is interrupted by a Carnival *batucada* (percussion samba) led by Repo. After initial reluctance, the picnickers begin to dance. Afro-Brazilian culture,

it is implied, eventually will triumph over racist ideology.

Another way in which Brazilian culture is figured as a mixed site is through the metaphor of garbage. For the late 1960s *udigudi* (underground) filmmakers, garbage captured the sense "of marginality, of being condemned to survive within scarcity, of being the dumping ground for transnational capitalism, of being obliged to recycle the materials of the dominant culture."[14] In an Afro-diasporic context, the garbage aesthetic evokes the ways in which blacks in the New World, largely deprived of social and economic power, have managed to transmogrify waste products into art, whether through the musical use of throwaway metal (the steel drums of Trinidad), the culinary use of throwaway parts of animals (soul food, *feijoada*), or the use in weaving of throwaway fabrics (quilting). All these aesthetics have in common a notion of discontinuity—a quilt is made of scraps exemplifying diverse styles and materials—whence their link with artistic modernism as an art of discontinuity and with postmodernism as an art of recycled trash

Macunaíma

Directed by Joaquim Pedro de Andrade

Brazil, 1969

(108 min.)

Courtesy Funarte–DECINE/CTAv

and pastiche. At the same time, garbage has a multitude of meanings that can be read literally (garbage as a source of food for poor people, as the site of ecological disaster, as the diasporized, heterotopic space of the promiscuous mingling of the rich and the poor, the industrial and the artisanal, the national and the international, the local and the global). Or garbage can be read metaphorically as social indictment—poor people treated like garbage, garbage as the dumping of pharmaceutical products or of canned television programs. Garbage can also be an allegorical text to be deciphered, so that the truth of a society can be read in its waste products.

In Brazilian art, syncretism has been an absolutely crucial thematic and aesthetic resource. Historically, Brazilian architects and artisans, many of them black, tropicalized the Iberian Baroque church style, for example, by turning grapes into pineapples. The Afro-Muslim architect Manoel Friandes, as Henry Drewal points out, infused the austere Christian exterior of the Church of Lapinha in Salvador with an "exuberant Islamic presence" through Moorish arches, decorative tiles, and Arabic script.[15] Brazilian cinema also uses the signs and tokens of syncretism, deploying multitemporal heterogeneity as a means of achieving a renovated aesthetic. The opening sequence of *Macunaíma*, for example, shows a family whose names are indigenous, whose epidermic traits are African and European and *mestiço*, whose clothes are Portuguese and African, whose hut is *mameluco*, and whose manner of giving birth is indigenous. Similarly, the tensions between Catholicism and Afro-Brazilian *candomblé* spiritualism in *The Given Word* are evoked through the manipulation of cultural symbols, setting in motion a cultural battle, for instance, between *berimbau* (an African instrument consisting of a long bow, gourd, and a string, played with wooden sticks) and a church bell, thus synecdochically encapsulating a larger religious and political struggle. *Tent of Miracles* (1977) counterposes opera and samba as a metaphor for the larger conflict between Bahia's white elite and its subjugated *mestiços*, between ruling-class science and Afro-inflected popular culture.

Brazilian cinema at its best orchestrates not an innocuous pluralism but rather a strong cultural counterpoint between in some ways incommensurable yet nevertheless thoroughly complicated cultures. The final shot of *Terra em Transe* (1967) brilliantly exemplifies this process. As we see the film's protagonist, Paulo, wielding a rifle in a Che Guevara-like gesture of quixotic rebellion, we hear a soundtrack composed of Villa-Lobos, *candomblé* chants, samba, and machine-gun fire. The mix is fundamentally unstable; the Villa-Lobos music never really synchronizes with the *candomblé* or the gunfire. We are reminded of Alego Carpentier's gentle mockery of the innocuous juxtapositions of the European avant-gardists—for example, Lautreamont's "umbrella and a sewing machine"—which he contrasts with the explosive counterpoints of indigenous, African, and European cultures thrown up daily by Latin American life and art.

Despite substantial obstacles, Brazilian cinema has accomplished an enormous amount. It has given some voice to people of color and provided glimpses of Brazilian history from a multicultural perspective. Nonetheless, Brazilian cinema has not yet managed to achieve the proud and open-ended synthesis typical of Brazilian popular music. Indeed, it has yet to become truly and consistently, as opposed to superficially and sporadically, polyphonic, not only in cinematic terms (the contrapuntal call-and-response play of track against track and genre against genre), but also in cultural terms (the interplay of socially generated voices). The overall trajectory from the white cinema of the silent period to the undoubtedly multicolored cinema of today does point to the progressive deployment of more social and cultural voices, even if that process has been less thorough-going than one might have hoped.

The challenge now is to go beyond the mere inclusion of individual representatives of diverse groups, beyond even a concern with positive and negative images, to present diverse community perspectives, to stage, as it were, the polyphonic clashes and harmonies of Brazilian cultural diversity. True cinematic polyphony will probably emerge only with the advent of political equality and cultural reciprocity among the nation's diverse communities. But until the advent of such a utopian moment, cultural and political polyphony can be evoked at least through the proleptic procedures of anticipatory texts, ones at once militantly imaginative and resonantly multivoiced, with their eyes and ears always open to the long-term possibilities of change. ■

CHECKLIST 8

BIOGRAPHIES

Checklist of the Exhibition

SILVANA AFRAM

Mulheres Negras (Black
Women of Brazil), 1986
Video with English subtitles
(25 min.)
Courtesy Women Make
Movies

SYLVIO BACK

Yndio do Brasil
(Our Indians), 1995
Video version of 35mm film
with English subtitles
(70 min.)
Courtesy of the artist

BRÍGIDA BALTAR

A coleta da neblina
(Collecting Mist),
1996–2001
DVD projection (3 min.)
Courtesy of the artist

ANNA BARROS

Como Pegar um Saci-Si
(How to Catch a Saci-Si),
1998
Computer animation
Courtesy of the artist

SANDRA CINTO

A ponte impossivel (The
Impossible Bridge), 1998
Automotive paint on wood
106¼ × 118⅛ × 19⅝ in.
(270 × 300 × 50 cm)
Collection of Ricardo
Trevisan

Untitled, 2001
Site-specific wall drawing
Acrylic and silver pen
Courtesy Galeria Casa
Triângulo, São Paulo

ORIANA DUARTE

Sopa do pedra
(Stone Soup), 1998
Video (60 min.)
Courtesy of the artist

*O gabinete de souvenirs
de A coisa em si*
(Souvenir Cabinet of the
Thing-in-Itself), 1998–2001
Embroidered maps,
music sheets, and souvenirs
Dimensions variable
Collection of the artist

ANNA BELLA GEIGER

Ideología (Ideology),
1973/1983
Video (5 min.)
Courtesy of the artist

*Mapas Elementales nº 1 e
nº 3* (Elemental Maps #1
and #3), 1976
Video (3 min. each)
Courtesy of the artist

Am. Latina, 1977
Graphite and colored pencil
on paper
23 × 37 in. (58.5 × 94 cm)
Collection of the artist

*Brasil nativo – Brasil
alienigena* (Native
Brazil – Alien Brazil), 1977
Twenty postcards
(photos by Luiz Carlos Velho)
Paper
4 × 5⅞ in.
(10 × 15 cm) each
The Museum of Modern Art
Library, New York

O pão nosso de cada dia
(Our Daily Bread), 1978
Paper bag and six postcards
(photos by Januário Garcia)
Paper
6¾ × 4¾ in.
(17 × 12 cm) each
Collection of the artist

Local da ação
(Place of Action), 1978
Video (5 min.)
Courtesy of the artist

Local da ação nº 2
(Place of Action #2), 1979
Engraving, etching, and
silkscreen
15⅜ × 15⅜ in.
(39 × 39 cm)
Collection of the artist

Local da ação nº 10
(Place of Action #10), 1980
Silkscreen and cliché
11⅜ × 19⅝ in.
(29 × 50 cm)
Collection of the artist

Local da ação nº 25
(Place of Action #25), 1991
Serigraph, engraving, and
cliché
24 × 39⅜ in. (61 × 100 cm)
Collection of the artist

*A linha imaginária
de Tordesilhas da série
Fronteiriços* (The Imaginary
Line of Tordesillas from the
Borderlines Series), 1993
Iron, encaustic, lead, copper,
and cliché
7⅞ × 23¼ × 4 in.
(20 × 59 × 10 cm)
Collection of the Museum of
Modern Art, Rio de Janeiro

*Orbis descriptio nº 7 da
série Fronteiriços*
(Description of the World #7
from the Borderlines Series),
1995
Iron, lead, copper, encaustic,
gold leaf, and cliché
4 × 24 × 16⅞ in.
(10 × 61 × 43 cm)
Collection of the artist

*Orbis descriptio nº 10
da série Fronteiriços*
(Description of the World
#10 from the Borderlines
Series), 1996
Iron, lead, copper, steel,
encaustic, silver leaf, and
cliché
4 × 24 × 17⅜ in.
(10 × 61 × 44 cm)
Collection of the artist

*Orbis descriptio nº 1321
da série Fronteiriços*
(Description of the World
#1321 from the Borderlines
Series), 1998
Iron, copper, steel,
encaustic, thread, and nails
18½ × 27⅛ × 4⅜ in.
(47 × 69 × 11 cm)
Collection of the artist

*Tordesilhas com equação
da série Fronteiriços*
(Tordesillas with Equator
from the Borderlines Series),
1999
Flandres plate, lead, metal
springs, and encaustic
6¾ × 20⅛ × 1⅛ in.
(17 × 51 × 3 cm)
Collection of the artist

Rolo nº 5 (Scroll #5), 1998
Mixed media on parchment
9 × 43¼ in. (23 × 110 cm)
Collection of the artist

Rolo com Opostos
(Scroll with Opposites),
2000
Mixed media
Scroll, fully opened:
41⅜ × 8¼ in.
(105 × 21 cm)
Lead plate, folded:
11 × 3⅛ in. (28 × 8 cm)
Etching: 11 × 5⅞ in.
(28 × 15 cm)
Collection of the artist

SANDRA KOGUT
Lá e Cá (There and Here),
1995
Video (25 min.)
Courtesy of the artist

SONIA LABOURIAU
Pássaros Migratórios
(Migratory Birds),
1992–2001
Site-specific installation
Urucum, seeds, binder,
water, glass, and nine
C-prints
Courtesy of the artist

NELSON LEIRNER
Santa Ceia
(The Last Supper), 1990
Crayon and colored pencil
on paper
31½ × 47¼ in.
(80 × 120 cm)
Collection of Graziela Strina
de Arruda

Santa Ceia
(The Last Supper), 1990
Mixed media
29⅞ × 37¾ in.
(76 × 96 cm)
Collection of Museum
of Contemporary Art,
Niterói, Brazil

Santa Ceia
(The Last Supper), 1990
Mixed media
30¾ × 68⅛ in.
(78 × 173 cm)
Collection of Plinio de Toledo
Arruda, São Paulo

Santa Ceia
(The Last Supper), 1990
Mixed media
19⅝ × 27½ in.
(50 × 70 cm)
Courtesy Galeria Luisa
Strina, São Paolo

LAURA LIMA
Video documentation of
series of Managed Actions:
Encapuzados
(Fighting Cows), 1996/1997
Mulher narcótica
(Doped Woman), 1997
RhR Integrants
(RhR Participants), 1999
Video
Courtesy of the artist

*Homem=carne/mulher=
carne* (Man=Flesh/
Woman=Flesh), 1999
Ink on paper
5 × 13 × ½ in.
(12.7 × 33 × 1.25 cm)
Collection of the artist

ANNA MARIA MAIOLINO
Arroz & Feijão (Rice and
Beans), 1979/2001
Site-specific installation
Five tables, sixteen chairs,
tablecloths, dinnerware,
silverware, glassware,
gauze, soil, rice, and beans
Courtesy Galeria Brito
Cimino, São Paulo

HUMBERTO MAURO
O descobrimento do Brasil
(The Discovery of Brazil),
1937
Video version of 16mm film
(62 min.)
Courtesy Estate of
Humberto Mauro

BETH MOYSÉS
Luta (Battle), 1998
Boxing gloves and
wedding lace
14⅛ × 13 × 11¾ in.
(36 × 33 × 30 cm)
Courtesy Galeria Thomas
Cohn, São Paulo

Memória do Afeto
(Memory of Affection), 2000
Video (7 min.)
Courtesy of the artist

MÔNICA NADOR
Video documentation
of *Paredes Pinturas*
(Painting Walls), 1998–99
Video (8 min.)
Courtesy of the artist

Untitled, 2001
Site-specific wall painting
Acrylic
Courtesy of the artist

NAZARETH PACHECO
Untitled, from the *Jóais*
(Jewelry) series, 1997–2001
Installation of twenty-five
to thirty pieces in Plexiglas
wall boxes
Crystal beads, cut stones,
surgical needles, razor
blades, scalpel blades,
fish hooks, lancets, and
X-Acto blades
Approx. 86⅝–90½ in. wide
(220–230 cm)
Collection of the artist

Untitled, 1997
Crystal beads, needles,
and acrylic
19⅝ × 15¾ × 2⅜ in.
(50 × 40 × 6 cm)
Collection of Museum
of Contemporary Art,
Niterói, Brazil

Untitled, 1998
Acrylic, crystal, and
stainless steel
13⅜ × 9⅞ × 9⅞ in.
(34 × 25 × 25 cm)
Courtesy Galeria Brito
Cimino, São Paulo

LYGIA PAPE
La nouvelle création
(The New Creation), 1967
Video (50 sec.)
Courtesy of the artist

*Poemas Visuais: Língua
Apunhalada* (Visual Poem:
Blood Tongue), 1968
Photograph and light box
70⅞ × 47¼ in.
(180 × 120 cm)
Courtesy Galeria Camargo
Vilaça, São Paulo

Video documentation
of *O Ovo* (The Egg), 1968
Video (3 min.)
Courtesy of the artist

Eat Me, 1975
Video (9 min.)
Courtesy of the artist

Catiti–Catiti, 1978
Video (10 min.)
Courtesy of the artist

ROSANA PAULINO

Ten drawings from *Models*
series, 1996–98
Ink, pastel, charcoal,
graphite, and acrylic on
paper
13 × 9⅜ in.
(33 × 24 cm)
13½ × 10⅝ in.
(34.4 × 27 cm)
and 24½ × 17½ in.
(62.3 × 44.5 cm)
Collection of the artist

*Auto retrato com máscara
africana I – Tarsila*
(Self-Portrait with an African
Mask I – Tarsila), 1998
Linocut
15 × 11 in. (38 × 28 cm)
Collection of the artist

*Auto retrato com máscara
africana II – Volpi*
(Self-Portrait with an African
Mask II – Volpi), 1998
Linocut
15 × 11 in. (38 × 28 cm)
Collection of the artist

Ten drawings from
untitled series
(Diário de uma doença)
(Illness Diary), 1999
Graphite, ink, watercolor,
and pastel on green
gessoed paper
15⅛ × 11⅜ in.
(38.3 × 29 cm) each
Private collection

ROSÂNGELA RENNÓ

Vera Cruz (True Cross), 2000
Video with English subtitles
(44 min.)
Courtesy of the artist

MIGUEL RIO BRANCO

*Nada levarei quando
morrer aqueles que mim
deve cobrarei no inferno*
(I Won't Take Nothing When
I Die Those Who Owe Me
Something Will Pay in Hell),
1979–81
DVD version of 16mm film
(20 min.)
Courtesy of the artist

Door into Darkness, 1995
Projection of seventeen
slides
Dimensions variable
Courtesy of the artist

REGINA SILVEIRA

Brazil Today, 1977
Book of six altered
postcards
Paper
4¼ × 6⅛ × ⅛ in.
(10.2 × 15.6 × .5 cm)
closed
Collection of the artist

Monudentro (Inside the
Monument), 1986–87/2001
Site-specific installation
Vinyl and carpeting
Courtesy Galeria Brito
Cimino, São Paulo

VALESKA SOARES

Untitled (from *Strangelove*),
1996
Lead, blown glass, wine,
and poison
Eleven pieces:
14⅛ × 9 × 3 in.
(36 × 23 × 7.5 cm) each
Collection of Patricia Phelps
de Cisneros, Caracas
Collection of José Antonio
Marton, São Paulo
Collection of the artist

HELENA SOLBERG

*Carmen Miranda:
Bananas Is My Business*,
1995
Video version of 35mm film
with English subtitles
(92 min.)
Courtesy Women Make
Movies

JANAÍNA TSCHÄPE

*He Drowned in Her Eyes
as She Called Him to
Follow: Wave*, 2000
Video version of DVD
(5 min.)
Courtesy of the artist

*He Drowned in Her Eyes
as She Called Him to Follow:
Medusa*, 2000
Video version of DVD (5 min.)
Courtesy of the artist

*He Drowned in Her Eyes
as She Called Him to Follow:
Moss*, 2001
Video version of DVD (5 min.)
Courtesy of the artist

ADRIANA VAREJÃO

*Proposta para uma
catequese: Parte I Diptico:
Morte e Esquartejamento*
(Proposal for a Catechesis:
Part I Diptych: Death and
Dismemberment), 1993
Oil on canvas
55⅛ × 94½ in.
(140 × 240 cm)
Collection Daniela
and Patrice de Camaret,
São Paulo

*Proposta para uma
catequese: Parte II Diptico:
Aparicao e Reliquias*
(Proposal for a Catechesis:
Part II Diptych: Apparition
and Relics), 1993
Oil on canvas
55⅛ × 94½ in.
(140 × 240 cm)
Collection Moisés and Diana
Berezdivin, Puerto Rico

Figura de Convite
(Entrance Figure), 1997
Oil on canvas
78¾ × 78¾ in.
(200 × 200 cm)
Private collection
Celia S. de Birbragher

*Testemunhas Oculares
X, Y e Z* (Eye Witnesses
X, Y and Z), 1997
Oil on canvas, porcelain,
photography, silver, crystal,
and iron
Three paintings:
33½ × 27½ in.
(85 × 70 cm) each
Three objects:
34⅝ × 6¼ × 9⅞ in.
(88 × 16 × 25 cm) each
Collection Frances Marinho,
Rio de Janeiro

SILVANA AFRAM

Born in São Paulo, 1960
Lives and works in São Paulo

Education

1998. M.A., communications, Escola de Comunicações e Artes, Universidade de São Paulo

1982. B.A., Faculdade de Comunicação Social Cásper Líbero

Projects

1986. Becomes manager-partner of Luares Produções e Comunicações, where she is a copywriter and an editor of sociocultural educational and academic texts

1984. Founds Lilith Video with Jacira Melo and Marcia Meireles, who together made many videos on gender issues until 1988. Afram also worked variously as a camerawoman, producer, editor, scriptwriter, and director on twenty-eight video productions and three weekly educational television series in São Paulo and Brasília

1983. Starts making videos at National TV in Brasília

Selected Films and Awards

1994. *O Seguro Morreu de Velho* (Prevention Is Better than Cure): best video, III Women's Latin American Video Festival, Quito

1990. *Os Technozeus* (The Technozeus): script award, National Popular Video Contest, Brazil

1989. *A Obscuridade da Minha Língua II* (The Darkness of My Language II): special mention, XVIII Festival International du Nouveau Cinéma et de la Vidéo, Montreal

1988. *Mulheres Negras* (Black Women of Brazil): second prize, Festival da Terra, Brazil

1987. *Mulheres Negras* (Black Women of Brazil): first prize, I Women's Video Festival, Brasília

1987. *Mulheres no Canavial* (Women in the Sugarcane Field): special jury award, I Women's Video Festival, Brasília

1987. *A Saúde Da Mulher Trabalhadora* (Working Women's Health): fourth prize, I Women's Video Festival, Brasília

SYLVIO BACK

Born in Blumenau, Brazil
Lives and works in Rio de Janeiro

The recipient of sixty-one national and international prizes, Sylvio Back is one of Brazil's most renowned filmmakers. A former film critic and journalist, he began directing motion pictures in 1962 and to date has directed and produced most of his thirty-five films, which include short and medium-length documentaries and nine full-length pictures. Also a poet and writer, he has published seventeen books (poetry, essays, and several screenplays), including erotic and satirical poems.

Selected Documentary Films

1995. *Yndio do Brasil* (Our Indians)

1991. *Rádio Auriverde* (Radio Brazil)

1987. *Guerra do Brasil* (The War of Brazil)

1982. *República Guarani* (Guarani Republic)

1980. *Revolução de 30* (The 1930 Revolution)

Fiction

1999. *Cruz e Sousa— O Poeta do Desterro* (The Banished Poet)

1976. *Aleluia, Gretchen* (Hallelujah, Gretchen)

1971. *A Guerra dos Pelados* (The War of the Skin Heads)

1968. *Lance Maior* (The Highest Bid)

Poetry

1999. *Boudoir* (Boudoir)

1995. *Yndio do Brasil: Poemas de Filme* (Our Indians: Poems from the Film)

1994. *A Vinha do Desejo* (Desire's Vineyard)

1988. *Moedas de Luz* (Coins of Light)

1986. *O Caderno Erótico de Sylvio Back* (The Erotic Notebook of Sylvio Back)

BRÍGIDA BALTAR

Born in Rio de Janeiro, 1959
Lives and works in Rio de Janeiro

Education

Architecture and history, Escola de Artes visuais do Parque Lage, Rio de Janeiro

Solo Exhibitions

2001. Galeria Nara Roesler, São Paulo

2001. Espaço Agora Capacete, Rio de Janeiro

1997. Joel Edelstein Arte Contemporânea, Rio de Janeiro

Group Exhibitions

2001. *Thread Unraveled,* El Museo del Barrio, New York City

2001. *Get that Balance,* Kampnagel KulturFabric, Hamburg

2001. *Arco das Rosas,* Casa das Rosas, São Paulo

2000. *O Século das Mulheres—Algumas Artistas*, Casa de Petrópolis, Rio de Janeiro

2000. *Novas Aquisições, Coleção Gilberto Chateaubriand,* Museu de Arte Moderna, Rio de Janeiro

1999. *Objeto dos anos 60 aos anos 90,* Instituto Itaú Cultural, São Paulo

1999. *Fundação em Conserto,* Fundação Progresso, Rio de Janeiro

1998. *Prêmio Brasília de Artes Visuais,* Museu de Arte de Brasília

1998. *Novas Aquisições, Coleção Gilberto Chateaubriand,* Museu de Arte Moderna, Rio de Janeiro

1997. *Panorama de Arte Brasileira '97,* Museu de Arte Moderna, São Paulo. Traveled to Museu de Arte Contemporânea, Niterói; Museu de Arte Moderna, Salvador; Museu de Arte Moderna, Recife

1997. *Apropriações,* Joel Edelstein Arte Contemporânea, Rio de Janeiro

1997. *Feminino,* Museu da República, Rio de Janeiro

ANNA BARROS

Born in São Paulo, 1931
Lives and works in São Paulo

Education

1996. Ph.D., communications and semiotics, Pontificia Universidade Católica, São Paulo

1990. M.F.A., Universidade de São Paulo

1984. B.F.A., Otis Art Institute, Parsons School of Design, Los Angeles

Solo Exhibitions

2000. *SCSC: quatro instalações,* Conjunto Cultural da Caixa, Brasília

1998. *Como Pegar um Saci-Si,* Galeria de Arte Valú Ória , São Paulo

1995. *Lumen-Essência,* Galeria Nara Rosler, São Paulo

Selected Group Exhibitions

1999. *Arte e Tecnologia no Centro-Oeste*, Galeria Jaime Câmara, Goiânia

1996. *Mulheres no Acervo do MAC*, Museu de Arte Contemporânea, Universidade de São Paulo

1996. *12 Artistas Pesquisadores da ANPAP*, Paço das Artes, São Paulo

Artist Biographies

Animated Films

2000. *Sibigrapi 2000,* Electronic Art Exhibition, Brazil

2000. *(Arte e Tecnologia)–Mostra de Vídeos–Investigações Eletrônicas,* Instituto Itaú Cultural, São Paulo

1999. *Invenção: Thinking the Next Millenium,* Instituto Itaú Cultural, in collaboration with ISEA (Inter-Society for the Electronic Arts), CaiiA-STAR (Centre for Advanced Inquiry in the Interactive Arts, University of Wales College, Newport, and Centre for Science, Technology and Art Research, University of Plymouth, United Kingdom), and *Leonardo* (journal published by ISAST/International Society for the Arts, Sciences and Technology)

1999. *Sibigrapi '99,* Electronic Art Exhibition, Brazil

1997. *Sibigrapi '97,* Electronic Art Exhibition, Brazil

1990. Dream Centenary–Computer Graphics Grand Prix 99, Aizu, Japan

SANDRA CINTO

Born in Santo André, Brazil, 1968
Lives and works in São Paulo

Selected Solo Exhibitions

2001. Tanya Bonakdar Gallery, New York City

2001. Centro Cultural São Paulo, São Paulo

1999. Bonakdar Jancou Gallery, New York City

1998. Galeria Casa Triângulo, São Paulo

1997. Capela do Morumbi, São Paulo

Selected Group Exhibitions

2001. *4ª Bienal do Barro de América,* Museo Alejandro Otero, Caracas

2001. *METRO: A Cidade em Você,* Centro Cultural Banco do Brasil, São Paulo

2001. *A Trajetória da Luz na Arte Brasileira,* Instituto Itaú Cultural, São Paulo

2000. *Obra Nova,* Museu de Arte Contemporânea, Universidade de São Paulo

2000. *Sandra Cinto e Albano Afonso,* Galeria Canvas, Porto

2000. *Summer Group Exhibition,* Paula Cooper Gallery, New York City

2000. *26ª Bienal de Pontevedra*

2000. *Elysian Fields,* Centre Georges Pompidou, Paris

1999. *ARCO '99,* Project Rooms, Madrid

1999. *Collectors Collect Contemporary: 1900–1999,* Institute of Contemporary Art, Boston. Traveled to Museum of Contemporary Art, San Diego

1999. *II Bienal de Artes Visuais do Mercosul,* Armazém do Porto, Porto Alegre

1999. *Território Expandido,* SESC Pompéia, São Paulo

1998. *XXIV Bienal Internacional de São Paulo*

1998. *Arte Contemporânea Brasileira: Um éentre Outrós,* Centro Cultural Banco do Brasil, Rio de Janeiro

1997. *Intervalos,* Paço das Artes, São Paulo

1996. *Projeto Antarctica Artes com a Folha,* Pavilhão Padre Manoel de Nóbrega, São Paulo

1996. *Ouro de artista,* Galeria Casa Triângulo, São Paulo

ORIANA DUARTE

Born in Campina Grande, 1966
Lives and works in Recife

Education

2000. M.A., communications and semiotics, Pontificia Universidade Católica, São Paulo

1990. B.A., industrial design, Universidade Federal de Pernambuco, Recife

Solo Exhibitions

1997. *A coisa em si* (The Thing-in-Itself), Instituto de Arte Contemporânea, Universidade Federal de Pernambuco, Recife

1995. *Playground,* Museu do Estado de Pernambuco, Recife

Group Exhibitions

2001. *Uma Geração em Trânsito* (A Generation in Transit), Centro Cultural Banco do Brasil, Rio de Janeiro

2001. *I Bienal do Cariri,* Juazeiro do Norte, Ceará

2000. *Salão Pernambucano de Artes Plásticas,* Observatório Cultural Malkoff, Recife

2000. *Projeto Rumos Visuais–Itaú Cultural: Arte e Política–Outros 500,* Instituto Itaú Cultural, São Paulo. Traveled to Fundação Joaquim Nabuco, Recife

2000. *BR 500,* Museu de Arte Contemporânea Americana, São Paulo

1999. *Panorama da Arte Brasileira '99,* Museu de Arte Moderna, São Paulo

1999. *Nordestes,* SESC/Pompéia, São Paulo

1999. *Os 90,* Paço Imperial, Rio de Janeiro

1998. *V Salão MAM–Bahia de Artes Plásticas,* Museu de Arte Moderna da Bahia, Salvador

1998. *Dragões e Leões,* Centro Cultural Dragão do Mar, Fortaleza

1998. *Instalações: Paulo Meira e Oriana Duarte,* Galeria de Arte UNAMA, Belém

1997. *XVI Salão Nacional de Artes Plásticas,* Museu de Arte Moderna, Rio de Janeiro

1997. *Mostra Ver e Verso Pernambuco,* Museu de Arte Moderna Aloísio Magalhães, Recife

1997. *Arte Contemporânea da Gravura/Brasil-Reflexão 97,* Museu Metropolitano de Arte, Curitiba

1997. *Grupo Camelo–Projeto Conexão II,* Núcleo de Arte Contemporânea da Universidade Federal da Paraiba, João Pessoa

1996. *Artistas Pernambucanos,* Galeria Metropolitana de Arte Aloísio Magalhães, Recife

ANNA BELLA GEIGER

Born in Rio de Janeiro, 1933
Lives and works in Rio de Janeiro

Education

1962. B.A., philosophy, Rio de Janeiro

1953–55. Studied art history at New York University and the Metropolitan Museum of Art, New York City

Selected Solo Exhibitions

1998. *No Princípio . . . ,* Paço Imperial, Rio de Janeiro

1998. *Skulpturen/Zeichnungen,* Galerie Bernd Slutzky, Frankfurt

1996–97. *Anna Bella Geiger: Constelações,* Museu de Arte Moderna, Rio de Janeiro. Traveled to Museu de Arte Moderno, São Paulo, and Museu de Arte Moderno, Salvador

1995. *Arte Contemporânea,* Joel Edelstein Arte Contemporânea, Rio de Janeiro

Selected Group Exhibitions

2001. *From the 70's,* Museo Nacional Centro Reina Sofia, Madrid

1999. *Circa 68,* Fundação Serralves, Porto

1998. *Idea de Logar,* Museo Nacional Centro Reina Sofia, Madrid

1998. *XXIV Bienal Internacional de São Paulo*

1997. *VI Bienal de La Havana,* Havana

1997. *I Bienal de Mercosul,* Porto Alegre

1995. *Adding It Up: Acquisitions 70–95,* Museum of Modern Art, New York City

1995. *Copie-Grafien-Bücher und Graphik,* Neues Museum Weserburg, Bremen

SANDRA KOGUT

Born in Rio de Janeiro, 1965
Lives and works in Rio de Janeiro

Sandra Kogut, one of the best-known personalities in Brazilian video art, has made a name for herself in the international cultural world through several exhibitions of her prize-winning work on film and video. Dedicated to the creation of performances, installations, and video works since 1984, she is seen today as a pioneering force in Brazilian video art. She has also been acclaimed for her work on film since 1990 and her multimedia creations since 1992. Kogut was part of the team that created *Brasil Legal,* a Globo TV program, and was artistic director of Globograph, a company specializing in new technology development.

Selected Films and Videos and Awards

1998. *Campos Neutrais* (The Neutrais Fields), filmed on the border between Brazil and Uruguay as part of the Borders project

1997. *Adieu monde ou l'histoire de Pierre et Claire* (Goodbye World, or The Story of Pierre and Claire): Prix Circom; jury prize, Estavar, France; silver medal, Leipzig Film Festival; mention, Grand Prix Vue sur les Docs, Marseille; mention, Festival of New Films, Split, Croatia; jury prize, Festival de Lisbonne, Portugal; Prix aux Rencontres Arts Plastiques d'Herouville, St. Clair, France; Grand Prix du Jury et Prix du Public, French Short Film Festival of New York; second prize, Hamburg Short Film Festival; prix, Ministry of Urban Development—Westphalie and Catholique Prize, Oberhausen Film Festival, Germany

1995. *Lá e Cá* (There and Here): prix, Oberhausen Film Festival, Germany; best short film, Kiev Film Festival, Ukraine; best short film, Film Festival de Montecatini, Italy

1993. *En Français:* grand prix, Oberhausen Film Festival, Germany

1991/1996. *Parabolic People:* main award, Deutscher Videokunstpreis, Germany; prize, Fotoptica International Video Festival, Brazil; prize, Festival Nouvelles Images de Locarno, Switzerland; grand prix, Festival Internacional de Cadiz, Spain

1990. *Vidéocabines São Caixas Pretas* (Video Booths Are Black Boxes): Sol de Prata, Rio Cine Festival, Brazil; best film, Jornada Paulista de V'deo, Brazil

1990. *What Do You Think People Think Brazil Is?:* director's choice award, 15th Annual Atlanta Video Festival; gold medal, International Film and TV Festival of New York; best video-art, Fotoptica International Video Festival, Brazil

1989. *Rio Today MAM,* for the reopening of the Museum of Modern Art, Rio de Janeiro; best documentary, Jornada Paulista de V'deo, Brazil

SONIA LABOURIAU

Born in Pasadena, California, 1956

Lives and works in Belo Horizonte

Education

1999–2001. M.A., literature and other semiotic systems, Universidade Federal de Minas Gerais, Belo Horizonte

1988. Graduate study in sculpture, installation, and performance, Art Institute of San Francisco

1984. Graduate study in art conservation, Centro de Conservação e Restauração de Bens Culturais Móveis, Escola de Belas Artes, Universidade Federal de Minas Gerais, Belo Horizonte

1976–83. B.F.A., visual arts, lithography, and drawing, Escola Guignard-Universidade Estadual de Minas Gerais, Belo Horizonte

Selected Solo Exhibitions

1998. *Feuilletables,* Performance, Galerie Anne de Villepoix, Paris

1997. *Telescópio,* Galeria Genesco Murta, Palácio das Artes, Belo Horizonte

1997. *Artista convidada do Programa de Exposições do Centro Cultural São Paulo*

1995. *Manuscrito,* Paço Imperial, Rio de Janeiro

Selected Group Exhibitions

2000. *The Collection of Latin American Art,* University of Essex Gallery, Colchester, England

1999. *Escultura Mineira,* public space installation, Tiradentes

1998. *Prêmio ICATU,* Paço Imperial, Rio de Janeiro

1998. *Interlacings,* Whitney Museum of American Art at Champion, Stamford

1997. *Panorama da Arte Brasileira '97,* Museu de Arte Moderna, São Paulo. Traveled to Museu de Arte Contemporânea, Niterói; Museu de Arte da Bahia, Salvador; Museu de Arte de Pernambuco, Recife

1997. *Escultura Mineira,* Museu de Arte da Pampulha, Belo Horizonte

1996. *Efeito Festival,* Galeria Pace, Belo Horizonte

1995. *Apropriação e Autoria,* Universidade Federal Fluminense, Niterói

NELSON LEIRNER

Born in São Paulo, 1932

Lives and works in Rio de Janeiro

Selected Solo Exhibitions

2000. *Fase Rio de Janeiro,* Galeria Paulo Darzé, Salvador

1999. *Clonagem,* Galeria Ana Maria Niemeyer, Rio de Janiero

1999. *Bolsa de Arte Porto Alegre*

1998. *Nelson Leirner, Uma Instalação,* Galeria Brito Cimino, São Paulo

1997. *Nelson Leirner, Uma Viagem,* Centro Cultural Light, Rio de Janeiro

Selected Group Exhibitions

2000. *Recortes,* Galeria Brito Cimino, São Paulo

2000. *Trajetória da Luz na Arte Brasileira,* Instituto Itaú Cultural, São Paulo

2000. *1ª Bienal de Artes do Cariri,* Juazeiro do Norte

2000. *Obra Nova,* Museu de Arte Contemporânea, Universidade de São Paulo

2000. *Arte e Erotísmo,* Galeria Nara Roesler, São Paulo

2000. *Os Anjos Estão de Volta,* Pinacoteca do Estado de São Paulo

2000. *A Arte do Papel,* Museu de Arte Contemporânea, Universidade de São Paulo

2000. *Um Oceano Inteiro Para Nadar,* Culturgest, Lisbon

2000. *Mostra do Redescobrimento Brasil+500 Anos,* Fundaçao Bienal de São Paulo

2000. *The Fifth Element, Money and Art,* Kunsthalle, Dusseldorf

1999. *Hierarquia,* Paço Imperial, Rio de Janeiro

1999. *Por que Duchamp?* Paço das Artes, São Paulo

1999. *XXXVIII Biennale di Venezia,* Venice

1999. *Panorama da Arte Brasileira '99,* Museu de Arte Moderna, São Paulo

1998. *II Prêmio Jonnie Walker de Artes Plásticas,* Museu Nacional de Belas Artes, Rio de Janeiro

1998. *Donações Recentes,* Museu de Arte Moderna, São Paulo

1998. *Iconoclastias Culturais,* Casa das Rosas, São Paulo

1998. *Re-figuração,* Museu de Arte Contemporânea, Universidade de São Paulo

1998. *Seleção Galeria Brito Cimino,* São Paulo

1997. Galeria Brito Cimino, São Paulo

1997. *Ao Cubo,* Paço das Artes, São Paulo

1995. *Infância Perversa,* Museu de Arte Moderna, Rio de Janeiro

LAURA LIMA

Born in Governador Valadres, 1971

Lives and works in Rio de Janeiro

Solo Exhibitions

2001. Galeria Casa Triângulo, São Paulo

1999. Galeria Casa Triângulo, São Paulo

1998. Casa Cultural, São Paulo

Selected Group Exhibitions

2000. *Fim de Milênio*, Museu de Arte Moderna, São Paulo

2000. *ARCO 2000*, Project Rooms, Madrid

1999. *Curadoria Vivia21, Laura Lima e Marssares*, Galeria do Poste, Niterói

1999. *Puller*, Fundação Progresso, Rio de Janeiro

1998. *XXIV Bienal Internacional de São Paulo*

1998. *Projeto Digestão*, Centro Cultural São Paulo

1998. *Ponto Cego*, Museu da Imagem e do Som, São Paulo

1998. *UProjeto Antarctica Artes com a Folha*, Galeria Casa Triângulo, São Paulo

1998. *'90s Generation: Projeto Antarctica com a Folha*, Pinacoteca no Parque, São Paulo

1998. *Objetos no Esphelho Estão Mais Próximos do que Parecem*, PUC, Rio de Janeiro

1998. *Dez Anos de Casa Tríangulo*, Galeria Casa Triângulo, São Paulo

1997. *Nove Anos de Casa Tríangulo*, São Paulo

1997. *25º Salão Nacional de Arte de Belo Horizonte*, Museu de Arte da Pampulha, Belo Horizonte

1997. *Intervalos*, Paço das Artes, São Paulo

1996. *Projeto Antarctica Artes a Folha,* Pavilhão Padre Manoel de Nóbrega, São Paulo

1996. *duo*, Espaço Livre, Niterói

ANNA MARIA MAIOLINO

Born in Scalea, Italy, 1942
Lives and works in Rio de Janeiro

Education

1971. Pratt Institute, New York City

1963. Escola Nacional de Belas Artes, Rio de Janeiro

1960. Escola Nacional de Belas Artes Cristobal Rojas, Caracas

Selected Solo Exhibitions

1999. *+ & -*, Gabinete de Arte Raquel Arnaud, São Paulo. Traveled to Galeria de Arte Celma Albuquerque, Belo Horizonte

1997. *Arte Contemporânea*, Joel Edelstein Arte Contemporânea, Rio de Janeiro

1997. *Projetos Especiais*, Funarte, Rio de Janeiro

Selected Group Exhibitions

2001. *Recortes*, Galeria Brito Cimino, São Paulo

2001. *Trajetória da Luz*, Instituto Itaú Cultural, São Paulo

2000. *Obra Nova*, Museu de Arte Contemporânea, Universidade de São Paulo

2000. *Beyond Preconception*, National Gallery, Prague

2000. *An Experiment: The Sixties Legacy*, International Curators Incorporated, New York City

1999. *The Third Eye,* Art in General, New York City

1999. *Book as Art XI*, National Museum of Women in the Arts, Washington, D.C.

1998. *XXIV Bienal Internacional de São Paulo*

1997. *inSITE '97*, San Diego

1995. *II Biennial, Barro de América*, Caracas

1995. *Inside the Visible— Begin the Beguine in Flanders*, Kanaal Art Foundation, Kortrijk, Belgium. Traveled to Institute of Contemporary Art, Boston; National Museum of Women in the Arts, Washington, D.C.; Whitechapel Art Gallery, London; and Art Gallery of Western Australia, Perth.

HUMBERTO MAURO

Born in Volta Grande, Minas Gerais, 1897
Died 1983

Probably the most famous director of early Brazilian film, Humberto Mauro, who was self-taught in the cinema arts, directed 260 short and feature-length films. He was a twenty-six-year-old with an engineering background when he first became interested in cinema, more for its technical possibilities than its intellectual ones. His life and work were a combination of creativity and persistence, as he lived through the major innovations that changed the movie industry over a century.

Selected Films

1964. *A Velha a Fiar*

1960. *Brasília*

1957. *Belo Horizonte*

1957. *Congonhas do Campo*

1956. *Brasilianas no.6— Manhà Na Roça*

1956. *Meus Oito Anos*

1950. *Eclipse*

1949. *Baía da Guanabara*

1945. *Brasilianas no.1— Chuá-Chuá e Casinha*

1944. *O Escravo— Carlos Gomes*

1940. *Bandeirantes*

1939. *Cidades Históricas de São Paulo*

1938. *Moinho de Fubá*

1937. *O descobrimento do Brasil*

1936. *Os Inconfidentes*

1936. *Os Lusíadas*

BETH MOYSÉS

Born in São Paulo, 1960
Lives and works in São Paulo

Education

2000. M.F.A., Universidade Estadual de Campinas

1993. B.F.A., Fundação Armando Álvares Penteado, São Paulo

Selected Solo Exhibitions

2001. Galeria Thomas Cohn, São Paulo

2000. *Memory of Affection*, Performance, International Day of Nonviolence Against Women, Avenida Paulista, São Paulo

1998. *Absence of Soul*, Intervention at Sé Cathedral, Galeria Thomas Cohn, São Paulo

1997. Thomas Cohn Contemporary Art, Rio de Janeiro

1996. *Ceiling of Pale Dreams*, Capela do Morumbi, São Paulo

Selected Group Exhibitions

2001. *White Mosaic by Sixty Women*, Performance, Centro Cultural Banco do Brasil, São Paulo

1999. *About Roses, Absence and Flames,* Cadiz

1999. *Extra Small, Extra Large*, Galeria Marina Potrich, Goiânia

1999. *Receptáculos*, Museu de Arte Contemporânea, Universidade de São Paulo

1998. *Preview 98*, Galeria Thomas Cohn, São Paulo

1998. *Sixty Women*, Fundação Memoria da América Latina, São Paulo

1998. *IV Contemporary Art Show*, Museu de Arte Moderno de Bahia, Salvador

1996. *IV Contemporary Art Show,* Vitor Meireles, Florianópolis

1995. *V Bienal Nacional de Santos—Artes Visuais,* Centro de Cultura Patrícia Galvão, Santos

1995. *4 at 144*, Galeria 144, São Paulo

MÔNICA NADOR

Born in Ribeirão Preto, 1955
Lives and works in São Paulo

Education

2000. M.F.A., Escola de Comunicações e Artes, Universidade de São Paulo

1983. B.F.A., Fundação Armando Álvares Penteado, São Paulo

Selected Solo Exhibitions

1996. *Parede para Nelson Leirner*, Museu de Arte Moderna, São Paulo

1995. Centro Cultural São Paulo

1995. Casa Thomas Jefferson, Brasília

1995. Fundação Cultural de Curitiba

Selected Group Exhibitions

2000. *Cutting Edge*, ARCO '00, Madrid

2000. *inSITE 2000*, San Diego and Tijuana

2000. *VII Bienal de La Havana*, Havana

2000. *Diálogo Arte Contemporânea Brasil/Equador*, Fundação Memoria da América Latina, São Paulo. Traveled to Centro Cultural de La Universidade Católica, Quito

2000. *Panorama das Artes*, Museu de Arte Moderna, Niterói. Traveled to Recife

2000. *III*, Galeria Brito Cimino, São Paulo

1999. *Panorama das Artes '99*, Museu de Arte Moderna, São Paulo

1999. *Ausência*, Museu de Arte Moderna, São Paulo

1998. *O Moderno e o Contemporâneo na Arte Brasileira: Coleção Gilberto Chateaubriand*, Museu de Arte de São Paulo

1998. Galeria Brito Cimino, São Paulo

1998. *Caminhos e Parceria*, SESC, Vila Mariana, São Paulo

1997. Galeria Brito Cimino, São Paulo

1997. *15 Artistas Brasileiros*, Museu de Arte Moderna, Rio de Janeiro. Traveled to Museu de Arte Moderna, Salvador

1997. *Ao Cubo*, Paço das Artes, São Paulo

1996. *Pequenas Mãos*, Paço Imperial, Rio de Janeiro. Traveled to Centro Cultural Alumni, São Paulo

1996. *15 Artistas Brasileiros*, Museu de Arte Moderna, São Paulo

1995. *United Artists*, Casa das Rosas, São Paulo

1995. *Das Vanguardas Européias e Modernismo Brasileiro à Visualidade Contemporânea*, Museu de Arte Contemporânea, Universidade de São Paulo

1995. *Anos 80: O Palco da Diversidade*, Museu de Arte Moderna, Rio de Janeiro. Traveled to Galeria de Arte, SESI, São Paulo

1995. *XI Mostra da Gravura Cidade de Curitiba*, Fundação Cultural de Curitiba

1995. *Galeria Luisa Strina: 20 Anos*, Museu de Arte, São Paulo

NAZARETH PACHECO
Born in São Paulo, 1961
Lives and works in São Paulo

Education
1999. M.F.A., Escola de Comunicações e Artes, Universidade de São Paulo

Solo Exhibitions
2000. Museu Universitário de Uberlândia

2000. Galeria Canvas, Porto

1999. Maison du Brèsil, Brussels

1999. Instituto de Cultura Brasileira, Berlin

1997. Galeria de Arte Valú Óri , São Paulo

Selected Group Exhibitions
2001. *Recortes*, Galeria Brito Cimino, São Paulo

2001. *Trajetória da Luz na Arte Brasileira*, Instituto Itaú Cultural, São Paulo

2001. *Espírito da Nossa Época*, Museu de Arte Moderna, São Paulo

2000. *XII Mostra da Gravura de Curitiba*, Anitiba

2000. *III,* Galeria Brito Cimino, São Paulo

2000. *Messagers de la Terre,* Rur'Art CRIPT Poitou-Charentes, Rouillé

2000. *Cutting Edge*, ARCO '00, Madrid

2000. *Ars Erótica-Sexo e Erotismo na Arte Brasileira*, Museu de Arte Moderna, São Paulo

2000. *Mujeres de las dos orillas São Paulo–Valencia*, Centro Valencià de Cultura Mediterrània, Valencia

1999. *Panorama de Arte Brasileira '99*, Museu de Arte Moderna, São Paolo

1999. *Acima do Bem e do Mal*, Paço das Artes, São Paulo

1999. *Sweet and Sour, Art & Public,* Geneva

1999. *A Vueltas con los Sentidos*, Casa da América, Madrid

1998. *XXIV Bienal Internacional de São Paulo*

1998. *Cutting Edge,* ARCO '98, Madrid

1998. *Feminino/Plural,* Museu Nacional de Belas Artes, Buenos Aires

1998. *Panorama de Arte Brasileira*, Museu de Arte Contemporânea, Niterói

1998. *Medidas de Si*, Museu de Arte Moderna, São Paulo

1998. *Arte de Expor Arte*, Museu de Arte Moderna, São Paulo

1998. *III Bienal Barro de América,* Maracaibo, Venezuela. Traveled to Museu Brasileiro da Escultura, São Paulo

1998. *Arte Brasileira no Acervo do Museu de Arte Moderna de São Paulo,* Centro Cultural Banco do Brasil, Rio de Janeiro

1997. *Cutting Edge*, ARCO '97, Madrid

1997. *Novas Aquisições*, Museu de Arte Moderna, Rio de Janeiro

1997. *Intervalos*, Paço das Artes, São Paulo

1996. *O Único, O Mesmo, O Afundamento*, Galeria de Arte Valú Ória, São Paulo

1996. *Nazareth Pacheco/Rosana Mariotto*, CEMIG, Belo Horizonte

LYGIA PAPE
Born in Friburgo, Rio de Janeiro
Lives and works in Jardim Botânico, Rio de Janeiro

Education
1980. M.A., philosophic aesthetics, Universidade Federal do Rio de Janeiro

Selected Solo Exhibitions
2001. Galeria Camargo Vilaça, São Paulo

2001. The Americas Society, New York City

2000. *3 Historias do Brasil: Artur Barrio, Antonio Manuel, Lygia Pape*, Museu Serralves, Porto

1999. *Vai e Vem: Sedução II*, Paço Imperial, Rio de Janeiro

1999. *Esculturas Volantes*, Galeria Canvas, Porto

1998. Museo Carrillo Gil, Mexico City

1997. Galeria Camargo Vilaça, São Paulo

1997. *Lygia Pape: Instalações*, Casa Joaquim Nabuco, Recife

1996. *Tteias*, Centro de Artes Fundaçao Calouste Gulbenkian, Lisbon

1996. *Lygia Pape*, Centro Cultural São Paulo

1995. *Esculturas*, Galeria Camargo Vilaça, São Paulo

Selected Group Exhibitions
2000. *Território Expandido*, SESC Pompéia, São Paulo

2000. *Um Oceano Inteiro para Nadar*, Culturgest, Lisbon

1999. *Cotidiano/Arte: A Técnica*, Instituto Itaú Cultural, São Paulo

1999. *Circa 68 (Caixa de Baratas e Eat Me)*, Museu de Serralves, Porto

1998. *Teoria dos Valores, (Livro do Tempo)*, Casa França-Brasil, Rio de Janeiro

1998. *"Out of Actions–Between Performance and the Object, 1949–1979,"* Museum of Contemporary Art, Los Angeles. Traveled to Vienna, Barcelona, Tokyo

1998. *XXIV Bienal Internacional de São Paulo*

1998. *Caixa Brasil, Fronteiras*, Instituto Itaú Cultural, São Paulo

1998. *Trinta anos de 68*, Centro Cultural Banco do Brasil, Rio de Janeiro

1998. *Camargo Vilaça BIS*, Galeria Camargo Vilaça, São Paulo

1997. *Tropicália*, Museu de Arte Moderna, Bahia

1997. *Palavreiro*, Galeria Sergio Milliet, Rio de Janeiro

1996. *Walking on the Soho Side*, Soho Art Festival, New York City

1996. *Impressões Itinerantes*, Palácio das Artes, Ouro Preto

1996. *Transparencias*, Museu de Arte Moderna, Rio de Janeiro

1996. *DESEXP(L)OS(IGN)IÇÃO*, Casa das Rosas, São Paulo

1995. *Livro-Objeto, A Fronteira dos Vazios*, Museu de Arte Moderna, São Paulo
1995. *Entre o desenho e a escultura*, Museu de Arte Moderna, São Paulo
1995. *Pape–Apollinaire*, Universidade Federal do Espirito Santo
1995. *Luar do Sertão: V Bienal Nacional de Santos*

ROSANA PAULINO
Born in São Paulo, 1967
Lives and works in São Paulo

Education
1998. London Print Workshop
1995. B.F.A., Universidade de São Paulo
1994. Studied printmaking, Museu Lasar Segall, São Paulo

Solo Exhibitions
2000. *Drawings: Program of Donations*, Centro Cultural São Paulo
1997. *Rosana Paulino: An Album of Drawings*, Galeria de Arte Contemporânea Adriana Penteado, São Paulo
1995. *A New Face in Hell*, Galeria de Arte Contemporânea Adriana Penteado, São Paulo

Selected Group Exhibitions
2001. *Fotografia não fotografia*, Museu de Arte Moderna, São Paulo
2000. *Mostra do Redescobrimento Brasil+500 Anos,* Fundaçao Bienal de São Paulo

2000. *Fotografia não fotografia*, Museo de las Artes, Universidad de Guadalajara, Mexico
2000. *Século XX: Arte do Brasil*, Centro de Arte Moderna José de Azeredo Perdigão, Fundação Calouste Gulbenkian, Lisbon
1999. *Bienal Internacional de Fotografia '99*, Centro de la Imagen, Mexico City
1999. *Brasileiro que nem eu, que nem quem?* Fundação Armando Alvares Penteado, São Paulo
1999. *Fotógrafos e fotoartistas na coleção,* Museu de Arte Moderna, São Paulo
1998. *Brasileiro que nem eu, que nem quem?* Palácio do Itamarati, Brasília
1998. *Heranças Contemporâneas II*, Museu de Arte Contemporânea, Universidade de São Paulo
1997. *Panorama das Artes Brasileira '97*, Museu de Arte Moderna, São Paolo
1997. *Salão Iemanja: Rosana Paulino, Pierre Verger e Paul Coultrier*, Universidade del Valle, Cali
1997. *Intervalos*, Paço das Artes, São Paulo
1997. *A Rota da Arte Sobre a Rota dos Escravos*, São Paulo
1997. *Imaginário Religioso*, Museu Rio Pardense, São José do Rio Pardo
1996. *Avesso do Avesso*, Paço das Artes, São Paulo
1996. *Salão de Artes de Jacareí '96*, Fundação Cultural de Jacareí, São Paolo
1995. *Gravura Paulista*, Galeria São Paulo

1995. *XI Mostra de Gravura da Cidade de Curitiba*
1995. *Novíssimos, A Produção dos 90*, Galeria Fotóptica São Paolo. Traveled to Funarte, Rio de Janeiro

ROSÂNGELA RENNÓ
Born in Belo Horizonte, 1962
Lives and works in Rio de Janeiro

Education
1997. Ph.D., art, Escola de Comunicações e Artes, Universidade de São Paulo
1987. Escola Guignard, Belo Horizonte
1986. Escola de Arquitetura, Universidade Federal de Minas Gerais, Belo Horizonte

Selected Solo Exhibitions
2001. *Ovacion y Silencio*, Galeria Juana Aizpuru, Madrid
2001. *Denkzeichen Project*, Alexander Platz, Berlin. Traveled to Museu do Chiado, Lisbon
2000. Galeria Módulo, Lisbon
1999. Australian Centre for Photography, Sydney
1997. *Vulgo*, Lombard Freid Gallery, New York City
1997. Galeria Luis Adelantado, Valencia
1996. *Cicatriz*, Museum of Contemporary Art, Los Angeles
1995. *HIpocampo*, Galeria Camargo Vilaça, São Paulo
1995. *In Oblivionem,* De Appel Foundation, Amsterdam

Selected Group Exhibitions
2001–2. *Politicas de la diferencia: Arte Iberoamericano fin de siglo*, Pinacoteca

do Estado de São Paulo. Traveled to Museo de Arte Contemporáneo de Caracas Sofia Imber, Museo de Arte Contemporâneo de México, Museo de Arte de Puerto Rico, Chicago Cultural Center
2001. *Bienal 50 Anos: Uma Homenagem a Ciccillo Matarazzo,* São Paulo
2001. *Brasil+500*, Museum of Modern Art, Oxford
2001. *II Berlin Biennale*
2000. *Brasil. Plural y Singular*, Museo de Arte Moderno, Buenos Aires
2000. *Der Anagrammatische der Körper und Seine Mediale Konstruktion,* Zentrum für Kunst und Medientechnologie, Karlsruhe
2000. *Mostra do Redescobrimento Brasil+500 Anos,* Fundaçao Bienal de São Paulo
2000. *Cá entre Nós*, Paço das Artes, São Paulo
2000. *Projeto Gazeta do Povo*, XII Mostra da Gravura, Curitiba
2000. *Mês Internacional da Fotografia de Curitiba*
2000. *Versiones del Sur*, Museo Nacional Centro de Arte Reina Sofia, Madrid
1999. *80 Anos de Arte no Brasil*, Museu de Arte Moderna, São Paulo
1999. *A Vueltas con los Sentidos*, Pabellón de Caballerizas, Casa de América, Madrid
1999. *II Semana Fernando Furlanetto de Fotografia*, Teatro Municipal de São João da Boa Vista
1999. *Contemporánea: Adquisiciones 1994–1998*, Museo Alejandro Otero, Caracas

1999. *The Anagrammatical Body*, Neue Galerie and Kunsthaus Mürzzuschlag, Graz
1998. *A Imagem do Som de Caetano Veloso*, Paço Imperial, Rio de Janeiro
1998. *Panorama de Arte Brasileira, Edição 97*, Museu de Arte Contemporânea, Niterói
1998. *Imagens Seqüestradas*, Museu de Arte Moderna, Rio de Janeiro
1998. *Transatlántico*, Centro Atlántico de Arte Moderno, Las Palmas, Canary Islands
1998. *The Garden of the Forking Paths*, Kunstforeningen, Copenhagen
1998. *Archiv X*, Offenes Kulturhaus, Linz
1997. *Hacer Memoria*, Museo Alejandro Otero, Caracas
1997. *Die Anderen Modernen*, Haus der Kulturen der Welt, Berlin
1997. *VI Bienal de La Havana*, Havana
1997. *Así Está la Cosa: arte objeto e instalaciones de Latinoamérica*, Cultural Center Art Contemporaneo, Mexico City
1996. *Novas Travessias: Recent Photographic Art from Brazil*, The Photographers' Gallery, London
1996. *Prospect 96*, Frankfurt Kunstverein, Frankfurt
1996. *96 Containers: Art Across the Oceans*, Langelinie, Copenhagen
1996. *Pushing Image Paradigms: Conceptual Manoeuvers in Recent Photography*, Portland Institute for Contemporary Art, Portland, Oregon
1996. Galeria Camargo Vilaça, São Paulo

1996. Christopher Grimes Gallery, Santa Monica

1996. *Mercosul Cultural,* Centro Cultural São Paulo

1996. *Sin Fronteras/Arte Latinoamericano Actual,* Museo Alejandro Otero, Caracas

1996. *Transparências,* Museu de Arte Moderna, Rio de Janeiro,

1996. *Ouro de Artista,* Galeria Casa Triângulo, São Paulo

1996. *Public Works,* Van Abbe Museum, Eindhoven

1995. *Espelhos e Sombras,* Centro Cultural Banco do Brasil, Rio de Janeiro

1995. *Fotografia Brasileira Contemporânea,* Centro Cultural Banco do Brasil, Rio de Janeiro

1995. *Revendo Brasília: Brasília neu Gesehen,* Haus der Kulturen der Welt, Berlin

1995. *Obsessions: From Wunderkammer to Cyberspace,* Foto Biennale, Enschede

MIGUEL RIO BRANCO
Born in Las Palmas, Canary Islands, 1946
Lives and works in Rio de Janeiro

Solo Exhibitions

1999. *Fundación "la Caixa,"* Centre Cultural, Barcelona

1999. Rena Bransten Gallery, San Francisco

1999. Galeria Módulo, Lisbon

1999. D'Amelio Terras Gallery, New York City

1998. Galerie Ghislaine Hussenot, Paris

1998. Galeria Camargo Vilaça, São Paulo

1998. Galería Oliva Arauna, Madrid

1998. London Projects, London

1997. *Nakta,* D'Amelio Terras Gallery, New York City

1996. *Mois de la Phot,* Galerie Agathe Gaillard, Paris

1996. *Santa Rosa,* Throckmorton Fine Art Gallery, New York City

1996. *Nakta*: I Bienal Internacional de Fotografia de Curitiba, Casa Vermelha, Paraná

1996. Joel Edelstein Arte Contemporânea, Rio de Janeiro

1996. Museu de Arte Moderna, Rio de Janeiro. Traveled to Museu de Arte Moderna, Salvador

1995. Galeria Luisa Strina, São Paulo

1995. *Out of Nowhere,* IFA Gallery, Stuttgart

Group Exhibitions

1999. *Carnaval,* Museo Extremeño Iberoamericanode Arte Contemporáneo, Badajoz

1999. Zeno X Gallery, Amberes

1999. *Biennal of Contemporary Art,* Tate Gallery, Liverpool

1998. *Mysterious Voyages,* Contemporary Museum, Baltimore

1998. *Exterminating Angel,* Galerie Ghislaine Hussenot, Paris

1998. *The Garden of the Forking Paths,* Kunstforen-ningen, Copenhagen

1998. *Roteiros, roteiros, roteiros, roteiros, roteiros, roteiros, roteiros, roteiros,* XXIV Bienal Internacional de São Paulo

1998. *Cor,* Centro Cultural Light, Rio de Janeiro

1998. *Amnesia,* Christopher Grimes–Track 16 Gallery, Santa Monica

1997. *Between the Eyes, the Desert,* inSITE '97, San Diego

1997. *Truce: Echoes of Art in an Age of Endless Conclusions,* SITE Santa Fe

1996. *Door into Darkness,* Prospect 96, Kunstverein, Frankfurt

1996. Galeria Camargo Vilaça, São Paulo

1996. *Excesso,* Paço das Artes, São Paulo

1996. *Out of Nowhere,* Foto Forum, Frankfurt

1995. *Panorama da arte brasileira,* Museu de Arte Moderna, São Paulo

REGINA SILVEIRA
Born in Porto Alegre, 1939
Lives and works in São Paulo

Education

1984. Ph.D., Escola de Comunicações e Artes, Universidade de São Paulo

1980. M.F.A., Escola de Comunicações e Artes, Universidade de São Paulo

1959. B.F.A., Instituto de Artes, Universidade Federal do Rio Grande do Sul, Porto Alegre

Selected Solo Exhibitions

2001. *Regina Silveira: Obras do Acervo,* Museu de Arte Moderna, São Paulo

2000. *Velox,* Galeria da Universidade de Brasília

2000. *Perpetual Transformation,* Art Museum of the Americas (OAS), Washington, D.C.

2000. *Equinócio,* Pavilhão das Cavalariças, Parque Lage, Rio de Janeiro

1999. *Desapariencias,* Galeria Gabriela Mistral, Santiago

1998. *Regina Silveira: Velox,* Galeria Brito Cimino, São Paulo

1998. *Velox,* Blue Star Art Center, San Antonio. Traveled to Museo de Arte Moderno, Buenos Aires

1997. *intro (re:fresh widow, r.s.),* Galeria Casa Triângulo, São Paulo

1997. *To Be Continued . . . ,* Northern Illinois University Art Museum, Chicago

1996. *Grafias,* Museu de Arte de São Paulo Assis Chateaubriand

1996. *Gone Wild* (in series *Inside/Out*), Museum of Contemporary Art, San Diego

1996. *Velox: Il Gabbiano,* La Spezia, Italy

1995. *Mapping the Shadows,* LedisFlam Gallery, New York City

1995. *Regina Silveira: Desenhos,* AS Studio, São Paulo

1995. Museu de Arte do Rio Grande do Sul, Porto Alegre

Selected Group Exhibitions

2001. *Rembrandt to Rauschenberg,* Jack Blanton Museum of Art, University of Texas, Austin

2001. *Esercizi di Stile,* Palazzina delle Arti, La Spezia, Italy

2000. *Obra Nova,* Museu de Arte Contemporânea, Universidade de São Paulo

2000. *1º Bienal Argentina de Grafica Latino Americana,* Museu Nacional del Grabado, Buenos Aires

2000. *Situações: Arte Brasileira–Anos 70,* Fundação Casa França Brasil, Rio de Janeiro

1999. *Passion for Wings,* National Aviation Museum, Ottawa

1999. *Homenaje Al Lápiz Como Instrumento de Libertad,* Museu José Luis Cuevas, Mexico City

1999. *II Bienal Mercosul,* Porto Alegre

1999. *Mastering the Millennium: Art of the Americas,* World Bank and Art Museum of the Americas (OAS), Washington, D.C.

1999. *Arte de Las Americas, El Ojo del Milenio,* Centro Cultural Ricoleta, Buenos Aires

1999. *100 Drawings,* P.S.1 Contemporary Art Center, Long Island, New York

1998. *XXIV Bienal Internacional de São Paulo*

1998. *Doações Recentes,* Museu de Arte Moderna, São Paulo

1998. *Figurações: 30 Anos de Arte Brasileira,* Museu de Arte Contemporânea, Universidade de São Paulo

1998. *Stelle Cadenti,* Bassano in Teverina, Italy

1998. *Horizonte Reflexivo,* Centro Cultural Light, Rio de Janeiro

1997. *Diversidade da Escultura Brasileira Contemporânea,* Instituto Itaú Cultural, São Paulo

1997. *Re-Aligning Vision: Alternative Currents in South American Drawing,* El Museo del Barrio, New York City. Traveled to Arkansas Art Center, Little Rock; Archer M. Huntington Art Gallery, Austin;

Museo de Bellas Artes, Caracas; Museo de Arte Contemporâneo, Monterrey, Mexico; and Miami Art Museum
1997. Museo de Bellas Artes, Caracas
1997. Museo de Arte Contemporáneo, Monterrey, Mexico
1996. *Arte Brasileira Contemporânea: Doações Recentes*, Museu de Arte Moderna de São Paulo
1995. *Prints*, Brooke Alexander Gallery, New York City
1995. *Livro-Objeto: A Fronteira dos Vazios*, Museu de Arte Moderna, São Paulo
1995. *Children's Corner*, Galeria Il Gabbiano, La Spezia, Italy
1995. *O Desenho em São Paulo: 1956–1995*, Galeria Nara Roesler, São Paulo

VALESKA SOARES
Born in São Paulo, 1957
Lives and works in
New York City

Education
Ph.D., arts, New York University
M.A., Pratt Institute, New York City
B. Arch., Universidade Católica, Rio de Janeiro
Postgraduate Specialization Diploma in history of art and architecture, Pontificia Santa Ursula, Rio de Janeiro

Selected Solo Exhibitions
2001. Galeria Camargo Vilaça, São Paulo
2000. LiebmanMagnan Gallery, New York City
2000. Art Gallery of Hamilton, Ontario
1999. *Pan American Series*, Museum of Contemporary Art, San Diego
1999. *Projeto Finep*, Paço Imperial, Rio de Janeiro
1999. Galerie Claudine Papillon, Paris
1998. *Vanishing Point*, Galeria Camargo Vilaça, São Paulo. Traveled to Christopher Grimes Gallery, Santa Monica
1998. *Vanity*, Portland Institute of Contemporary Art, Portland, Oregon
1998. *Histories*, Public Art Fund, New York City
1997. *Personagens*, Galeria Luis Adelantado, Valencia
1996. *Strangelove*, Galeria Camargo Vilaça, São Paulo
1996. Laumeier Sculpture Park Museum, St. Louis, Missouri
1996. Christopher Grimes Gallery, Santa Monica
1995. *Discontinuous Teasers*, Window Project, New Museum of Contemporary Art, New York City

Selected Group Exhibitions
2001. *Elusive Paradise: The Millennium Prize*, National Gallery of Canada, Ottawa
2000–2001. *UltraBaroque*, Museum of Contemporary Art, San Diego; Modern Art Museum of Fort Worth; San Francisco Museum of Modern Art; Art Gallery of Ontario, Toronto; Miami Art Museum; Walker Art Center, Minneapolis
2000–2001. *Arcadia*, National Gallery of Canada, Ottawa
2000. *Fricciones*, Museo Nacional Centro de Arte Reina Sofia, Madrid
2000. *Good Art Is Good Business*, Bronx Museum, New York
2000. *Greater New York*, P.S.1 Museum, Museum of Modern Art, New York City
2000. *inSITE 2000*, San Diego and Tijuana
2000. *Shoes*, TZ Art Gallery, New York City
1999. *Dobles Vides*, Barcelona Maritime Museum
1999. *A Vuelta con los Sentidos*, Casa de America, Madrid
1999. *Um e Outro*, Centro Cultural Banco do Brasil, Rio de Janeiro
1999. *La Metamorfose de las Manos*, Centro Cultural Mar del Plata
1999. *Not There*, Rena Bransten Gallery, San Francisco
1999. *Der brasilianische Blick: Sammlung Gilberto Chateaubriand*, Haus der Kulturen der Welt, Berlin. Traveled to Ludwig Forum für Internationale Kunst, Aachen; Kunstmuseum Heidenheim
1998–99. *Amnesia*, Contemporary Arts Center, Cincinnati. Traveled to Biblioteca Luis Arango, Bogota; Christopher Grimes–Track 16 Gallery, Santa Monica; and Contemporary Art Museum, Tampa
1998. *Desde el Cuerpo: alegorias de lo Feminino*, Museo de Bellas Artes de Caracas, Caracas
1998. *Amnesia, Fronteiras*, Instituto Itaú Cultural, São Paulo
1998. *XXIV Bienal Internacional de São Paulo*
1998. *Anos 90: Coleção Gilberto Chateaubriand*, Museu de Arte Moderna, Rio de Janeiro. Traveled to Haus der Kulturen der Welt, Berlin
1997. *You Are Here*, Royal College of Art, London
1997. *Esto es: Arte Objecto y Instalación de Iberoamerica*, Centro de Arte Contemporaneo, Mexico City
1997. *Life's Little Necessities: 2nd Johannesburg Biennale*
1997. *Art Foundry Editions: Santa Fe at Knoedler*, Knoedler and Company, New York City
1996. *6 Women in Red*, Galeria Luis Serpa, Lisbon
1996. *Collective Soul*, Galeria Marabini, Bologna
1996. *To Live Is to Leave Traces*, Hospicio de Las Cabanas, Guadalajara
1996. *The Tailor's Dummy*, Christopher Grimes Gallery, Santa Monica
1996. *Visions*, Rhona Hoffman Gallery, Chicago
1996. *Camargo Vilaça Bis*, Galeria Camargo Vilaça, São Paulo
1996. *Pequenas Mãos*, Paço Imperial, Rio de Janeiro. Traveled to Centro Cultural Alumni, São Paulo
1996. *Transparências*, Museu de Arte Moderna; Paço Imperial, Rio de Janeiro
1995. *Dark Room*, Stark Gallery, New York City
1995. *La Habana–São Paulo: Junge Kunst aus Lateinamerika*, Haus der Kulturen der Welt, Berlin
1995. *The Education of the Five Senses*, White Columns, New York City. Traveled to Palazzo Pamphili, Rome
1995. *Longing and Belonging*, Site Santa Fe, New Mexico
1995. *Espelhos e Sombras*, Centro Cultural Banco do Brasil, Rio de Janeiro
1995. *Brasil na Bienal*, Galeria da Universidade Federal Fluminense, Niteroi

HELENA SOLBERG
Born in Brazil
Lives and works in the United States

Helena Solberg is an award-winning filmmaker who has directed and produced many short dramatic and documentary films. Most of her films, which examine social, political, and women's issues, concentrate on Latin America and its relationship with the United States.

Selected Films and Awards
1995. *Carmen Miranda: Bananas Is My Business*, with David Meyer
1990. *The Forbidden Land*: Bronze Apple, National Education Film Festival
1987. *Made in Brazil*
1986. *Home of the Brave*: blue ribbon, American Film Festival; honorable mention, Global Village Film Festival
1986. *Portrait of a Terrorist*
1983. *Chile: By Reason or by Force*
1982. *The Brazilian Connection*
1981. *From the Ashes . . . Nicaragua Today*: Emmy; Silver Hugo, Chicago Film Festival; best documentary, Global Village Film Festival; red ribbon, American Film Festival
1977. *Simplemente Jenny*: blue ribbon, American Film Festival

1975. *The Double Day*, released at the Mexico International Women's Year Conference: jury recommendation, Manheim Film Festival

1974. *The Emerging Woman*, the official film of the American Bicentennial Commission: blue ribbon, American Film Festival

JANAÍNA TSCHÄPE
Born in Dachau, Germany, 1973
Lives and works in New York City

Education
1998. M.F.A., School of Visual Arts, New York City
1994. Artists-in-Residence Program, Museu de Arte Moderna, Salvador Bahia
1992–98. Fine arts studies, Hochschule für Bildende Kunst, Hamburg

Selected Solo Exhibitions
2002. Museum of Fine Arts, Dominican Republic
2001. Galeria Camargo Vilaça, Sao Paulo
2001. Museo Nacional Centro de Arte Reina Sofia, Madrid
2000. *1,2,3 Catherine Bastide*, Brussels
1998–99. *Entering the Space That Produces Liquid*, Jensen Gallerie, Hamburg. Traveled to Clinica Aesthetica, New York City
1996. Galeria Sergio Porto, Rio de Janeiro

Selected Group Exhibitions
2001. *My Generation*, 24-Hour Video Art, Atlantis Gallery, London

2001. *Geração em Trânsito*, Centro Cultural Banco do Brasil, Rio de Janeiro
2000. *Personal Permanent Records*, Blue Starr, Houston. Traveled to Museum of the Americas (OAS), Washington, D.C.
1999. *Sei Artisti per Goethe, Eine Italienische Reise*, ACC, Weimar
1998. *Der brasilianische Blick: Sammlung Gilberto Chateaubriand*, Haus der Kulturen der Welt, Berlin. Traveled to Ludwig Forum für Internationale Kunst, Aachen; Kunstmuseum Heidenheim
1997. *Dimensão da Arte Contemporânea Brasileira*, Museu de Arte Contemporânea, Universidade de São Paulo
1996. *Hamburger Börse, Studenten der HFBK*, Hamburg
1996. *Dialogo*, Museu de Arte Moderna, Rio de Janeiro
1996. *Viva Brazil*, Museo de Arte Contemporaneo, Santiago
1995. *Corpo sobre Corpo*, Museu de Arte Moderna, Rio de Janeiro
1995. *Objetos e Instalações*, Museu de Arte Moderna, Salvador

ADRIANA VAREJÃO
Born in Rio de Janeiro, 1964
Lives and works in Rio de Janeiro

Selected Solo Exhibitions
2001. Victoria Miro Gallery, London
2001. Galeria Pedro Oliveira, Porto

2001. Centro Cultural Banco do Brasil, Rio de Janiero
2001. Centro Cultural Banco do Brasil, Brasília
2000. Lehmann Maupin Gallery, New York City
2000. Galeria Camargo Vilaça, São Paulo
2000. Bildmuseet, Umea
1999. *Alegria*, Galeria Camargo Vilaça, São Paulo
1998. Galeria Soledad Lorenzo, Madrid
1998. Pavilhão Branco, Instituto de Arte Contemporânea, Lisbon
1997. Galerie Ghislaine Hussenot, Paris
1997. Museo de Arte Contemporaneo Sofia Imber, Caracas
1996. Galeria Camargo Vilaça, São Paulo
1996. Galerie Barbara Farber, Amsterdam
1995. Annina Nosei Gallery, New York City

Selected Group Exhibitions
2001. *Idéia Coletiva,* Galeria Camargo Vilaça, São Paulo
2000. *Biennale,* Sydney
2000. *Raw,* Victoria Miro Gallery, London
2000. *Novas Aquisições da Coleção Gilberto Chateaubriand*, Museu de Arte Moderna, Rio de Janeiro
2000. *Brasil 2000,* Culturgest, Lisbon
2000. *UltraBaroque,* Museum of Contemporary Art, San Diego; Modern Art Museum of Fort Worth; San Francisco Museum of Modern Art; Art Gallery of Ontario, Toronto; Miami Art Museum; Walker Art Center, Minneapolis

2000. *Mostra do Redescobrimeto Brasil+500 Anos,* Fundação Bienal de São Paulo
1999. *First Liverpool Biennial of Contemporary Art,* Tate Gallery, Liverpool
1999. *Cinco Continentes e uma Cidade*, Museo de la Ciudad de México, Mexico City
1999. *Inconfidência Mineira: Imagens da Liberdade*, Secretaria de Estado da Cultura, Belo Horizonte
1998. *Desde el Cuerpo: alegorias de lo feminino*, Museu de Bellas Artes, Caracas
1998. *XXIV Bienal Internacional de São Paulo*
1998. *Situacionismo un Grupo de Fotografias*, Galeria OMR, Mexico City
1998. *Der brasilianische Blick: Sammlung Gilberto Chateaubriand*, Haus der Kulturen der Welt, Berlin. Traveled to Ludwig Forum für Internationale Kunst, Aachen; Kunstmuseum Heidenheim
1997. *A Arte Contemporânea da Gravura Brasil: Reflexão 97*, Museu Metropolitano de Arte, Curitiba
1997. *Asi Esta La Cosa: arte objeto y instalaciones de America Latina,* Centro Cultural de Arte Contemporaneo, Mexico City
1997. Whitechapel Art Gallery, London
1996. *New Histories,* Institute of Contemporary Art, Boston
1996. *Excesso*, Paço das Artes, São Paulo
1996. *96 Containers: Art Across the Oceans*, Copenhagen

1996. Galerie Ghislaine Hussenot, Paris
1996. *Avant-premiére d'un Musée: Le Musée d'Art Contemporain de Gand*, Institut Néerlandais, Paris
1995. *1st Johannesburg Biennale*
1995. *La Habana–São Paulo: Junge Kunst aus Lateinamerika*, Haus der Kulturen der Welt, Berlin
1995. *TransCulture, XXXXVI Biennale di Venezia,* Palazzo Giustiniani Lolin, Venice. Traveled to Benesse Haouse Naoshima Contemporary Art Museum, Okayama City
1995. *Mostra da Gravura*, Museu Municipal de Arte, Curitiba
1995. Fundação Romulo Maiorana, Belém
1995. Museo Carrillo Gil, Mexico City

Notes

INTRODUCTION
By Franklin Espath Pedroso
Pages 18–19

1. Emily Dickinson. *Uma centena de poemas* (São Paulo: T. A. Queiroz, 1985). Translated by Aíla de Oliveira Gomes.

VIRGIN TERRITORY
By Susan Fisher Sterling
Pages 20–33

1. Edward J. Goodman, *The Explorers of South America,* revised ed. (Norman: University of Oklahoma Press, 1992), 14. Goodman's description is borrowed from Jaime Cortesão, *A carta de Pero Vaz de Caminha* (Rio de Janeiro: Edições Livros de Portugal, 1943).
2. Ibid., 14. This narrative is a condensed version of Goodman's narrative.
3. Paulo Roberto Pereira, "Caminha's Letter and the Brazil Utopia," *Letter from Pero Vaz de Caminha/Carta de Pero Vaz de Caminha, Mostra do Redescobrimento* (São Paulo: Associação Brasil+500 Anos Arte Visuais, 2000), 37.
4. Goodman, 14–18. Goodman discusses other possible discoverers of Brazil, including Amerigo Vespucci.
5. Pereira, 37; Daniel Boorstin, *The Discoverers* (New York: Vintage, 1985), 241–44.
6. See Boorstin, 241–43, on the debate over whether a fourth continent was possible. Until the time of Columbus's voyage, Ptolemaic-Christian doctrine specified three continents—Europe, Asia, and Africa—which were connected to one another and surrounded by very little water. Another commonly held belief was that there were no large land masses below the equator.
7. Peter Winn, *Americas: The Changing Face of Latin America and the Caribbean* (Berkeley: University of California Press, 1999), 69.
8. Ibid.
9. Catherine de Zegher, "Introduction: Inside the Visible," *Inside the Visible* [exhibition catalogue] (Boston: Institute of Contemporary Art, Kanaal Art Foundation, and MIT Press), 22.
10. Ibid.
11. Thomas McEvilley, "Enormous Change at the Last Minute," *Artforum* (December 1991): 86.
12. Winn, 296.
13. Dan Cameron, "Between the Lines," *Rosângela Rennó* (São Paulo: Galeria Camargo Vilaça, 1995), n.p.
14. David William Foster, *Gender and Society in Contemporary Brazilian Cinema* (Austin: University of Texas Press, 1999), 61.
15. Luiza Interlenghi, "Cartography and Dislodgment: Image and Word," in *Anna Bella Geiger: Constelações* (Rio de Janeiro: Museu de Arte Moderno), 83.
16. Guy Brett, "The Logic of the Web," *Lygia Pape: Gávea de Tocaia* (São Paulo: Cosac and Naify Edições, 2000), 307.
17. Rosana Paulino, "Corpus Aridus," *Rosana Paulino: Album de desenho* (São Paulo: Galeria Adriana Penteado), 16.
18. Winn, 316. This comment was made in 1989 by Benedita da Silva, the first black woman elected to Brazil's congress and one of Brazil's five federal deputies.
19. Anna Maria Maiolino, unpublished installation notes for *Arroz & Feijão* (Rice and Beans), 3.
20. Winn, 295.
21. Agnaldo Farias, "The End of Art According to Nelson Leirner," in *Nelson Leirner: A Retrospective* (São Paulo: Paço das Artes, 1994), 164.
22. Ligia Canongia, "About the Question of the Theme," in *Miguel Rio Branco* (Rio de Janeiro: Museu de Arte Moderno, 1996), n.p.

THE HISTORY OF THE PRESENT
By Berta Sichel
Pages 34–45

1. Bill Ashcroft, *Post-Colonial Transformation* (London: Routledge, 2001), 16.
2. Ibid., 128.
3. This point of view is defended by the vast majority of historians, sociologists, and thinkers, including the well-known Brazilian sociologist Gilberto Freire.
4. The colonial discourse has been discussed in a number of books. Edward Said's *Orientalism: Western Conceptions of the Orient* (London: Penguin, 1991) is a primary source on the subject.

5. Ashcroft, 16. For Ashcroft, European imperialism continues to affect most of the world to the present day.
6. Homi K. Bhabha, *The Location of Culture* (London: Routledge, 1994), 37.
7. Arjun Appadurai, *Modernity at Large: Cultural Dimensions of Globalization* (Minneapolis: University of Minnesota Press, 1996), 197.
8. See Robert Stam, *Tropical Multiculturalism: A Comparative History of Race in Brazilian Cinema and Culture* (Durham: Duke University Press, 1997). Stam's essay published in this catalogue is adapted from the final chapter of the book.
9. Appadurai, 197.
10. Op. cit.
11. Unlike the use of the term *modernism* in U.S. art criticism, which encompasses a set of tendencies and approaches far too broad and diverse, and as distinct from modernism in other Latin American countries, Brazilian *Modernismo* was influenced by the French avant-garde of the 1920s. It was simultaneously a rebellion against tradition and a search for a national aesthetic consciousness.
12. Today Oiticica has been "rediscovered" partly through the efforts of Catherine David, former *Documenta* curator, but mostly through the work of Brazilian curators and scholars who knew the artist well. Ten years after his death in 1980 he became a cult figure for European critics and curators. Only then was he officially acknowledged in Brazil.

13. Frederico de Moraes, "Brazil: International Languages," in *Brazil Projects* [exhibition catalogue] (New York: PS1, 1986).
14. On that occasion Waldemar Cordeiro contacted the magazine *Ad-arquitetura e decoração*, which featured material from the exhibition in its November–December 1957 issue (no. 20), acting as a catalogue for the show. The accompanying texts were written by Cordeiro, Décio Pignatari, Augusto de Campos, Haroldo de Campos, and Ferreira Guilar. Concrete poems and photographs of the paintings and sculptures were also included.
15. The violent political interruption of the 1960s stultified what was then the most innovative facet of the nation's art, culture, and social life: the tropicalization of music, which was closely connected to the work of Oiticica and Cinema Novo.
16. Frederico de Moraes, *Do conceitual à arte contemporânea* (São Paulo: Cadernos História da Pintura no Brasil, Instituto Itaú Cultural, 1994), 5.
17. For example, Marlyse Meyer has looked into the role of women as readers of romances and the importance of the literary salons that existed from the beginning of the twentieth century until the late 1930s, in which women were active participants. Feminist studies also examined the literary informal economy that developed on the fringe of traditional historiography. One theme that has emerged from these studies, most of which

focused on the nineteenth century or the first decades of the twentieth century, is the formation of national identity and the different ways in which women and men writers approach the ideologies of nationality.
18. All of these artists' work has been shown at the National Museum of Women in the Arts in the exhibitions *UltraModern: The Art of Contemporary Brazil* (1994) and *Inside the Visible* (1996).
19. In *Virgin Territory,* Leirner exhibits his series *Santa Ceia* (The Last Supper), discussed by the Brazilian curator Agnaldo Farias in this catalogue.
20. All of these, with the exception of Jac Leirner, joined 137 other artists in the groundbreaking exhibition *Como vai você Geração 80?,* held at the School of Visual Arts, Parque Lage, Rio de Janeiro, in July 1984.

SYLVIO BACK
Barracks Indians
By Sylvio Back
Pages 50–53

1. Nelie Sá Pereira, *Major Luiz Thomaz Reis— o cinegrafista de Rondon (pesquisa e filmografia)* (Rio de Janeiro: Departamento de Documentação e Divulgação da Embra-filme, 1982).
2. Antonio Carlos de Souza Lima, "O governo dos índios sob a gestão do SPI," in Manuela Carneiro da Cunha, *História dos índios do Brasil* (São Paulo: Fapesp, SMC, Companhia das Letras, 1992).

ORIANA DUARTE
Noumenon: The Thing-in-Itself
By Moacir dos Anjos
Pages 60–61

1. Melo Neto, ed. João Cabral, *Obra Completa* (Rio de Janeiro: Nova Aguilar, 1994).

ANNA BELLA GEIGER
A Sense of Constellation
By Fernando Cocchiarale
Pages 62–65

1. For example, the postcards *O Pão Nosso de Cada Dia* (Our Daily Bread) (1978), *Brasil nativo–Brasil alienigena* (Native Brazil–Alien Brazil) (1977); the videos *Mapas Elementales nº 1, nº 2 e nº 3* (Elemental Maps #1, #2 and #3) (1976), *Novos Atlas nº 1 e nº 2* (New Atlas #1 and #2) (1975–76); the primers *História do Brasil* (History of Brazil) (1975), *Admissão à Geografia* (Test on Geography) (1974), *Os Dez Mandamentos* (The Ten Commandments) (1974), and *Uma Pequena Lenda Brasileira* (A Little Brazilian Legend) (1974).

SONIA LABOURIAU
From Without to Within/ From Within to Without
By Ricardo Basbaum
Pages 68–69

1. Urucum is a red pigment extracted from the seeds of *Bixa orellana* and was originally used by indigenous South American people for cooking and body painting;

it was widely employed in Brazilian cooking.
2. Sonia Labouriau, 1992.

LAURA LIMA
The Artist as Predator
By Ricardo Basbaum
Pages 74–75

1. N. Katherine Hayles has proposed a distinction between *embodiment* and *incorporation,* configuring the body "as a cultural construct and the experiences of embodiment that individual people within a culture feel and articulate and an 'inscription' [that] is normalized and abstract . . . a system of signs operating independently of any particular manifestation." See N. Katherine Hayles, *How We Became Post-Human: Virtual Bodies in Cybernetics, Literature, and Informatics* (Chicago: University of Chicago Press, 1999).

ANNA MARIA MAIOLINO
Rice and Beans
By Berta Sichel
Pages 76–79

1. Suzanne Preston Blier, "Ritual," in *Critical Terms for Art History,* eds. Robert Nelson and Richard Shiff (Chicago: University of Chicago Press, 1966), 193.
2. Tony Godfrey, *Conceptual Art* (London: Phaidon Press, 1998), 276.

NAZARETH PACHECO
A Lacerating Reality
By Tadeu Chiarelli
Pages 86–89

1. The text "Objectos dependentes" (Dependent Objects) has been published twice: for the brochure produced for the artist's one-person show held at Centro Cultural de São Paulo in 1990 and for the brochure produced for her one-person show at Galeria Macunaíma, IBAC, Rio de Janeiro, in 1991.

REGINA SILVEIRA
Recapturing History
By Susana Torruella Leval
Pages 102–5

1. Marta Rossetti Battista, "Bandeiras de Brecheret: Historia de um monumento, 1920–53" (São Paulo: DHP, 1985).
2. Conversation with Regina Silveira, New York, November 14, 1991.

ADRIANA VAREJÃO
Travel Chronicles
By Rina Carvajal
Pages 116–19

1. Conversation with the artist, August 9, 1996.

GEOGRAPHIC CONTINGENCIES. SPACE AND MEMORY
By Pedro P. Geiger
Pages 122–29

1. *The American Heritage Dictionary of the English Language,* 4th ed. (2000), defines *mare clausum* as "a navigable body of water, such as a sea, that is under the jurisdiction of one nation and closed to all others."
2. Bertha K. Becker, "Brasil—Tordesilhas, Ano 2000," *Território* 7 (1999): 7–9.
3. A. Dupont, quoted in Jean Luc Piveteau, "Le territoire est-il un lieu de memoire?" *L'Espace Geographique* 24, no. 2 (1995): 116.
4. George Louis Leclerc de Buffon, cited in Antonello Gelbi, *The Dispute of the New World* (Pittsburgh: University of Pittsburgh Press, 1973).
5. See Pedro P. Geiger, "América, América," in *Geografia e Meio Ambiente no Brasil,* eds. Bertha Becker, Antônio Christofoletti, Faní Koifman, and Pedro P. Geiger (São Paulo: Editora HUCITEC, 1995), 23–24.
6. Denis E. Cosgrove, *Social Formation and Symbolic Landscape* (London and Sydney: Croom Helm, 1984), 8–9.
7. See Gilles Deleuze, *A lógica do sentido,* 4th ed. (São Paulo: Editora Perspectiva, 1998), 260–62.
8. Candice Vidal e Souza, *A pátria geográfica, sertão e litoral no pensamento social, Brasileiro* (Goiânia: Universidade Federal de Goiás, 1997), 45.
9. Deleuze, 5.
10. Ibid., 7.
11. Caio Prado Júnior, *Formação do Brasil contemporâneo* (São Paulo: Brasiliense, 1942), 365.
12. See Prado Júnior, *História econômica do Brasil* (São Paulo: Brasiliense, 1945).
13. Prado Júnior, *Formação do Brasil contemporâneo,* 370–71.
14. See David Wilkinson, "Cities, Civilizations and the Oikumenes, I," *Comparative Civilizations Review* 27 (Fall 1992): 51–87.
15. See Immanuel Wallerstein, *The Modern World System: Capitalist Agriculture and the Origin of the European World Economy in the Sixteenth Century* (New York: Wiley, 1974).
16. The hegemony of the "central civilization" is a myth whose intrinsic value comes from the events that began with the Roman Empire, was centered in Europe and the Mediterranean basin, and was ruled by the Christian faith.
17. Deleuze, 267
18. Ibid.
19. Ibid., 265–69.
20. Jean-Luc Piveteau, "Le territoire est-il un 'Lieu de memoire,'" *L'Espace Geographique* 24, no. 2 (1995): 114.
21. Ibid., 113.
22. Ibid., 114.
23. Translation by Oscar Seidlin.
24. Becker, 20.
25. Ibid.

ETHNIC IDENTITIES IN BRAZIL
By Giralda Seyferth
Pages 132–37

1. Emílio Willems, "Immigrants and Their Assimilation in Brazil," in T. L. Smith and A. Marchant, eds., *Brazil: Portrait of Half a Continent* (New York: Dryden Press, 1951).
2. See estimates by J. F. Carneiro in *Imigração e colonização no Brasil* (Rio de Janeiro: Faculdade Nacional de Filosofia, Cadeira de Geografia do Brasil, Publicação Avulsa, 1950), 2, and Manuel Diegues Júnior in *Imigração, urbanização, industrialização* (Rio de Janeiro: CBPE/INEP, 1964).
3. Diegues Júnior, 26.
4. Max Weber, *Economia e sociedade* (Brasília: Editora da Universidade de Brasília, 1991), 268–73, discusses the formation of these ethnic collectivities.
5. Roberto Gron, *Negócios e famílias: armênios em São Paulo* (São Paulo: Editora Sumaré, 1992).
6. Regarding these two categorizations, a pretense of pluralism has been claimed systematically since the 1930s, an ideal that recognized Brazil not as a nation but as a state containing different ethnicities and nationalities.
7. Willems, *A aculturação dos alemães no Brasil* (São Paulo: Companhia Editora Nacional, 1946).
8. Diegues Júnior, 54.
9. Giralda Seyferth, "Os paradoxos da miscigenação," in *Estudos Afro-asiáticos,* 1991, 20.
10. See Willems, *A aculturação dos alemães no Brasil,* and Diegues Júnior, *Imigração, urbanização, industrialização.*
11. Willems, "Immigrants and Their Assimilation in Brazil."
12. Giralda Seyferth, "Racismo e identidade nacional: paradoxos e utopias," in 19 *Ciência Hoje,* no. 109 (1995).
13. Oracy Nogueira, *Tanto preto quanto branco* (São Paulo: T. A. Queirós, 1985).

BEYOND THE IDENTITY PRINCIPLE: THE ANTHROPOPHAGY FORMULA
By Suely Rolnik
Pages 138–45

1. Pierre Lévy, lecture at Unisinos, Porto Alegre, 1999.
2. Fernando Pessoa, *Livro do Desassossego* (The Book of Disquiet), vol. 2 (Lisbon: Atica, 1982), 241, n. 495.
3. Oswald de Andrade, "Brasil-Wood Poetry Manifesto" [1924], in *The Anthropophagy Utopia,* in *The Complete Works of Oswald de Andrade* (São Paulo: Globo, 1990).
4. Oswald de Andrade, "Anthropophagist Manifesto" [1928], in *The Anthropophagy Utopia,* in *The Complete Works of Oswald de Andrade* (São Paulo: Globo, 1990).
5. Darcy Ribeiro, *O Povo Brasileiro. A formação e o sentido do Brasil* (São Paulo: Companhia das Letras, 1995).

6. De Andrade, "Anthropophagist Manifesto" [1928].

7. Ibid.

8. Ibid.

9. Lygia Clark, "A propósito da magia do objeto" [1965], in *Lygia Clark, Arte Brasileira Contemporânea* series (Rio de Janeiro: Funarte, 1980).

10. Hélio Oiticica, "Eden" [1969], in *Hélio Oiticica* (Paris: Réunion des Musées Nationaux, Editions du Jeu de Paume, 1992).

11. De Andrade, "Anthropophagist Manifesto" [1928].

12. Two buildings constructed by Deputy Sergio Naya used sea sand to lower construction costs. One of the buildings collapsed during the 1998 Carnival, causing the death of eight people. The second was demolished after the accident following a court decision. Two months later the deputy was removed from office.

13. Ribeiro, *O Povo Brasileiro*.

14. De Andrade, "Anthropophagist Manifesto" [1928].

15. De Andrade, "The March of the Utopias" [1953], in *The Anthropophagy Utopia*, in *The Complete Works of Oswald de Andrade* (São Paulo: Globo, 1990).

BRAZILIAN CINEMA: RACE AND REPRESENTATION
Robert Stam
Pages 146–57

1. For more on Bakhtinian theories and their relevance for the media, see Robert Stam, *Subversive Pleasures: Bakhtin, Cultural Criticism and Film* (Baltimore: Johns Hopkins University Press, 1989).

2. Carl N. Degler, *Neither Black Nor White: Slavery and Race Relations in Brazil and the United States* (New York: Macmillan, 1971), 122

3. In 1975 the Congress of Brazilian Women made the following statement about the mulatta figure: "Brazilian black women inherited a cruel legacy: that of being the object of pleasure of the colonizers. It is the fruit of this cowardly crossing of blood that is now proclaimed the 'only national product worthy of export: the Brazilian mulatta.' But if the quality of the 'product' is said to be high, the treatment she receives is extremely degrading and disrespectful." Quoted in Abdias de Nascimento, *O Genocídio do Negro Brasileiro* (Rio: Paz e Terra, 1978), 61–62.

4. See Teófilo de Queiroz Jr., *Preconceito de Cor e a Mulata na Literatura Brasileira* (São Paulo: Atica, 1975), 122.

5. Quoted in Abdias de Nascimento, *Quilombismo*, 239.

6. Muniz Sodré, "Mulata da Melhor Mulataria?" *Isto É* (November 23, 1977): 46.

7. See Ella Shohat and Robert Stam, *Unthinking Eurocentrism: Multiculturalism and the Media* (London: Routledge, 1994).

8. Quoted in Flora Sussekind, *O Negro como Arlequim: Teatro e Discriminacao* (Rio de Janeiro: Achiame, 1982).

9. See Zelbert Moore, "Reflections on Blacks in Contemporary Brazilian Popular Culture in the 1980s," in *Studies in Latin American Popular Culture*, vol. VII (1988).

10. Carlos Hasenbalg and Nelson do Valle Silva, "As Imagems do negro na publicidade," in *Estrutura Social, Mobilidade, e Raça* (Sao Paulo: Vértice, 1988), 185–88.

11. See Amelia Simpson, *Xuxa: The Mega-Marketing of Gender, Race and Modernity* (Philadelphia: Temple University Press, 1993).

12. For more on Zelig, see Robert Stam and Ella Shohat, "*Zelig* and Contemporary Theory: Meditation on the Chameleon Text," *Enclitic*, vol. IX, nos. 1–2 (1987).

13. Sussekind, 17.

14. Ismail Xavier, *Allegories of Underdevelopment: From the "Aesthetics of Hunger" to the "Aesthetics of Garbage."* Ph.D. diss., New York University, 1982.

15. Henry Drewal, "Sign, Substance, and Subversion in Afro-Brazilian Art," in Arturo Lindsay, ed., *Santeria Aesthetics in Contemporary Latin American Art* (Washington, D.C.: Smithsonian Institution Press, 1996), 266.

Contríbutors

Aracy Amaral, a historian and critic, is a professor on the faculty of Architecture and Urbanism, University of São Paulo.

Moacir dos Anjos is chief curator at the Museum of Modern Art Aloísio Magalhães (MAMAM), Recife.

Ricardo Basbaum is an artist and writer based in Rio de Janeiro.

Ivana Bentes is a researcher and critic in film and the visual arts and teaches at the School of Communication, Federal University of Rio de Janeiro.

Ligia Canongia is a critic and art historian in Rio de Janeiro.

Katia Canton is professor of contemporary art at the University of São Paulo and curatorial director of its Museum of Contemporary Art.

Rina Carvajal is an art historian and independent curator in New York.

Tadeu Chiarelli is professor of art history in the Fine Arts Department, University of São Paulo.

Fernando Cocchiarale is curator at the Museum of Modern Art, Rio de Janeiro, and professor of aesthetics, PUC-RIP and the School of Visual Arts, Parque Lage.

Ania Corcilius is an artist living in Hamburg, Germany, and editor of the journal *SuperUmbau*.

Agnaldo Farias is professor of art history at the University of São Paulo at São Carlos and curator of the Instituto Tomie Ohtake.

Celso Fioravante is a journalist and art critic in São Paulo.

Pedro P. Geiger is a geographer retired from the Brazilian Institute of Geography and Statistics, Rio de Janeiro.

Hernani Heffner is a Cinédia scholar and curator of documentation and research for the Film Library, Museum of Modern Art, Rio de Janeiro.

Arnaldo Jabor is a filmmaker and writer living in São Paulo.

Lisette Lagnado is an independent curator who works as an arts consultant for the Instituto Itaú Cultural, São Paulo.

Susana Torruella Leval is director of El Museo del Barrio, New York City.

Vik Muniz is an artist living in Brooklyn, New York.

Franklin Espath Pedroso is associate chief curator for BrasilConnects, São Paulo.

Suely Rolnik is a psychoanalyst, writer, and director of the Contemporary Subjectivity Ph.D. Program, Catholic University of São Paulo.

Giralda Seyferth is a professor in the Graduate Program in Social Anthropology, National Museum of the Federal University of Rio de Janeiro.

Berta Sichel is the director of the Film and Video Department, Museo Nacional Centro de Arte Reina Sofia, Madrid.

Robert Stam is a professor in the Department of Cinema Studies, New York University.

Susan Fisher Sterling is chief curator, National Museum of Women in the Arts, Washington, D.C.